THEORY OF PROSODY

IN

EIGHTEENTH-CENTURY ENGLAND

By

PAUL FUSSELL, Jr.

ARCHON BOOKS
1966

106426

To

P. F. and W. S. F.

PREFACE

To an observer in the mid-nineteenth century, "prosody" was "a word scarcely proper to be spoken within hearing of the ladies, a necessary evil of academic days, a subject which pedantry itself seldom dreams of obtruding on ears polite,"[1] and to many twentieth-century students of literary history, prosodic investigation has seemed at best a fruitless endeavor bearing little relation to the operative processes of poetic creation and serving primarily as an exhibition of the investigator's incapacity for dealing with more vital affairs. It need hardly be pointed out that in the eighteenth century, prosodic theorizing was an activity in which many of the finest minds of the period participated: prescriptive and descriptive prosodic theorizing occupied the hours of Thomas Gray, Allan Ramsay the Younger (son of the poet and court painter to George III), Samuel Johnson, Thomas Sheridan, and Charles Burney; and the widespread interest in verse structure drew prosodic treatises from a horde of minor out-at-elbows schoolmasters, penny-a-line critics and Grub-Streeters, and genteel country curates. Even Thomas Jefferson somehow found time to pen a hurried essay on the subject. If prosodic theorizing did not quite attain the acceptability of gaming as an indoor sport, it may certainly be said to have been one of the topics of the day: the fact that more than one hundred writers contributed to prosodic theory during the century indicates something of the public interest in prosodic investigations.

A sound education in the theory of prosody, both ancient and modern, was assumed to be the Augustan poet's absolute minimum of preparation for his career. Johnson, surveying Young's poetic achievement, is taken aback to discover that Young "seems never to have studied prosody, nor to have had any direction but from his own ear." "But [Johnson hastens to add] with all his defects, he was a man of genius and a poet."[2] Augustine had found ample evidence of God's design in the principles of verse structure; Boethius had had recourse to the laws of verse for illustrations of the operation of a universal metaphysic; in a related way, the more positivistic eighteenth century often connected prosody with rules of conduct and with associationist aesthetic theory, and took delight in assuming certain correspondences between a poet's accustomed regularity of stress and his habitual adherence to fixed principles of ethical behavior. As Lord Kames put it in 1762, "the music of verse merits more attention than it has been honored

---

[1] Coventry Patmore, "English Metrical Criticism," *North British Review,* XXVII (1857), 127.
[2] George Birkbeck Hill, ed., *Lives of the English Poets* (Oxford, 1905), III, 399.

with. It is a subject intimately connected with human nature."[3]   An age which was accustomed to surveying human nature from China to Peru and to studying man from every accessible vantage point did not let slip the opportunity of seeking principles of moral right and wrong in such a commonplace commodity as verse structure.

As the century advanced, however, the study of versification gradually came to seem of less importance, and during the nineteenth century it generally retired from the drawing-room and the coffee house to find tenuous refuge in the university and the learned society. The genesis of theories of unpremeditated art and the excitement engendered by the discovery of fresh poetic subject-matter near the end of the eighteenth century forced prosody into a position of minor importance from which, indeed, it has never risen. Although the middle of the nineteenth century witnessed a revival of interest in the musical analogy, and although various quantitative revivalists such as Robert Bridges attracted some attention to prosody early in our own century, as a study furnishing material for broader generalizations in the areas of ethics and metaphysics, prosody ("the Gay Science" one modern scholar rather wistfully calls it[4]) has never regained the high position it occupied during the Renaissance and the eighteenth century.

Something should be said here of the scope and purpose of this monograph. I have tried to examine every available prosodic treatise produced from 1657 to the beginning of the nineteenth century, and in addition to locate relevant prosodic opinions in the works of those who did not develop their attitudes towards verse structure into whole and coherent separate works. The writings which make a direct contribution to the metrical theory of the century range from the most banal grammar-school texts to abstruse dissertations having to do more with theoretical mathematics than with any sort of poetry. Since I have had to be rather inflexibly selective in my treatment of theoretical aspects, I have directed most of my attention to eighteenth-century theories of the rhythmical structure of the heroic line, to the theory of poetic contractions, and to the eighteenth-century foundations of what was to become "romantic" prosody. Limitations of space have prevented me from treating (1) the controversy over the nature of accent and quantity; (2) the eighteenth-century theory of the nature of rhyme; (3) the theory of line integrity; and (4) the theory of the cesura: no consideration of eighteenth-

---

[3] *Elements of Criticism* (Basel, 1795), II, 249.
[4] Robert Frederick Brewer, *Orthometry: The Art of Versification and the Technicalities of Poetry* (revised ed.; Edinburgh, 1912), p. 280.

century prosodic theory can of course pretend to any completeness which is obliged to neglect these four topics.

One difficulty encountered immediately by any student of these materials is the ambiguity of the basic documents themselves: it is frequently impossible to know whether a prosodist is laying down prescriptive ideals for verse or is simply providing objective descriptive comments on the *données* of contemporary verse. This uncertain wavering between prescriptive and descriptive activity breeds confusions and contradictions in the work of many of the prosodists; where I have been unable to resolve or interpret contradictions, I have been silent, and I trust that the reader will not allow himself to become unduly concerned as he observes some prosodists advancing quite contradictory opinions in different sections of their works.

Believing with Johnson that "what has been longest known has been most considered, and what is most considered is best understood,"[5] I have not scrupled to employ the traditional foot terminology, although I am aware of its limitations. Certain other terms, however, may require some explanation. I have used the term "syllabism" to refer to a theory of the poetic line which takes the number of syllables in the line to be its primary structural basis. In the same way, the term "accentualism" refers to a theory of the line which considers the number of stresses to be its fundamental prosodic skeleton. I have found the designations "conservative," "liberal," and "radical" useful to suggest certain broad groups into which the prosodic theorists seem to range themselves.

For his patience with this work and for countless heartening acts of kindness performed outside the line of duty, I am grateful, as are many students of the English eighteenth century, to Professor George Sherburn of Harvard University. I should also like to thank Professor Walter Jackson Bate of Harvard for his lively interest and provocative suggestions. Professors Pauline Aiken, Dorothy Bethurum, Augusto Centeno, and H. M. Smyser, all of Connecticut College, have been good enough to read the manuscript and to make helpful criticisms. I am indebted to the Trustees of the British Museum for permission to cite Allan Ramsay the Younger's unpublished essay on versification, to Mr. Alastair Smart of the University College of Hull for sharing with me his knowledge of Ramsay, and to Professor W. R. Irwin of the State University of Iowa for his encouragement. I must thank

---

[5] *The Works of William Shakspeare, with the Corrections and Illustrations of Dr. Johnson, G. Steevens, and others, revised by Isaac Reed* (3rd Amer. ed.; Boston, 1810), I, 26.

Connecticut College for financial assistance in the publication of this work, Mackie Jarrell for help with proofs, and my wife for an amiable job of typing.
New London, Conn.   P. F., JR.
July, 1953

TABLE OF CONTENTS

CHAPTER I

THE CODIFICATION OF SYLLABISM AND STRESS REGULARITY

1. *The March towards Metrical Perfection*

The idea of progress, a notion implicit in many of the most characteristic intellectual tendencies of the Renaissance, is intimately connected with the development and codification of what the Restoration hailed as the New Prosody. The outcome of the civil war had represented, to most of the literate, a triumph of the forces of irregularity, and the wits who returned from France upon the restoration of Charles II were not slow to infuse poetic and prosodic theory with the political-social concept of progressive refinement and to exhibit a consciousness of a very recent victory over barbarity, disharmony, and irregularity.

The various "imitations" of Boileau's *L'Art Poétique* produced from 1680 to 1710 reveal both the influence of the idea of progress on the formulation of conservative prosodic theory in the eighteenth century and the debts of this New Prosody to French practice: Fairfax's name was customarily substituted for Villon's in these brief versified literary histories, Spenser became the "parallel" of Marot, Davenant was regarded as occupying a place in the English march towards refinement corresponding to that of Ronsard in the French literary progress, and Waller came to be considered the British Malherbe. This continual paralleling of English and French literary history during the Restoration could not but reinforce the notion that, if French and English poetry were "advancing" along the same lines, French and English prosody too had a certain common relationship.[1]

There were indeed a few dissenters, but, like some anti-progressivists of later days, their feeble voices were barely heard. Samuel Woodford, in his *Paraphrase upon the Canticles* (1679), ventured to suggest rather testily that "changing we have been from *Chaucer's* time downward with a Witness, however it be call'd Refining."[2] But this timid demurrer from a mere versifier of the Scriptures was drowned out by the immense roar of approbation for the prosody of Denham and Waller. Dryden delivers the keynote address for the proponents of the refined prosody: " . . . the excellence and dignity

---

[1] René Wellek, *The Rise of English Literary History* (Chapel Hill, 1941), p. 40.
[2] *A Paraphrase upon the Canticles* (London, 1679), sig. C3.

of [rhyme] were never fully known till Mr. Waller taught it; he first made writing easily an art."[3] Rymer[4] and Dennis join the chorus; Waller, Dennis says, "was the first who us'd our Ears to the Musick of a just Cadence."[5] Addison's poem "An Account of the Greatest English Poets" is typical in its disparagement of Chaucer's and Spenser's prosody as "barbarous" and its assumption that Waller was the first refiner of English prosody.

Johnson confidently felt that the prosodic technique attained by Waller "perhaps will never be obsolete";[6] and since the refinement of English metric was considered an accomplishment to which the effort of many centuries had contributed, little prosodic development was expected in the career of a poet like Waller: Johnson considers it a virtue that Waller's prosodic principles were so "fixed" that "His versification was in his fi.st essay such as it appears in his last performance."[7] Once having reached a state of prosodic perfection, Waller could, after all, go no further.

Milton was generally pitied for having been obliged to write too soon to profit from this enlightened movement towards metrical smoothness and regularity; Johnson allows Milton's verse a certain "harmony" (a word always synonymous with "regularity of stress" to Johnson), but adds that Milton's prosody is "harmonious" only "in proportion to the general state of our metre in Milton's age." If Milton "had written after the improvements made by Dryden, it is reasonable to believe that he would have admitted a more pleasing modulation of numbers into his work."[8] The connection in Johnson's mind between prosodic regularity and the recent triumph over "harshness" and barbarism in manners and customs may be seen in his diction here: "The new versification, as it was called, may be considered as owing its establishment to Dryden; from whose time it is apparent that English poetry has had no tendency to relapse to its former savageness."[9] From Johnson's choice of words like "relapse" and "savageness," one can gain some understanding of the social implications of the rise of syllabism and stress regularity, and also some comprehension of one reason why the "official" prosody of the eighteenth century was defended with such tenacity by early reviewers of

[3] W. P. Ker, ed., *Essays of John Dryden* (Oxford, 1926), II, 86.

[4] See *A Short View of Tragedy; Its Original, Excellency, and Corruption. With some Reflections on Shakespear and Other Practitioners for the Stage* (London, 1693), p. 79.

[5] J. E. Spingarn, ed., *Critical Essays of the Seventeenth Century* (Oxford, 1908-1909), III, 153. ("The Impartial Critick").

[6] Hill, ed., *Lives*, I, 250-251.

[7] *Ibid.*, I, 251.

[8] *Ibid.*, I, 318.

[9] *Ibid.*, I, 421.

Hunt, Scott, Coleridge, and Keats; as will be seen, the association of verse structure with the political ideas of its makers was a concept still very much alive at the beginning of the nineteenth century, and a literary generation terrified by the French Revolution and its repercussions on the British political scene instinctively saw in the rise of a more free and varied prosody a lurking and sinister Jacobinism.

The idea of progress was indeed almost as much alive during the latter part of the eighteenth century as it had been at the Restoration, and most of the conservative prosodic theorists joined Johnson in the attempt to stave off any revision of the notion that metrical improvement must terminate in a refined fixity. In 1762, Daniel Webb finds that "the forming and perfecting our versification" is the most powerful stimulus to the final improvement of the English tongue itself.[10] Sir John Hawkins, writing in 1776, believes that "the natural course and order of things" is "ever towards perfection," and he finds this as true of music as of physics and mathematics.[11] In 1783, Hugh Blair proclaims bluntly, "Waller first smoothed our Verse; Dryden perfected it."[12] And as late as 1804, William Mitford is happy to award Pope the distinction of being "the last refiner of English versification," who carried metrical technique "to a perfection beyond which the language cannot go."[13] The almost incalculable influence of this prevailing progressivist supposition must be kept in mind if the character, virtues, and deficiencies of syllabic prosody, the official prosody of the eighteenth century, are to be rightly understood.

2. Sources, Influences, and the English Tradition

The two most influential streams of prosodic tradition flowing into England during this period were, of course, the French and the ancient; during the earlier decades of the century, these two metrical traditions served to reinforce the stability of English syllabism and stress regularity, and to establish this metrical system as the normal one. The "new tonality" and the unique "rhetorical and metrical skeleton" available in the works of Boileau and his followers in France were quickly absorbed into English metrical practice,[14] and the purely syllabic structure of the French alexandrine, with

---

[10] *Remarks on the Beauties of Poetry* (London, 1762), pp. 56-57.

[11] *A General History of the Science and Practice of Music* (London, 1776), I, xli.

[12] *Lectures on Rhetoric and Belles Lettres* (2nd ed.; London, 1785), III, 112.

[13] *An Inquiry into the Principles of Harmony in Language, and of the Mechanism of Verse, Modern and Antient* (2nd ed.; London, 1804), p. 88.

[14] See A. F. B. Clark, *Boileau and the French Classical Critics in England, 1660-1830* (Paris, 1925), pp. 451-452.

its inevitable medial cesura, was often regarded as the exact, almost God-given model for the general structure of the English line. Thomas Gray, with an air of merely summing up a popular commonplace, calls the school of Waller, Dryden, Addison, Prior, and Pope the *"School of France,"*[15] and Thomas Sheridan, looking back in 1775 on the prosodic accomplishments of the previous hundred years, asserts that the English prosodists have either "indolently adopted the rules of prosody laid down by our neighbours [*i.e.,* the principles of French syllabism]; or, where they would not answer, have had recourse to those of the ancients."[16] The "rules of prosody laid down by our neighbours" are substantially those advanced by the Abbé Du Bos in 1719. Four main rules are to be observed by the manufacturer of French verses, Du Bos points out. "In the first place, our verse must be composed of a certain number of syllables, according to the kind of verse." Secondly, every line of four, five, or six feet must have a well-marked cesura. Thirdly, apocope is to be used freely to minimize ugly vowel-gaping ("hiatus") between words. "And lastly, we must rhime."[17] Indeed, the only difference between the structure of French and English verse was often considered to be the matter of the alternate disposal of accents in English poetry, and even this difference between the two prosodies was frequently overlooked.

Two ancient line-forms offered themselves as especially convenient models for imitation: the first was the quantitative dactylic-spondaic hexameter, about the true metrical nature of which violent controversies have been traditional since the very earliest stages of English prosodic theorizing. The second classical form available for prosodic parallels was the quantitative iambic-spondaic line, which had been felt, by critics of the Silver Age, to be "purer" the closer it approached a structure of six iambic feet. Allan Ramsay the Younger, arguing here in favor of a regular iambic line in English uncontaminated by any dissyllabic substitution, has instinctive recourse to Horatian authority: "This practice, of admitting Spondees into Iambic verse prevailed very much amongst the ancient poets, both Greek and Roman; but Horace, who knew what belonged to good Poetry as well as any of them, did not approve of it, but says, that those Iambic verses were most admired and *celebrated* which preserved the *vivacity* natural to the Iambics by using

---

[15] Paget Toynbee and Leonard Whibley, edd., *Correspondence of Thomas Gray* (Oxford, 1935), III, 1124.

[16] *Lectures on the Art of Reading. In Two Parts. Containing Part I. The Art of Reading Prose. Part II. The Art of Reading Verse* (2nd ed.; London, 1781), p. 192.

[17] Thomas Nugent, trans., *Critical Reflections on Poetry, Painting and Music* (London, 1748), I, 263.

them unmixed with other feet."[18] Thomas Warton announces that "An
Alexandrine entirely consisting of Iambic feet, answers precisely to a pure
Iambic verse of the antients."[19] A practitioner of English verse who made
too frequent deviations from the expectedly regular iambic structure by daring
occasionally to substitute a different dissyllabic foot in any but the first position could always be certain of a scornful reception among certain of the
conservative prosodists who had pretensions to classical learning.[20] While
the influence of contemporary French prosodic theory made itself felt on the
limitation of the English heroic line to "a certain number of syllables," and
thus served as a sanction against the use of trisyllabic substitution, the influence of classical prosody, with its general principle that little or no substitution be employed except for comic purposes, bolstered the English conservative prosodists' conviction that the English heroic line was more "pure" (and
thus more virtuous) the less dissyllabic substitution it exhibited. Thus the
two cardinal points of the conservative prosodic tradition in the eighteenth
century, syllabism and stress regularity, found authoritative sanction in the
two non-English traditions which most powerfully shaped the course of
eighteenth-century English literature in general.

It should not be forgotten, however, that the Restoration's obsession with
the strict syllabic limitation of the English line was, in part, a theoretical
codification of a gradual tendency towards syllabism and stress regularity
which had been under way in English poetry at least from the time of
Chaucer.[21] It is erroneous to think of the New Prosody as the result of a
series of sudden theoretical ukases promulgated by prosodic theorists and
tamely accepted by the poets. A great deal of evidence supports the assertion
that Shakespeare's prosody is, except perhaps in his very last plays, almost
as syllabic as the Augustans',[22] and it has been accepted for over half a
century that Milton's prosody is primarily syllabic;[23] in fact, Milton may even

[18] "An Enquiry into the Principles of English Versification" (British Museum Add.
MS. 39,999), fol. 19, n.
[19] Observations on the Faerie Queene of Spenser (London, 1754), p. 260.
[20] J. A. Symonds believes that Johnson's intimate acquaintance with classical prosodic
principles was the main impulse behind his hostility to substitution in English verse.
(Blank Verse [London, 1895], p. 82).
[21] See George R. Stewart, Modern Metrical Technique as Illustrated by Ballad Meter,
(1700-1920) (New York, 1922), p. 19; Charlton M. Lewis, Principles of English Verse
(New York, 1906), p. 32; and S. Ernest Sprott, Milton's Art of Prosody (Oxford, 1953),
p. 46.
[22] See E. A. Abbott, Shakespearian Grammar (London, 1870), pp. 344-429; G. D.
Willcock, "Passing Pitefull Hexameters: A Study of Quantity and Accent in English
Renaissance Verse," MLR, XXIX (1934), 16; and Helge Kökeritz, Shakespeare's Pronunciation (New Haven, Conn., 1953), pp. 25-31.
[23] See Lewis, Principles, pp. 32-33; Egerton Smith, The Principles of English Metre

have considered the element of stress in his verse very much the way we consider the element of quantity (or the element of assonance) in modern English poetry: that is, as an effective embellishment, but by no means a major structural element.[24] What happened in the field of prosodic theorizing in the Restoration was that the syllabic principle, which "had to great poets like Milton been mainly a self-imposed regulative principle, to set a check on structural laxity," apparent all too often in the blank verse of the Jacobean drama, "became elevated into a positive and fundamental law."[25] Puttenham, as early as 1589, was theorizing in very much the same direction as the Restoration and Augustan syllable-counters, and it seems likely, as Thomas Gray noted, that Donne in his Satires was composing primarily decasyllabically, with the very slightest structural concern for the position of stresses.[26] Instead of regarding eighteenth-century conservative prosody, then, in both its theoretical and practical aspects, as a unique system foreign to what preceded and followed it, and as a metrical ideal foisted in an underhanded and somehow unpatriotic manner on the defenseless English poets, it will be more in accordance with the facts to think of the theory of syllabism and stress regularity in this century as an approximately equal compound of indigenous and non-English elements. The movement did draw a great deal of sustenance from French and classical theory and practice, but mainly incidentally and, as it were, for reasons of respectability.

3. Some Restoration Theorists and "Improvers"

Before considering the contributors to the syllabic theory themselves, it may be noted that the term "numbers" throughout the century has usually

---

(Oxford, 1923), pp. 38, 113-114, and 302; Max Kaluza, *A Short History of English Versification, from the Earliest Times to the Present Day* (A. C. Dunstan, trans., London, 1911), p. 314; Robert Bridges, *Milton's Prosody, with a Chapter on Accentual Verse and Notes* (rev. final ed.; Oxford, 1921), pp. 4-5; and Sprott, *Milton's Art of Prosody*, pp. 47, 48, and 66.

[24] See Willcock, "Passing Pitefull Hexameters," p. 18. S. Ernest Sprott finds that "only half of Milton's . . . lines [in *PL*] can show to the ear five accents." (*Milton's Art of Prosody*, p. 106). It has been suggested by Paull Franklin Baum that the "fit quantity of Syllables" which Milton mentions in his note on the verse of *PL* refers, not to the varied length of the vowels, as in quantitative prosody, but simply to the proper number of syllables per line. (*The Principles of English Versification* [Cambridge, Mass., 1929], p. 143, n. 1). William Jackson, writing near the end of the eighteenth century, uses "quantity" to mean the number of syllables in a line. (*Thirty Letters on Various Subjects* [London and Exeter, 1783], II, 106, 108). Sprott, on the other hand, believes that Milton by "fit quantity" means the length and weight of syllables, not the number. (*Milton's Art of Prosody*, p. 44). See below, notes 63, 118.

[25] Smith, *Principles*, pp. 117-118.

[26] Edmund Gosse, ed., *The Works of Thomas Gray in Prose and Verse* (New York, 1885), I, 340, n. 1.

a direct reference to a count of the number of syllables in a line. Bede and Augustine had used *"numeri"* to mean a count of the number of syllables in a foot (or sometimes a count of the feet themselves),[27] but to most of the conservative theorists in the eighteenth century, "numbers" carried connotations of strict decasyllabism.[28] The matter is put succinctly in 1763 by the anonymous author of an essay on versification in the *British Magazine:* "Rhythmus, or number, is certainly essential to verse, whether in the dead or living languages; the real difference between the two is this: the number in the ancient verse relates to the feet, but in modern poetry to the syllables."[29] And in the prosodic material scattered through Dryden's works, "numbers" most often refers to the number of syllables in a line.[30] The eighteenth-century conservative prosodists thus appropriated the classical term for meter in general, but narrowed its meaning and gave to it an arithmetical turn expressive of the Newtonian intellectual climate under which the theory of syllabic prosody received its most rigid formulations. This mathematicism had, of course, a strong effect on all the eighteenth-century arts involving temporal repetition; the mere title of a work published in 1688 by Thomas Salmon, *A Proposal to Perform Music in Perfect Mathematical Proportions,* gives an indication of the general intellectual bent of the conservative prosodists.

It is appropriate that a remark by Thomas Hobbes should be one of the earliest statements of syllabism in the period. The prefaces to Davenant's *Gondibert* (1651) have long been recognized as having given the first formal expression to some of the most characteristic Augustan poetic conventions, and it is significant that Hobbes, in his answer to Davenant's Preface, feels the necessity of calling approving attention to the structure of Davenant's line, "wherein the syllables . . . are ten."[31] An early expression of the Restoration prosodists' delight in the other main conservative principle, strict

[27] Israel Baroway, "The Accentual Theory of Hebrew Prosody: A Further Study in Renaissance Interpretation of Biblical Form," *ELH,* XVII (1950), 120.

[28] See T. S. Omond, *English Metrists, Being a Sketch of English Prosodical Criticism from Elizabethan Times to the Present Day* (Oxford, 1921), p. 29; and Smith, *Principles,* p. 112.

[29] Peter Cunningham, ed., *The Works of Oliver Goldsmith* (New York, 1881), III, 361; and see p. 362. This essay has been attributed to both Goldsmith and Smollett, but seems to be by neither. See A. Dwight Culler, "Edward Bysshe and the Poet's Handbook," *PMLA,* LXIII (1948), 880, and Caroline Tupper, "Essays Erroneously Attributed to Goldsmith," *PMLA,* XXXIX (1924), 325-342.

[30] R. D. Jameson, "Notes on Dryden's Lost Prosodia," *MP,* XX (1923), 248. And see above, n. 24.

[31] Sir William Davenant, *Gondibert: An Heroick Poem* (London, 1651), p. 76.

regularity of stress, followed not long after. One "J. D." (not, apparently, John Dryden, although Dryden owned a copy of the work[32]), in his preface to Joshua Poole's *English Parnassus* (1657), pronounces the line

> Though death doth consume, yet vertue preserves

"harsh," and emends it to

> Though death doth ruine, vertue yet preserves.[33]

The unbearable irregularities in the original line are, of course, a pyrrhic foot in the second position which is "compensated" by a following trochee, and a trochee in the fourth position. These are sufficient, however, to give to the line a suggestion of triple cadence, the slightest hint of which in works pretending to seriousness or elevation was anathema to the conservative prosodists. "J. D." goes on to point the moral: "This discovers of what consequence the exact observation of the accent is, which, like right *time* in *Musick,* produces harmony, the want of it harshnesse, and discord."[34] Here we find "harmony," as in Johnson, used with the meaning "strict alternation of accented and unaccented syllables." "J. D." is the first of the Restoration prosodists to employ the musical analogy, and he no doubt would have been sorely troubled if he could have foreseen that this apparently innocent illustration was, later on, to help furnish one of the major premises of "romantic" metrical theory, namely, the assumption of approximate temporal equality among the constituent time units of both poems and musical compositions.

An examination of the numerous prosodic comments made by Dryden and scattered throughout his essays, prefaces, and letters reveals that Dryden was essentially a strict syllabist in theory, but that the concept of accent was also fairly well developed in his prosodic thinking. One of the greatest losses to English prosodic study is that of Dryden's "English *Prosodia,* containing all the mechanical rules of versification," the "materials" for which Dryden said he had collected;[35] if any of this treatise ever was actually written, it surely would be a valuable addition to English prosodic theory. Even without the *Prosodia,* however, one is able to discover that, to Dryden, "The English verse, which we call heroic, consists of no more than ten syllables."[36] The ancients, he maintains, had two advantages over the moderns: they were not obliged to rhyme, "and were less constrained in the quantity of every syllable,

---

[32] Culler, "Edward Bysshe and the Poet's Handbook," pp. 859-860.
[33] *English Parnassus: Or, a Helpe to English Poesie* (London, 1657), sig. A5v.
[34] *Ibid.*
[35] Ker, ed., *Essays,* II, 217.
[36] *Ibid.,* II, 112; see also p. 218. Cf. Sprott, *Milton's Art of Prosody,* p. 47.

which they might vary with spondees or dactyls."[37]   An equal number of syllables in every line results in what Dryden calls "equality of numbers," and this "equality" Dryden regards as a relatively recent improvement in English versification.[38] Dryden's intimate acquaintance with the principles of classical versification led him to emphasize that English verse is composed of feet (although only dissyllabic ones, to be sure), and he thus escaped the extreme syllabic position, which holds that the number of syllables, as in French prosody, is the sole structural criterion for the formation of the English line, and that stress either does not exist or is of such minor importance as to constitute a mere "beauty" and to have no fundamental contribution to make to the syllabic backbone of the line.[39]

One can perceive by now, from examining the views of a few theorists of the Restoration, the nature of the heroic line as it was generally understood: it was to be a line of ten syllables, with the stresses (where these were recognized) falling on the alternate syllables.[40] Such a line was the embodiment of "harmony"; variation in the number of syllables through trisyllabic substitution was not recognized at all, and variation in the position of the stresses could be undertaken only at the poet's extreme peril.[41] "Discord," with all its associations with the metrical and moral disorder of the Jacobean drama, and with its inevitable suggestion of the harsh and broken music of a

---

[37] Ker, ed., *Essays,* I, 12.

[38] *Ibid.,* II, 259.

[39] See Jameson, "Notes on Dryden's Lost Prosodia," p. 252; see also p. 248.

[40] Strict syllabic limitation and, occasionally, regular alternation of stresses are also advanced by the following: Thomas Rymer, "Preface" to translation of Rapin's *Reflections,* in Spingarn, ed., *Critical Essays,* II, 167; Samuel Woodford, *Paraphrase upon the Canticles,* sig. B6; Isaac Watts, *The Art of Reading and Writing English* (3rd ed.; London, 1726), pp. 66-67; John Newbery, *The Art of Poetry on a New Plan: Illustrated with a Great Variety of Examples from the Best English Poets; and of Translations from the Ancients* (London, 1762), I, 9 (Goldsmith is sometimes thought to have had a hand in this revision of *The Art of Poetry Made Easy* [London, 1746]) ; Thomas Percy, *Reliques of Ancient English Poetry: Consisting of Old Heroic Ballads, Songs, and Other Pieces of our Earlier Poets* (London, 1765), II, 269, and n.; James Burnett, Lord Monboddo, *Of the Origin and Progress of Language* (Edinburgh, 1774-1792), II, 385, 390; Hugh Blair, *Lectures on Rhetoric and Belles Lettres,* III, 105; John Scott, *Critical Essays on Some of the Poems of Several English Poets* (London, 1785), pp. 97-98; Lindley Murray, *English Grammar, Adapted to the Different Classes of Learners. With an Appendix Containing Rules and Observations for assisting the More Advanced Students to Write with Perspicuity and Accuracy* (1st Amer. ed.; Boston, 1800), p. 199; and John Walker, *Elements of Elocution. Being the Substance of a Course of Lectures on the Art of Reading; Delivered at Several Colleges in the University of Oxford* (London, 1781), II, 148.

[41] Samuel Wesley offers a succinct statement of the mechanics of this prosodic system:
> If I our *English Numbers* taste aright,
> We in the grave *Iambic* most delight:

civil war still too fresh in the memories of poets and prosodists alike, was waiting as a trap for the careless poet if he should unluckily place a stressed syllable in any but an even-numbered position in the line.

Some Restoration "improvements" of Shakespeare furnish interesting exhibits of this regularistic sensibility in action. Nahum Tate, redacting *Richard III* and confronted with the line

Prevent it, resist it, stop this breach in time,
(IV, i, 148)

is unable to countenance the initial amphibrach which swells the line to a total of eleven syllables. He is able to eliminate the "discord" by the simple expedient of dropping one word:

Prevent, resist it, stop this breach in time.

Tate's line is now absolutely regular both in number of syllables and position of stresses, and is thus fit to be delivered on the Restoration stage. Pope, incidentally, found this particular metrical improvement of Tate's highly satisfactory, and included it in his edition of Shakespeare.[42]

Sir William Davenant, "editing" *Hamlet,* feels impelled to omit the "indeed" from

Indeed, I heard it not: it then draws near the season,
(I, iv, 5)

and thus to reduce a thirteen-syllable line to one of eleven syllables, which, although not quite "harmonious," was felt to be occasionally useful if restricted to dramatic poetry which approached the colloquial.[43] Again, Davenant finds in *Hamlet*

If once I be a widow, ever I be a wife,
(III, ii, 213)

a line of twelve or thirteen syllables, depending on the degree of the reader's contraction of "ever I." The editor smoothes the line to

If once I widow be, and then a wife,

doing away at once with the excessive number of syllables and the suggestion

---

Each *second* Syllable the Voice should *rest,*
Spondees may serve, but still th'*Iambic's* best:
Th'unpleasing *Trochee* always makes a *Blot,*
And lames the *Numbers;* or, if this forgot,
A strong *Spondaic* should the *next* succeed,
The feeble *Wall* will a good Buttress need:
            (*An Epistle to a Friend Concerning Poetry* [London, 1700], p. 14).

[42] Hazelton Spencer, *Shakespeare Improved: The Restoration Versions in Quarto and on the Stage* (Cambridge, Mass., 1927), p. 263.

[43] *Ibid.,* p. 179.

of an anapest in what was before the fifth foot.[44]

In 1687, a "Person of Quality" produced a version of the first book of the *Faerie Queene* in "heroick numbers," and the first four lines of the resultant product, *Spenser Redivivus,* indicate the way regularization of the position of stresses went hand in hand with the purging of "Gothick" diction and the Augustan tendency towards increased generality of description:

> A Worthy Knight was Riding on the Plain,
> In Armour clad, which richly did contain
> The gallant Marks of many Batels fought,
> Tho' he before no Martial Habit sought.[45]

Spenser's lines had read:

> A Gentle Knight was pricking on the plaine,
> Y cladd in mightie armes and siluer shielde,
> Wherein old dints of deepe wounds did remaine,
> The cruell markes of many a bloudy fielde.
>
> (I, i, 1-4)

In the third line here, the spondee in the second position and the trochee in the fourth are felt to be too violent an interruption of the regular flow of stresses, and they are consequently smoothed out. It is interesting to notice that the redactor also omits the expletive "did" in the same line; the "feeble aid" of such auxiliaries was felt to be a blemish long before Pope cleverly condemned their use.[46]

4. Edward Bysshe

The name of Edward Bysshe, together with those of Joshua Steele, Sidney Lanier, and Robert Bridges, is certainly one of the best known in the history of English prosodic theory; execration has been heaped on Bysshe's head by literary and prosodic historians alike, and to those intent on demonstrating what was wrong with eighteenth-century prosodic writing, the name of Bysshe has come most readily to hand. Edward Bysshe was a Sussex man and may have been one of Shelley's ancestors. ("Which would be humorous," Saintsbury comments.[47]) In 1702, Bysshe published *The Art of English Poetry,* which consists of three separate sections. First comes *"Rules* for making VERSES," which offers Bysshe's prosodic creed; this is followed by a collection of "the most Natural, Agreeable, and Sublime *THOUGHTS,"* extracted

[44] *Ibid.*   106426

[45] See F. W. Bateson, *English Poetry: A Critical Introduction* (London, 1950), p. 166, n. 1.

[46] In the *Essay on Criticism,* II, 146.

[47] *A History of English Prosody* (London, 1906-1910), II, 573, n. 1.

from "the best *ENGLISH* POETS,'' and the whole is concluded by a rhyming dictionary which furnished the foundation for all subsequent aids of the same kind. (In fact, the "Vocabulary of Rhymes" in *Webster's Collegiate Dictionary* [edition of 1947] is "based ultimately and essentially on Bysshe."[48]) *The Art of English Poetry* was an extremely popular work, and new editions were called for in 1705, 1708, 1710, 1714, 1718, 1724, 1737, and 1762.[49] As late as 1757, the book was still being used by schoolboys as a *vade mecum* for the manufacture of English verses. Hogarth's print of "The Distressed Poet" (1736) depicts a shabby versifier in the act of composing "Poverty, a Poem" in a garret, his copy of Bysshe open beside him.[50] Samuel Richardson availed himself of Bysshe's collection of *"THOUGHTS"* for sentiments for his characters to deliver: there are at least three borrowings from Bysshe's second section in *Pamela,* five in *Sir Charles Grandison,* and a total of 43 in *Clarissa.*[51] Smollett probably owned a copy, for Jery Melford in *Humphry Clinker* uses Bysshe's very words when he opines that "[our verses] are reckoned by the number of syllables," whereas those of the ancients were constructed according to the number of feet.[52] Goldsmith owned two copies of Bysshe,[53] and Blake put his copy (or at least the middle section of it) to rather extraordinary uses: "On an August morning in 1807, wrote William Blake, 'My Wife was told by a Spirit to look for her fortune by opening by chance a book which she had in her hand; it was Bysshe's "Art of Poetry." ' When she happened on a most licentious passage by Aphra Behn concerning sexual enjoyment, Blake professed himself 'so well pleased with her Luck that I thought I would try my own,' but the *Sortes Bysshianae,* unwilling to oblige a second time, gave him only a description of an oak tree in a storm."[54]

Copies of Bysshe's book were also owned by Johnson, Bulwer-Lytton, Coleridge, Byron, and Rossetti.[55] There must have been few literary persons during the eighteenth century who did not occasionally have recourse to *The Art of English Poetry,* although, judging from the varying degrees of contempt in which it was held by Walpole, Oldys, Fielding, and Sir Walter

[48] Culler, "Edward Bysshe and the Poet's Handbook," p. 867.

[49] *Ibid.,* p. 861. A useful facsimile reprint of Part I of Bysshe's 3rd ed. (1708) is A. Dwight Culler's edition of *The Art of English Poetry* (Augustan Reprint Society, Publication No. 40; Los Angeles, 1953).

[50] Culler, "Edward Bysshe and the Poet's Handbook," p. 864.

[51] *Ibid.,* pp. 870-871.

[52] *Ibid.,* p. 881.

[53] Henry Austin Dobson, *Eighteenth-Century Vignettes, First Series* (World's Classics ed.; London, 1923), p. 164.

[54] Culler, "Edward Bysshe and the Poet's Handbook," p. 864.

[55] *Ibid.,* p. 866; p. 864.

Scott, among others, it must never have been the thing to do to admit publicly to ownership of the book.[56] Charles Gildon, writing in 1721, dwells angrily on Bysshe's influence with the poetry-reading public, especially with the younger and less well-educated readers, and describes Bysshe's book as one "too scandalously mean to name, which, by the arts of the *booksellers* concerned, has spread, by many editions, thro' all England, and corrupted, or at least continued the corruption of the young readers and lovers of poetry."[57] Again, Gildon reveals the wide dispersal and influence of *The Art of English Poetry:* "The plausibility of his title has carried off so many impressions, as have made it with the ignorant, the *Standard* of Writing."[58]

Bysshe's influential work is important as the first systematic formulation and presentation of the principles of the system of syllabic prosody into which most English verse since the fourteenth century had been gradually settling. Bysshe's fantastic popularity is partly to be explained by the fact that he was the first to offer what seemed a sound and comprehensive explanation of the prosodic phenomena of the English line; when Bysshe is accused of simply applying the principles of French metric to English poetry, it should be remembered that the poetry itself had for decades earlier been approaching a condition for the explanation and elucidation of which French prosodic theory was both readily available and eminently suitable. Du Bos's rules for French verse were, as I have shown, capable of explaining all the characteristics of the contemporary English line except the disposition of accents. The fact that we are able to understand that Bysshe's prosody "explained" nothing at all is largely beside the point; what is of importance is that the early eighteenth-century ear, at least up until Gildon's attempted refutation of Bysshe in 1718, found little in the metrical structure of English verse that Bysshe's treatise did not sufficiently cover. If Bysshe understates the role of accent, it is not primarily because the French theorists had neglected accent, but because Bysshe, together with the bulk of his readers, was so little aware of the structural importance of accent in English poetry that he felt it not worth wasting time on. As it happens, Bysshe did practically translate a French work, Claude Lancelot's *Quatre Traitez de Poësies, Latine, Françoise, Italienne, et Espagnole* (1663), and reproduce it as his first section; from Lancelot's treatment of Spanish prosody, Bysshe appropriated most of his rules

[56] *Ibid.,* p. 864.

[57] *The Laws of Poetry, as Laid Down by the Duke of Buckinghamshire in his Essay on Poetry, By the Earl of Roscommon in his Essay on Translated Verse, and by the Lord Lansdowne on Unnatural Flights in Poetry, Explain'd and Illustrated* (London, 1721), p. 72.

[58] *The Complete Art of Poetry. In Six Parts* (London, 1718), I, 93.

for the position of the cesura in English, and from Lancelot's section on French prosody *("Breve Instruction")*, Bysshe derived almost all the rest of his prosodic system, including his syllabic explanations of English verse structure.[59] Gildon was the first to tax Bysshe with merely laying French theory over English practice,[60] but Gildon did not think of asking why Bysshe's French system had seemed to its early readers such a wholly satisfactory explanation of English meter.

As has been said, "The syllable is the 'Faith' of Bysshe's creed":[61] "The structure of our verses," Bysshe begins, "whether Blank, or in Rhyme, consists in a certain Number of Syllables; not in Feet compos'd of long and short Syllables, as the Verses of the *Greeks* and *Romans."*[62] Throughout, "due Number of Syllables"[63] is the main structural basis of the line. Lines of blank verse are lines "where the Measure [*i.e.*, the "due" number of syllables] is exactly kept without Rhyme."[64] Bysshe does mention accent, but his rejection of foot prosody prevents him from promulgating the usual rule that the accent must fall on every even syllable of the heroic line. Instead, Bysshe substitutes a system of three "main" or "prevailing" accents in the heroic line, which must invariably fall on the second, fourth, and sixth syllables; the customary stresses on the eighth and tenth syllables are strangely neglected.[65] A reading of "J. D.'s" contribution was apparently fresh in Bysshe's mind when he wrote that the observation of his rules for the placement of the "prevailing" three stresses on the second, fourth, and sixth syllables, "like . . . right Time in Musick, will produce Harmony; the Neglect of them Harshness and Discord." Bysshe consequently finds Davenant's lines

> None think Rewards render'd worthy their Worth,

and

> And both Lovers, both thy Disciples were,

completely devoid of "the Sound of . . . Verse," since the first has stresses

---

[59] Culler, "Edward Bysshe and the Poet's Handbook," p. 877. T. S. Omond, ignorant of Bysshe's enormous debt to Lancelot, makes the interesting point—and one not at all vitiated by his ignorance of Bysshe's source—that Bysshe's system is actually merely a more definite statement of the notions of English metric which the Elizabethan grammarians had been advancing. Bysshe's having had recourse to the French treatise for the best existing explanation of English verse structure does not alter the fact that the English metric which needed explanation was, for all practical purposes, a French one. (See *English Metrists,* p. 32).

[60] *Complete Art of Poetry,* I, 93, 293.

[61] Saintsbury, *History,* II, 538.

[62] *Art of English Poetry* (4th ed.; London, 1710), p. 1.

[63] *Ibid.,* p. 12. Cf. Milton's "fit quantity."

[64] *Ibid.,* p. 35.

[65] *Ibid.,* p. 6.

on the fifth and seventh syllables, and the second has an accent on the third. The lines may be "mended" by these alterations:

> None think Rewards are equal to their Worth,

and

> And Lovers both, both thy Disciples were.[66]

But these few strictures about the wrong placement of accent are not, I think, sufficient to prove that Bysshe "obviously desiderated alternation of stressed and unstressed syllables."[67] What Bysshe really "desiderated," we shall never know, but what he stated to be the quintessence of the English line in the *Art of English Poetry* was the number of syllables it contained; the matter of the proper placement of his three most important accents was put forth in his work as a secondary consideration.[68] Bysshe plainly approves of English lines which are as regular in stress as possible (much the way moderns permit themselves to be pleased by "vowel music" and the like, not as a structural ideal but as an embellishment), but he is restrained from making strict alternation of stressed and unstressed syllables the prime basis of the line by his desire to reject the classical foot system; he and his contemporary readers were left with the number of syllables as the "defining principle,"[69] and, until the work of Charles Gildon appeared in 1718, the English poetic line was generally felt to have been sufficiently defined when its "due" number of syllables was asserted.

The popularity of Bysshe's work began to wane around 1765,[70] but it continued, until the beginning of the nineteenth century, to serve as the generally accepted explanation of the major phenomena of English verse structure. Bysshe succeeded in codifying ("mummifying," Saintsbury says[71]) in a brief and easily comprehended form the early eighteenth-century conservative theory of prosody; he "seems, somehow or other, to find himself expressing what everybody had been thinking more or less confusedly for more than a generation; and what almost everybody was to think it proper to think for more than one or two generations more."[72] And as a recent commentator puts it, Bysshe's *"Rules* for making VERSES,"* "although wrong, unoriginal, and perverse, have an importance far beyond their merit. . . . for they took a metrical criticism which was hesitating uncertainly between three different

---

[66] *Ibid.,* pp. 5-6.
[67] Smith, *Principles,* p. 113.
[68] See Culler, ed., *The Art of English Poetry,* pp. ii-iii.
[69] Culler, "Edward Bysshe and the Poet's Handbook," pp. 872-873.
[70] *Ibid.,* p. 862.
[71] *History,* II, 541.
[72] *Ibid.,* II, 537.

prosodic systems, the quantitative, the accentual, and the syllabic, and by formulating for the first time a complete, explicit *prosodia,* they confirmed it in the one it was already favoring, the syllabic system of the French."[73] This is well said, but one would want to be a little more certain that modern metrical theorists have succeeded admirably in elucidating metrical aspects of genuinely contemporary poetry before censuring Bysshe for being "wrong." Bysshe was generally right, I believe, in so far as he restricted himself to examining the poetry of his contemporaries; it can hardly be considered Bysshe's fault that most of his contemporaries were already producing verse which lent itself admirably to explanation along French lines, nor should it be thought the result of a failing of Bysshe's that eighteenth-century prosody is neither nineteenth nor twentieth-century prosody. A sober examination of the efforts of some who have sought to "explain" the metrical practice of the 1940's and 1950's by reference to the work of Kipling, Masefield, and Noyes[74] will show that Bysshe at least had the will to face the verse of his contemporaries, and it is not evident that he performed much more ludicrously than most modern metrists do when confronted by the work of Ezra Pound.

5. *The Solidification of Conservative Principles*

Bysshe's treatise supplied the need for a handy formulation of English prosodic theory for a number of years. Between 1702 and 1718, we come upon little except generalized pleas for even greater regulation, especially in the lyric. William Coward, for example, in 1709, calls for some specific rules to control the type of feet permitted in lyric verse:

> LYRIC with us is nothing but a song,
> Wrote with what Numbers we imagine fit.[75]

The idea of composers of lyrics using whatever feet they please strikes Coward as a lax and dangerous business, and he feels the need of some modern Horace to lay down the prosodic law for the regulation of stress variation in the lighter *genres.*

Nine years after this reactionary performance, Charles Gildon, apparently envious of Bysshe's reputation as pre-eminent prosodist of Great Britain, entered the lists against him. Matthew Green has helped perpetuate Gildon's

---

[73] Culler, "Edward Bysshe and the Poet's Handbook," p. 878.

[74] See, *e.g.,* Evelyn H. Scholl, "English Metre Once More," *PMLA,* LXIII (1948), 293-326.

[75] *Licentia Poetica discuss'd: or, the True Test of Poetry. Without which it is Difficult to Judge of, or Compose, A Correct English Poem* (London, 1709), p. 81.

name in *The Spleen:*

> Nothing is stol'n: my Muse, though mean,
> Draws from the spring she finds within;
> Nor vainly buys what Gildon sells,
> Poetic buckets for dry wells.
>
> (13-16)

Green was referring primarily to the sixth and last section of Gildon's *Complete Art of Poetry* (1718), a section containing the customary collection of "beautiful" thoughts from the "best *English* poets." The other five parts of Gildon's book are in dialogue form, and the fifth dialogue contains most of the matter which is of interest here. Gildon's major effort is to discredit Bysshe by any available means, and he chooses to differ with Bysshe by preferring foot prosody to Bysshe's predominantly syllabic system. Gildon is well aware, in a way that some modern critics have not been, that Bysshe was emphasizing the number of syllables as the primary criterion of the English line, and that Bysshe was intentionally understating the structural role of accent.[76] Gildon inquires with mock incredulity whether Bysshe actually believes that "an *English Verse* can be made without any regard to the *Length* or the *Shortness* of the Syllables? This would banish Prose entirely, and make every ten Syllables an *Heroic* Verse, than which nothing can be more false and absurd."[77] ("Length" and "Shortness," of course, in Gildon as in many others, mean substantially "stressed" and "unstressed."[78]) Gildon recognizes the theoretical possibility of a trisyllabic foot in English, but often scans as if no such foot actually exists.[79] Despite Gildon's forceful attempt to consider the English line in terms of feet, and consequently to suggest the structural office of accent in English verse, the prosodic field was still Bysshe's for a good many years, and syllabism continued for a time to offer itself as the readiest explanation of the line.

Another effort to apply the concept of feet, however, was made by Alexander Malcolm in his *Treatise of Musick* (1721). Attempting a rebuttal of Isaac Vossius, the Dutchman, who had been saying that English verse was constructed according to the Bysshian "certain number of syllables" with no attention to the position of stresses,[80] Malcolm argues, "Now, what a rash and unjust Criticism is this! . . . 'Tis true, we don't follow the metrical Composition of the Ancients; yet we have such a mixture of strong and soft, long

---

[76] See *The Complete Art of Poetry,* I, 267-303.
[77] *Ibid.,* I, 294.
[78] *Ibid.,* I, 299.
[79] *Ibid.,* I, 267-303.
[80] See *De Poematum Cantu et Viribus Rythmi* (London, 1673).

and short Syllables, as makes our Verse slow, rapid, smooth, or rumbling, agreeable to the subject."[81] It was becoming more plain every year that such onomatopoeic and representative-meter effects as those which Dryden's translation of the *Aeneid* had accustomed readers to look for were not wholly to be explained in terms of the purely syllabic theory.

Around 1743, the Scot James Thomson received from his friend George Lyttelton some help in the composition of "Autumn" for *The Seasons,* and the resulting few lines of blank verse are interesting prosodically, set contrastingly as they are in the midst of lines of a different character. Lyttelton's eleven lines ("Autumn," 207-217) contain only three feet which are not iambs; one of these is the universally sanctioned initial trochee, and the other two are pyrrhics in the third position.[82] This extreme regularity of stress (there is much less variation here than in the bulk of Pope's couplet verse) indicates that Lyttelton held the view of the structure of blank verse which most of his contemporaries shared. For it was generally believed that, deprived of the regular recurrence of rhyme, blank verse had to compensate for this loss of a regularizing device by displaying a more regular pattern of stresses than the heroic couplet required. There had to be, in other words, at least one rhythmical phenomenon which recurred with sufficient regularity to be very strongly marked; in the absence of the regularly beating "chime" of rhyme, the stresses were the only material the poet had left to enable him to produce the desired effect of an exactly regular recurrence. Variations, even as rare and innocent as those in Lyttelton's "Autumn" blank verse, were generally regarded by the conservatives as "licenses." Lyttelton also suggested that Thomson replace the line

> Unbounded, tossing in a flood of corn
> ("Autumn," 42)

with one of his own more regular composition, which read,

> O'er waving golden fields of ripened corn.

But Thomson preferred to retain his stress variety.[83]

A convenient way to examine the metrical expectations of the extreme syllabist and regularist school is to inspect one of the greatest mementos of this complex of dead aesthetic presuppositions, Richard Bentley's edition of

[81] *A Treatise of Musick. Speculative, Practical, and Historical* (Edinburgh, 1721), p. 604.

[82] J. L. Robertson, ed., *The Seasons and The Castle of Indolence* (Oxford, 1891), pp. 320-321. And see G. C. Macaulay, "Thomson and Pope," *The Athenaeum*, Oct. 1, 1904, p. 446.

[83] Robertson, ed., *Seasons*, p. 316.

Paradise Lost, which appeared in 1732. Bentley's prosodic "emendations" reveal that he expects two things of the English blank verse line: decasyllabic purity and absolute stress regularity in the iambic pattern. Bentley is completely innocent of the concept of "unity in variety," which was becoming the fashionable way in some quarters to justify Milton's stress variations. To Bentley, a Miltonic line is the better the closer it approaches perfect conformity with the two interlocking ideals of regularity; one wonders in what interesting way Bentley read Milton's note on the verse, with its specific mention of "apt numbers" (*i.e.,* numbers varied according to the sense).

A very few examples are enough to show Bentley's method of proceeding. He finds Milton's line

> Created hugest that swim th'Ocean stream
> (I, 202)

"very absonous," and suggests in its stead,

> Of all the Kinds that swim the Ocean stream.[84]

Even the new hiatus in the fourth foot of Bentley's line, surely enough to offend the ears of most classical scholars, is apparently preferable to Milton's pyrrhic and spondee in the third and fourth places. Bentley prints Milton's

> Thus *Belial* with words clothed in Reason's garb
> (II, 226)

with a stress carefully marked over "with," and then pronounces that "This is harsh Measure, and Accent unnatural." He would prefer it to read,

> *Thus* HE *with Words* ARRAY'D *in Reason's garb.*[85]

This stressing of "with" indicates that Bentley's ear had become so accustomed to the regular iambic pattern that he was unable to read a line from *Paradise Lost* or apprehend its cadence, and, as will be seen shortly, Bentley was only one among hundreds with the same aural difficulty. It should be evident from this exhibition of Bentley's that what we observe here is in reality not a superficial matter of a mere metrical theory unconnected with the more central aesthetic positions of the age, but is instead part of a total rhythmical complex with its roots deep in the psychology and even perhaps the physiology of these prosodic conservatives. A scholar like Bentley, one of the most learned men of his time, in his anxiety to behold evidence of temporal regularity where it does not necessarily exist, is here to be seen paying almost no attention to the meaning of Milton's lines, and laying a strong stress on a word which almost never takes it in English, and which by no mere mistake could

---

[84] *Milton's Paradise Lost. A New Edition* (London, 1732), p. 10.
[85] *Ibid.,* p. 45.

be conceived of as taking it in this line. The nature and rationale of this anxiety of Bentley's will become, I hope, clearer soon.

Bentley proceeds thus through *Paradise Lost,* correcting "bad accent" wherever it seems not sufficiently in accord with the pure iambic pattern. In just such a way, it has been suggested, a "neo-classical" twenty-first or twenty-second century which finds triple time "harsh" will perhaps "versify" Rossetti and other Victorians, and seek to rework the rhythmical bases of modern poetry (whatever they may prove to be) so that it will be at least comprehensible to readers whose rhythmical expectations will have altered drastically from the Victorians' and ours.[86] The spectacle of Bentley going about his bizarre work is not, I believe, simply an occasion for the exercise of rage or jocularity; it is a challenge to discover the basis and significance of this particular prosodic sensibility, and to see if a partial explanation can be found in the more general aesthetic theories of the century.

Typical as Bentley is of the class of highly conservative stress-regularists who flourished well into the nineteenth century, it is reassuring to recall that his edition of Milton was almost universally damned,[87] and that the extreme prosodic sensibility which Bentley represented was never in a completely stable and unquestioned position of rule, even during the syllabic prosody's palmiest days. Johnson's gentlemanly remark that Bentley was "perhaps better skilled in grammar than in poetry"[88] is, in fact, one of the kindest things that have ever been said of the man and of his edition of *Paradise Lost;* the contemporary reception of Bentley's work was one of immense hostility and outrage. There were many who held a "theoretical" view of absolute stress regularity in blank verse, but there were few who had not been persuaded to permit certain "licenses" in practice, and there were fewer still who could watch without anger the prosodic emendation of a secure classic by a scholar with apparently nothing whatever of the poetic in him.

For the delectation of those, however, who did demand an almost absolute regularity of stress in their blank verse, Richard Glover produced his dreary epic *Leonidas* in 1737. Perhaps the extremists had had their tastes

---

[86] Stewart, *Modern Metrical Technique,* p. 63.

[87] See James Henry Monk, *The Life of Richard Bentley, D.D., . . . With an Account of his Writings* (London, 1830), pp. 577-588. J. W. Mackail says that "It was received, first with a feeling akin to stupefaction, and then with an universal roar of anger or derision." (*Bentley's Milton* [British Academy Warton Lecture on English Poetry, XV; London, 1924], p. 5). *Milton Restor'd and Bentley Deposed* (London, 1732), which has been erroneously attributed to Swift, has, oddly enough, no comment to make on Bentley's metrical emendations, but mocks only his strictures on obscurity, hyperbole, and the like.

[88] Hill, ed., *Lives,* I, 181.

whetted by Bentley's regularization of Milton's prosody; at any rate, the blank verse of *Leonidas* displays an almost total regularity of accent, with only very occasional initial trochees and even more rare internal pyrrhics for variation. Despite the fact that the poem contains over 5000 lines almost unvaried by the use of any feet other than iambic, *Leonidas* was widely read (no doubt mainly for its political tendencies), and a year after its publication, Henry Pemberton stepped forth with an "appreciation" of (among other things) Glover's prosody in *Observations on Poetry, Especially the Epic: Occasioned by The Late Poem upon Leonidas* (1738).

To Pemberton, "the slightest variation of accenting is . . . a positive blemish."[89] He is accordingly gratified to be able to report that "The author of Leonidas appears to have been very attentive to the just measure of his verse."[90] Pemberton conceives of the heroic line as a line of ten syllables with every even-numbered syllable "receiving some degree of emphasis" and "pronounced in a longer time [!] than the rest."[91] Pemberton, like "J.D.," and obviously not searching very deeply into its real implications, uses the poetry-music analogy to support his view that an occasional trochee in an iambic line, except when used initially, disturbs "the equality of the movement"[92] and "renders the verse less perfect."[93] "In all verses distinguishably melodious," Pemberton asserts, "we shall on examination find the just measure always to have been observed."[94] Needless to say, "just measure" means here "absolute regularity of stress." The very minute amount of variety Pemberton's ear does crave is supplied by Glover's "varied" employment of words of different lengths. No matter how regularly the stresses fall, Pemberton is convinced that the verse can be so diversified by "the different relations of the words to the feet" as "not to offend by any insipid similarity."[95] Pemberton also believes in the ability of the varied cesura to impart such variety that there is no necessity whatever to employ any substitution.[96] This is Bentleyism with a vengeance, but so few prosodists disagreed immediately with Pemberton (or indeed even noticed his work) that one may assume that theoretical stress regularity could be regarded by the less extreme critics as something rather

[89] Omond, *English Metrists,* p. 48.
[90] *Observations on Poetry, Especially the Epic: Occasioned by The Late Poem upon Leonidas* (London, 1738), p. 134.
[91] *Ibid.,* p. 130.
[92] *Ibid.,* p. 114.
[93] *Ibid.,* p. 131.
[94] *Ibid.,* p. 133.
[95] *Ibid.*
[96] *Ibid.,* pp. 133-134.

harmlessly "academic," and dangerous only when it occasioned the deface-
ment of works of which they had grown fond.

William Benson, in his *Letters Concerning Poetical Translations, and
Virgil's and Milton's Arts of Verse* (1739), chooses to ally himself with
Gildon against Bysshe, and to prefer the conception of a certain number of
feet to that of a certain number of syllables. Had Benson permitted trisyllabic
feet, the way would perhaps have been open to a breaking, at least on the
theoretical level, of the syllabic limitation, and to an early gesture towards a
rudimentary "equal-time" theory. The timid Benson, however, fails to press
his point, except to intimate that there might be a foot used in the English
heroic line with more than two syllables.[97] Even then, one suspects that all
Benson has in mind is the use of hendecasyllabic lines in verse other than
dramatic.

It would be fatiguing and unrewarding to discuss the prosodic theories
contained in the multitude of school grammars produced during the century.
They are almost without exception devoid of originality, one author merely
copying his predecessor and adding new exercises for the use of pupils. The
notion of the English line set forth in Thomas Dilworth's *New Guide to the
English Tongue* (1740) is typical enough in its catechistic form and Bysshian
matter to represent the whole school-grammar *genus:*

> Q. *What is a* Verse?
> A. . . . in Poetical Writings, it conveys unto us an Idea of a certain
> Number of *Syllables* artfully compacted in one Line, to gratify
> the Ear.[98]

It will be seen that no matter in what precise shape the Bysshian conception
presents itself, the formula "a certain number of syllables" is sure to appear
as the major condition of the definition.

James Harris, writing in 1744, rings an interesting variation on the
Bysshian syllabic definition: "An *English Heroic* verse," Harris announces
with the air of a man who has just made a discovery vital to the future development of English prosodic theory, "consists of ten *Semipeds,* or Half-
feet."[99] But call the syllables what he will, Harris is still safely within the
fold of syllabism and stress regularity.

It was during the 1740's that the theory of syllabic prosody received its
first telling opposition. My purpose at present, however, is only to indicate

---

[97] *Letters Concerning Poetical Translations, and Virgil's and Milton's Arts of Verse.
&c.* (London, 1739), p. 15.
[98] *A New Guide to the English Tongue. In Five Parts* (Boston, 1770), p. 89.
[99] *Three Treatises. The First Concerning Art. The Second Concerning Music, Painting, and Poetry. The Third Concerning Happiness* (London, 1744), p. 92, n. "e."

something of the nature of the theories of syllabism and stress regularity, and to show how the theories tended, through unexamined repetition, to solidify into an extremely inelastic body of conventional reactions and uninvestigated presuppositions. Despite the very cogent attacks on the whole syllabic system which began at about this time, the syllabists for well over a half century more were to advance their theories with an almost total unconcern for the ever-increasing harassment they were receiving from various dissenters and prosodic radicals.

Edward Manwaring's *Of Harmony and Numbers, in Latin and English Prose, and in English Poetry* (1744) repeated a great many ideas advanced earlier in his *Stichology* (1737) and *An Historical and Critical Account of the Most Eminent Classic Authors in Poetry and History* (1737). Manwaring approaches English verse in much the same way as he does classical: he first assumes *a priori* that prosodic practice is fundamentally rational and reducible to a set of definite rules and readily apprehensible principles of order; he then recommends that "in reading the Poets we . . . enquire after these Principles, and where-ever these Principles are contradicted and violated, we are to look upon the Poetry as absurd and vitious."[100] Here again is a suggestion of the familiar association of prosodic predictability with reason and with moral rectitude which Johnson was to help dignify to the status of a coherent and almost self-contained ethic of prosody. Manwaring sometimes appears to reject both Bysshe's syllabism and Gildon's foot prosody, but he really does little more than parrot Harris' banal conception of "half Feet."[101] In *Of Harmony and Numbers,* Manwaring returns to the official Bysshian formulation, and indicates that he has been proceeding all along in terms of ten syllables, "which is the Measure of *English* Heroic Poetry."[102] Perhaps the best indication of Manwaring's prosodic sensibility, and that of a great many of his fellow conservatives, can be given by his statement "all Poetry partakes of the Elements of Geometry and Musick"; in fact, "the best Interpreters of poetical Numbers are those who apply the Rules of Musick and Geometry to Poetry."[103] Equipped in this way for an examination of some typically stress-varied lines in *Paradise Lost,* it is not surprising to find Man-

[100] *Stichology: or, a Recovery of the Latin, Greek, and Hebrew Numbers. Exemplified in the Reduction of all Horace's Metres, and the Greek and Hebrew Poetry* (London, 1737), p. 38.
[101] *Of Harmony and Numbers, in Latin and English Prose, and in English Poetry* (London, 1744), p. 37.
[102] *Ibid.,* p. 42.
[103] *Stichology,* p. 74.

waring adjudging them "no Poetry."[104]

6. Samuel Johnson

The most distinguished literary sensibility to ally himself with the conservative prosodic tradition in the eighteenth century was Samuel Johnson. Johnson customarily makes a rigid distinction between theoretical and practical prosodic ideals: in his theory, he will be found to prefer the absolutely regular pure iambic line, but, faced with a poem of obvious merit written in "mixed" iambic measure (that is, with an occasional dissyllabic substitution), he will generally accept the situation manfully. In his own words, "The heroick measure of the *English* language may be properly considered as pure or mixed. It is pure when the accent rests upon every second syllable throughout the whole line. . . . The repetition of this sound or percussion at equal times, is the most complete harmony of which a single verse is capable, and should therefore be exactly kept in distiches. . . . "[105] It may be noticed here that Johnson, perhaps inadvertently, uses the phrase "percussion at equal times," which, if extended logically, could have served a prosodist of less conservative tastes as a hint towards the development of an equal-time, and ultimately accentual and anti-syllabic, theory of prosody. As "harmony" in Johnson's words above can be taken to mean "theoretical stress regularity," so "dissonance" comes to serve as a useful description of the result of an internal trochaic substitution.[106] It is mainly Milton's substitutions, even those which are read purely dissyllabically and consequently do not offend any canon of syllabic limitation, which are behind Johnson's continual suspicion of that poet's prosody. "He has indeed," Johnson says, "been more attentive to his syllables than to his accents."[107] Milton thus falls into "dissonance" too often by forgetting that "harmony is the end of poetical measures."[108] Johnson also uses the word "harsh" not so much to refer to ugly collocations of consonants as to serve as a virtual synonym for "irregular in stress." Writing of *Samson Agonistes*, Johnson says, "The versification is in the dialogue much more smooth and harmonious than in the parts allotted to the chorus, which are

---

[104] *Of Harmony and Numbers*, pp. 49-50.

[105] *The Rambler. In Four Volumes* (12th ed.; London, 1793), II, 184-185. (No. 86, Sat., Jan. 12, 1751). In the same essay, however, Johnson maintains that "to preserve the series of sounds untransposed in a long composition, is not only very difficult, but tiresome and disgusting; for we are soon wearied with the perpetual recurrence of the same cadence." Johnson permits the "mixed" measure in blank verse, but (the first foot excepted) no more than one dissyllabic substitution is to be allowed per line.

[106] *Ibid.*, II, 188.

[107] *Ibid.*, II, 197. (No. 88, Sat., Jan. 19, 1751).

[108] *Ibid.*, II, 207. (No. 90, Sat., Jan. 26, 1751).

often so harsh and dissonant, as scarce to preserve, whether the lines end with or without rhymes, any appearance of metrical regularity."[109]

The brief Prosody prefixed to Johnson's *Dictionary* (1755) has been called "the second most influential document in eighteenth-century metrical criticism,"[110] the first in importance being, of course, Bysshe's *Art of English Poetry*. Johnson's remarks on meter in the *Dictionary* served to buttress further what Bysshe had codified, and to supply the second half of the century, as Bysshe had the first, with a stable and authoritative body of conservative prosodic standards.

The definition of versification which opens the section on prosody in the *Dictionary* has the true Bysshian ring: "VERSIFICATION is the arrangement of a certain number of syllables according to certain laws."[111] Johnson goes on to deny, as Dryden had, the existence of a trisyllabic foot in English: "The feet of our verses are either iambick . . . or trochaick. . . . "[112] Theoretical stress regularity is required, but it is plain that, in practice, Johnson was willing to permit the more genteel variations. "In all [iambic] measures," he writes, "the accents are to be placed on even syllables; and every line considered by itself is more harmonious, as this rule is more strictly observed."[113] The phrase "considered by itself" is an indication that Johnson was quite aware of his distinction between theoretical prosody and its practical applications.

It has been noticed by neither of the two most competent modern historians of prosodic theory[114] that Johnson came to feel the unsatisfactoriness of this attempt to retain the concept of absolute stress regularity by relegating it to an untouchable theoretical sphere; Johnson's rule advancing theoretical stress regularity cited above is generally quoted alone to expose his prosodic authoritarianism in as unfavorable a light as possible. Few have taken the trouble to read what Johnson felt it necessary to add to this rule for iambic measures in the fourth edition of the *Dictionary* (1773), the first reprinting of the work to contain any revisions. In this revised version, Johnson adds to the words "every line considered by itself is more harmonious, as this rule is more strictly observed," the warning, "The variations necessary to pleasure

---

[109] *Ibid.*, III, 208. (No. 140, Sat., July 20, 1751). Note that Johnson defines "smooth" in the *Dictionary* as "Equal in pace; without starts or obstructions." Internal trochaic substitution would be a perfect example of "obstruction."

[110] Culler, "Edward Bysshe and the Poet's Handbook," p. 881.

[111] *A Dictionary of the English Language* (London, 1755), sig. N1ᵛ.

[112] *Ibid.*

[113] *Ibid.*, sig. O.

[114] *I.e.*, Saintsbury and Omond.

belong to the art of poetry, not the rules of grammar."[115] Since Johnson feels that he is here merely treating the principles of prosody as they form a part of the larger system of English grammar, bare rules are sufficient, and the inevitable exceptions are to be looked for elsewhere. Now whether this *caveat* added to the fourth edition of the *Dictionary* is evidence of a general reconsideration of his basic theory, or whether it was merely inserted to help quiet the ever-increasing clamor which his original stress-regularity rule had aroused in the camp of the prosodic liberals, it is impossible to tell.[116] It does seem unlikely that a thinker devoted to the propagation of "fixed principles" should publicly indicate that some of his were losing their requisite rigidity. Johnson's 1773 disclaimer is certainly an indication, whatever its real motivation, that he was publicly and officially willing to recognize certain irregularities in meter if they were plainly the result of conscious art and were not simply evidence of a fatuous search for novelty or an immoral indulgence in an "amiable" loosening of the universally esteemed prosodic bonds. But to Johnson, these irregularities, in prosody as in morality, are still "licenses," and "Our versification admits of few licenses. . . . "[117]

Taken together, Johnson's scattered prosodic judgments served to impart to a system still essentially Bysshian a needed rehabilitation, and the added weight which the theory of syllabism and stress regularity received from Johnson's support gave it a respectability in the latter half of the century almost as formidable as that which it had maintained during the first fresh excitement over "the French way of writing."

7. *Post-Johnsonian Conservatism*

From Johnson's massive theorizings down to the irresponsible and shallow blusterings of William Kenrick is a great step indeed, but Kenrick's purely automatic reference to "an Arithmetical Quantity of Syllables"[118] as the basis of the English line in one of his facetious miscellanies reveals that the same syllabism was conceived as governing the poetic productions of Grub Street as was thought to be, at times, a manifestation of Divine Law in

---

[115] *Dictionary* (6th ed.; London, 1785), sig. h4v.

[116] It seems likely that an acquaintance with John Rice's *Introduction to the Art of Reading with Energy and Propriety* (London, 1765) may have caused Johnson to add the new sentence in his revision of the *Dictionary*. Rice is extremely caustic throughout about Johnson's authoritarianism, and he devotes particular attention to the specific passage which Johnson later felt in need of revision.

[117] *Dictionary* (6th ed.), sig. h6.

[118] *The Kapélion, or Poetical Ordinary; Consisting of a Great Variety of Dishes in Prose and Verse; Recommended to all who have a good Taste or keen Appetite* (London, 1753), p. 13. Cf. Milton's "fit quantity."

more respectable quarters. In Kenrick's *New Dictionary of the English Language* (1773), the favored disposition of stresses is roughly Johnsonian: "The harmony of English versification evidently arises from a pleasing diversification [*i.e.,* strict alternation] of . . . accented and unaccented syllables, conformable to the arbitrary rules laid down in the particular species of verse. . . . "[119] Even with this theoretical commitment to regularity, however, Kenrick is forced to recognize the prosodic effectiveness of *Comus* and *Paradise Lost;* he contrives to praise the versification of these works by the device of considering them works of "genius" and consequently "superior to all artifice."[120] The interesting aesthetic implications of this position apparently gave Kenrick no uneasiness. In fact, the very difficulty of "explaining" the versification of poets who wrote before the codification of theories of stress regularity forced many minds better than Kenrick's into a condition which can be best described as one of prosodic schizophrenia.

Kenrick is one of the few contributors to English prosodic theory to use the word "monotony" in a frankly non-pejorative sense: " . . . the harmony of poetic numbers," he writes, " . . . must be consistent with an accentual monotony."[121] "Monotony," at least in reference to rhythmical phenomena, was simply the fittest term to describe what struck Kenrick as desirable; he would be very much surprised to discover what a century and a half of gradual shifts in rhythmical tastes has done to the concept of monotony.

The ear of Thomas Warton proved to be as delighted by a pattern of stress regularity as the ear of Johnson. To Warton, Spenser's alexandrine in the *Faerie Queene*

Yet was admired much of fooles, women, and boys
(V, ii, 30)

"would be much improved in its harmony" if changed to

Yet was admired much of women, fooles, and boys.[122]

And Lord Kames also finds that "precise rules" and "certain inflexible laws" govern the construction of English verse; the "number and variety" of the component syllables are the bases of the line, "and in some measure the order of [their] succession."[123] The count of the syllables in the line is, in fact,

---

[119] *A New Dictionary of the English Language* (London, 1773), p. 52.
[120] *Ibid.*
[121] *Ibid.,* p. 53.
[122] *Observations on the Faerie Queene,* p. 259.
[123] *Elements of Criticism,* II, 249.

the very first thing to be regarded.[124] We are hardly swept off our feet by Kames's assertion that "Every line [in heroic verse] consists of ten syllables, five short and five long. . . ."[125] Kames is prepared to admit so little variation that he actually sees English verse excluding "the bulk of polysyllables," for lamentably few of these display the requisite strict alternation of stressed and unstressed syllables. Thus, words such as "magnanimity" and "impetuosity" are specifically interdicted for poetic uses, since they fail to conform to the perfect iambic pattern.[126] (It would be interesting to know if any credulous readers of the *Elements of Criticism* actually tried to carry out this rule in their verses; if this desire to reject non-iambic polysyllables should ever be discovered to have been at all widely shared, it would surely open fascinating vistas for the investigation of mid-century poetic diction conventions.) Thus, lines varying at all from the pure iambic norm are, to Kames, simply "faulty."[127] *Paradise Lost* contains, expectedly, "many careless lines."[128]

Daniel Webb is another who permits no trisyllabic feet to sully the purity of the iambic line, which plainly "consists of five feet, or ten syllables."[129] Webb finds it unbelievable that an alexandrine could ever consist of more than twelve syllables,[130] and to his ear, "[heroic] verse is never more musical than when it consists intirely of iambics: . . . two trochees in succession have an ill effect."[131] Even Pope is too careless of his stresses for Webb, who cites a line from the *Essay on Criticism* to show the "ill effect" of contiguous trochees.[132] The following line, presumably because of its initial pyrrhic, is without "division" of "movements":

And with a pale and yellow melancholy.

It is incapable of being reduced to "proportion"; its "rhythmus" is "dissolved," and it "falls into relaxations"; in short, it is "prosaic."[133]

Thomas Tyrwhitt, the editor of Chaucer, writes in 1775 that "we are not to expect from Chaucer that regularity in the disposition of his accents, which the practice of our greatest Poets in the last and the present century has taught us to consider as essential to harmonious versification."[134] Although the exist-

---

[124] *Ibid.*, II, 253.
[125] *Ibid.*, II, 270-271.
[126] *Ibid.*, II, 273.
[127] *Ibid.*, II, 301.
[128] *Ibid.*, II, 314.
[129] *Observations on the Correspondence between Poetry and Music* (London, 1769), p. 102, and n. "l."
[130] *Ibid.*, p. 149, n. "n."
[131] *Ibid.*, p. 107, n. "o."
[132] *Ibid.*
[133] *Ibid.*, p. 112.
[134] *The Canterbury Tales of Chaucer. To which are added, An Essay upon his*

ence of *L'Allegro* and *Il Penseroso* forces from Tyrwhitt the admission that tetrameter lines may vary the number of syllables "without much prejudice to the harmony of the verse," he is unable to make the easy transference of the same principle to the inviolate pentameter, with which "no such liberty can be taken"; "I have no conception myself," he writes, "that an heroic verse, which wants a syllable of its complement, can be musical, or even tolerable."[135] Thus powerfully had the notion of syllabic regularity infused the theory of the heroic line; the fact that the pentameter line was generally considered reserved for elevated or serious subjects had much to do with keeping its structure sacrosanct and more impervious to prosodic change than that of some other forms. The attempted stubborn retention against all radical onslaughts of at least one line-form in which little or no variation could be allowed was the reaction of most conservative theorists to the attacks they began to receive in increasing volume from the forties on. With his attention fixed on the number of syllables in the line, it will seem very natural that Tyrwhitt should have been one of the first to discover that the thirteenth-century *Ormulum* is composed syllabically.[136]

Statesmen as well as scholars manifested this regularistic temper, and it is interesting to find Thomas Jefferson helping to spread English syllabism back to one of its areas of origin. Around 1789, Jefferson, in a letter to M. de Chastellux, set about to explain the principles of English versification to his French acquaintance: carried on and on by his desire to make everything clear, he swelled his letter into a virtual formal prosodic essay which should be better known than it is. Admirers of Jefferson may be thankful that this letter on English versification has been kept out of sight until comparatively recent times, for it must be said, with all possible reverence for Jefferson's manifold achievements in other areas than letters, that this essay on prosody would hardly bring credit to a schoolboy's literary sensibility. There could be no more striking instance of the operation of the so-called "cultural lag" in American affairs during the eighteenth and subsequent centuries than this performance of Jefferson's, which, with no indication that its author is aware of the existence of any other prosodic system, out-Bysshes

---

Language and Versification; an Introductory Discourse; and Notes (London, 1775-1778), IV, 104-105.

[135] *Ibid.*, IV, 81-82, n. William Mitford also praises the syllabically irregular lines of *L'Allegro*, and then immediately proceeds: "This is a variety wholly inadmissable in heroic verse. The five-footed measure, with such deficiency in the first foot, so wants the necessary balance, that it can neither associate with complete five-footed verses, nor stand as a verse by itself." (*An Inquiry into the Principles of Harmony*, p. 113).

[136] *Canterbury Tales*, IV, 64-65, n.

Bysshe and forces even Bentley to permit another absolute stress-regularist to share his pedestal. In Jefferson's defense, however, it can be pointed out that this essay was not the public performance of a man of letters; it is instead a relatively informal effusion by an amateur; and it can hence be of great value in representing some of the rhythmic presuppositions of the more-or-less common readers of the period, those, that is, who on normal occasions would consider the subject of prosody one of no particular concern of theirs, no matter how much they might be addicted to keeping up with the new poetry.

The range of Jefferson's poetic reading, as revealed in his illustrative citations, gives some indication of the condition of literate public taste in eighteenth-century America: he refers to Milton, Addison, Pope, Swift, Gray, Shenstone, Cunningham, Langhorne, Armstrong, Young, Moss, and Hopkins, with Shenstone supplying the bulk of the quotations.

Only three kinds of verse exist for Jefferson. There is iambic or "even" verse (since every even-numbered syllable receives a stress), trochaic or "odd" verse, and anapestic or "trisyllabic" verse.[137] "The English poet," he then explains, " . . . must so arrange his words that their established accents shall fall regularly in one of these three orders."[138] Jefferson, assuming that absolute regularity of stress is ubiquitous in English verse, suggests that the foreign student may learn the proper accentuation of any word in English simply by locating an appearance of the word in any English poem, by determining the "measure" of the poem, and then by pronouncing the word as the stress pattern of the measure dictates. The eager student of the English tongue need have only one caution in using this method: he must be wary of the first foot, since it might conceivably turn out to be a trochee. Conversely, if the foreigner is in doubt as to the meter of any English poem, he need merely ascertain the pronunciation of any of its polysyllabic words in a good pronouncing dictionary, examine the pattern of stresses as they reveal themselves in the line from which this key word is taken, and his problem is solved. Jefferson does admit that, very rarely, the learner may commit a negligible error; he can make none at all, however, in dealing with anapestic verse, "decent" examples of which will exhibit no substitution whatever.[139] I shall demonstrate later on what effect presuppositions such as these had on Jefferson and many others when they read verse aloud.

As late as 1795, the Bysshian system is still forging powerfully ahead

---

[137] Andrew A. Lipscomb, ed., *The Writings of Thomas Jefferson* (Washington, 1903-1905), XVIII, 421.
[138] *Ibid.*, XVIII, 418-419.
[139] *Ibid.*, XVIII, 431-435.

and even gathering momentum; Adam Smith avails himself of an Italian authority for the reinforcement of his own views on stress regularity: "Ruscelli observes, that in the Italian Heroic Verse the accent ought to fall upon the fourth, the sixth, the eighth, and the tenth syllables; and that if it falls upon the third, the fifth, the seventh, or the ninth syllables, it will spoil the verse. In English, if the accent falls upon any of the above-mentioned odd syllables, it equally spoils the verse."[140] The indulgence towards the beginning of the line here is worth notice; the use of the initial trochee for variety had become so widespread in English poetry as to produce virtually a unique type of line, consisting, practically, of a dipodic unit comparable to the classical choriambus, followed by a strong cesura and three iambic feet.

At the very close of the century, the syllabist and stress-regularist tradition was, if anything, stronger and more extreme, at least in its theoretical aspects, than at many earlier points in the century; the events in France had influenced thinking in other areas than political theory, and the conservatives, whether in politics, religion, or literature, were marshalling their resources against the tides of irregularity and subversion which they saw imminently sweeping through England from France. The national culture which had once served to contribute laws for the much-needed regulation of English poetry was now, the conservatives felt, the source of all unspeakable licenses, and the reactionaries, in prosody as well as in other areas, fought the forces of insubordination and disorder by taking up more and more extreme positions.

The Reverend Mr. Joseph Robertson, who produced an *Essay on the Nature of the English Verse, With Directions for Reading Poetry* in 1799, is a good representative of these reactionary prosodic theorists who are determined to make no compromise whatever with the radicals. Despite the date of Robertson's work, he concludes with the Popian injunction "FOLLOW NATURE,"[141] with "NATURE" meaning precisely what it had meant in the *Essay on Man,* roughly, that is, "whatever is," or whatever has legitimate, objective, and universal existence. Robertson assumes that Milton was composing according to the pure iambic pattern with no variations of stress whatever, and he writes that "Milton frequently lays an accent on insignificant particles," citing these lines, thus italicized, in support of his criticism:

Thus Belial *with* words cloth'd in reason's garb.

---

[140] *The Works of Adam Smith* (London, 1811), V, 327. ("Of the Affinity between Certain English and Italian Verses").

[141] *An Essay on the Nature of the English Verse, With Directions for Reading Poetry* (London, 1799), p. 134.

(Bentley's similar treatment of this line will be recalled.)

> Thy ling'ring, *or* with one stroke *of* this dart.
>
> Yet fell. Remember, *and* fear *to* transgress.
>
> And dust shalt eat all *the* days *of* thy life.[142]

Like Bentley, Robertson is simply disabled from reading *Paradise Lost* by the fact that the pure iambic pattern has taken such possession of his mind and ear that he is no longer capable of being made aware of any other arrangement of stresses when he reads a line of verse. With readers like Robertson (and there were a very great many of them among the educated classes, more, I think, than has been hitherto realized) deciding on the merits of productions like *Christabel* and *The Ancient Mariner,* the wonder is not that the early accentual poems of Coleridge, Scott, Hunt, and others were thoroughly damned by most of the public organs, but instead that many readers of the new poetry were actually able to make the discovery that the new meters were not regular syllabically, for an ear which "hears" absolute stress regularity in Milton's most freely varied lines will tend to "hear" absolute stress regularity in any poetry.

Robertson continues: "There is perhaps no reason, why we should suppose, that a false position of the accent is more allowable in English poetry, than false quantity in the works of Homer or Virgil."[143] "False" position of accent is, of course, any stress which varies from the absolutely regular iambic pattern. Robertson is so anxious to hear regularity that he persuades himself that Young, in the following line, "lays the accent on the first syllable" of "caprice":

> For caprice is the daughter of success.[144]

It will be noted that it is to avoid a recognition of the virtually anapestic movement of the first part of this line that Robertson stresses "cáprice," and there can be little doubt that he also gave strong accents to both "is" and "of" here. Triple time was considered "low" by most of the conservative theorists, and it was apparently better not to give it the encouragement which recognition of it would imply. Like a rustic intruder at a fashionable social function, triple time was to be ignored if it appeared in serious works, in the hope, presumably, that it would eventually go away.

Even an initial trochee in a heroic line is not recognized by Robertson, for, of Garth's line

> Biggotted to this idol we disclaim,

142 *Ibid.,* p. 60.
143 *Ibid.,* p. 61.
144 *Ibid.,* p. 68.

Robertson's only explanation is that Garth surely intended "biggotted" to be pronounced "big-gót-ted."[145] Robertson reveals himself as Jefferson's British counterpart when he points out that a knowledge of the measures of English verse is the best aid to "the young reader" in learning the correct pronunciation of Greek and Roman names of heroes, countries, and the like;[146] like Jefferson's "foreigner," this young reader has only to determine the measure of the poem in which the classical name appears, and he can be assured that the word is inserted in the line in such a way as to "fit" precisely the pure iambic pattern.

The views about the nature of the English poetic line which I have been surveying were not held by Englishmen alone; they were assumed to be self-evident truth by most French writers of the period, and William Mitford suggests that respectable English verse was considered necessarily syllabic as far away as Rome.[147]

8. The Persistence of the Syllabic Tradition, and Some Conjectures

The extra momentum which the syllabic and stress-regularity tradition received from the prosodic reactionaries during the period of the French Revolution served to carry the conventional theory along well into the nineteenth century and even into the twentieth. Mitford is to be found delivering purely Bysshian sentiments in 1806;[148] George Gregory rejects feet and clings to the "number of syllables" in 1808;[149] John Carey, the author of such works as *Scanning Exercises for Young Prosodians* and the schoolmasterly *Learning Better than House and Land, A Moral Tale for Youth,* emphasizes the syllabic limitation of the English line in 1816;[150] and in 1827, William Crowe indicates that the number of syllables is to him the major structural basis of the line and much more important even than the criterion of alternating accents.[151] Goold Brown, an American grammarian, was severely taken to task by Poe[152] for advancing, as late as 1845, this anti-trisyllabic-substitution definition: "Versification is the art of arranging words into lines of corre-

[145] *Ibid.,* p. 70.

[146] *Ibid.,* p. 76.

[147] *An Inquiry into the Principles of Harmony,* p. 296.

[148] *Ibid.,* pp. 90-93.

[149] *Letters on Literature, Taste, and Composition, Addressed to His Son* (Philadelphia, 1809), pp. 227-228.

[150] *Practical English Prosody and Versification, A New and Improved Edition* (London, 1816), pp. 1-2; 49-50, n.

[151] *A Treatise on English Versification* (London, 1827), p. 199.

[152] In "The Rationale of Verse." See John H. Ingram, ed., *The Works of Edgar Allen Poe* (3rd ed.; Edinburgh, 1883), III, 219-265.

spondent length, so as to produce harmony by the regular alternation of syllables differing in quantity."[153] Pure French syllabism, undiluted by any perception of the structural office of stress in English verse, is still being put forth by B. Van Dam and C. Stoffel in *Chapters in English Printing, Prosody, and Punctuation,* published at Heidelberg in 1902.[154] An examination of I. A. Richards' *Practical Criticism* (1929) will reveal that a great many readers of verse are at this very moment expecting "a certain number of syllables" in every English poetic line.[155] And, unconscious and innocent as it is, the use by some modern literary scholars of such terms as "octosyllabic" and "deca-syllabic" indicates how deeply into the modern psyche notions of syllabism have penetrated;[156] such terms as these may be employed with validity if one is referring to frankly syllabic or accentual-syllabic verse, but they serve only to breed future syllabists when used to describe verse in which trisyllabic substitution occurs.

It is somewhat strange that during the eighteenth century the blending of the purely syllabic French system with the more stress-conscious English tradition should have worked towards the promulgation of regularity of accents; we should rather expect that all this excessive emphasis on the number of syllables (sometimes, after the genuine French manner, without any concern for the number or position of stresses) would have helped divert attention more than it did from the matter of the placement of stresses in alternating positions. As one modern metrist has pointed out, however, although the purely syllabic criterion does not necessitate such a law, it un-doubtedly involves, in some way not entirely clear, a tendency towards alter-nation of stressed and unstressed syllables.[157] Perhaps the necessity, in a syllabic system, of unconsciously "counting off" the syllables as they pass, in order to perceive the rhythmic equality of the lines, prompts the reader or hearer to organize the syllables subjectively into groups of two, simply to facilitate the counting process. In much the same way, the human ear, ap-parently always alert for the opportunity to create some form of order from the sounds presented to it, organizes the continual, unvaried "tick, tick, tick, tick" of a watch or clock into more easily apprehensible units of two beats, and the familiar *"tick,* tock, *tick,* tock" rhythm is heard: here, the human

---

153 *Institutes of English Grammar* (New York, 1862), p. 235.
154 See Scholl, "English Metre Once More," p. 293.
155 *Practical Criticism: A Study of Literary Judgment* (New York, 1929 and later printings), p. 171 (Protocol 13·62); p. 158 (Protocol 12·51); pp. 170-171 (Protocol 13·61).
156 See Smith, *Principles of English Metre,* p. 113.
157 *Ibid.*

ear does all the stressing and "tocking," and thus "reads into" the dull and unaesthetic ticking of the clock a pattern which, since it owes its existence to a human creative act, although one so automatic as to be wholly unconscious, is an artistic one, and can supply the sort of pleasure which it is in the nature of artistic patterns to give.[158] Thus the single units of a syllabic system of prosody, if imported into the poetry of a language which, like English, is characterized by strong accents, would tend in time to be unconsciously "organized" by their hearers into the groups (*i.e.,* dissyllabic feet) of a virtually accentual-syllabic system. In matters of this sort, conjecture is bound to be hazardous, but it is surely conceivable that pure French syllabism underwent the transmutation to the English theory of combined syllabism *and* absolute alternation of stresses by some such subtle process as that sketched above.

The eighteenth-century tendency towards regularity of stresses does not manifest itself only in the more formal verse of the period: even street broadsides and other varieties of purely popular poetry, the authors of which read not a word of all this prosodic theorizing, reveal the same prevailing rhythmical temper which found itself gratified by equality of syllabic numeration and strict alternation of accents. This situation has been found to be the result of "the power of classical criticism to impose upon verse [of all levels] a standard of regularity,"[159] but it seems, perhaps, better explained by the power of the century's habitual appreciation of certain types of rhythm at the expense of others. The "classical" criticism and the conservative prosodic theorizing should be regarded as manifestations (or, if one prefers, even as symptoms) of the passion for rhythmical regularity, but not as its cause.

I have sought in this chapter to provide a mere historical outline of the origin and persistence of that theoretical prosodic tradition in the eighteenth century for which I have found the designation "conservative" a useful description. I have attempted to furnish a background against which other eighteenth-century contributions to English metrical theory may be considered and evaluated. It should not be assumed that everyone was a syllabist, even during the period of syllabism's real reign, practically as well as theoretically, from about 1660 to 1740. But syllabism and the theory of stress regularity were established as the official prosody until roughly the end of the

---

[158] See Catherine Ing, *Elizabethan Lyrics: A Study in the Development of English Metres and their Relation to Poetic Effect* (London, 1951), pp. 200-201. Cf. Sprott, who speaks of "the modern psychological theory that rhythm is as it were imposed upon experience by the selective, organizing human mind." (*Milton's Art of Prosody,* p. 111).

[159] Stewart, *Modern Metrical Technique,* p. 24.

century ("The syllable-counters had triumphed," Omond laments[160]), and the moral and aesthetic assumptions on which this conservative theory was based were so intimate a part of the age's temper that it finally required men with rare and admirable powers of detachment to escape their age's unconscious assumptions and to begin, relatively early, the formulation and codification of that rhythmical complex which must be approached through the concept of romantic prosody.

[160] *English Metrists,* p. 31.

CHAPTER II

THE ETHICS AND AESTHETICS OF STRESS REGULARITY

1. *The Search for Principles of Stability*

The theory of syllabism and stress regularity, the formulation of which I have traced, was not without its strong ethical and aesthetic implications, as indeed is every prescriptive theory of verse structure, no matter how purely mechanical or incidental it may appear. For the art of versification, or of "verse," is an act involving serious philosophical considerations. Whether a versifier of the conservative stamp chooses to order the static materials of experience according to certain pre-existing principles, or whether a more liberal maker of verse chooses to allow the natural organization (or disorganization) of what strikes him as "experience" to give the law to his verse structure, and thus to a part of his total theory of aesthetic order, most versifiers (and most prosodists) will be found to be proceeding in accordance with certain often-unconscious assumptions about the nature of the universe and the nature of man's condition in it. In the same way that every different worldview will possess its own unique prosody, so every distinct prosodic system will be discovered, I think, to proceed ultimately from its own metaphysical, ethical, and aesthetic suppositions. The history of prosody is thus inseparable from the history of ideas, so-called, and an effort to produce one prosody which, laid over the manifold phenomena of English verse structure from Chaucer to the present time, can somehow explain everything seems as fatuous as a similar tendency, occasionally met with, to neglect a consideration of historical contexts in the study of literature in general. To assume that Shakespeare was a democrat, Swift a sentimentalist, and Johnson a dog-lover, simply because one modern reader happens to be all these things, is hardly more preposterous than to assume that eighteenth-century prosodic theory represents somehow an embarrassing dry season in the continued triumphal progress of English metrical theory towards its predestined glorious fruition in the late nineteenth and early twentieth centuries. And yet this is the implication that most modern metrical theorists and historians present us with.[1] Modern prosody, ripped from its historical context, will surely appear as ridiculous

---

[1] See, *e.g.*, Saintsbury, *History of English Prosody*, and Omond, *English Metrists*, *passim*.

two centuries from now as eighteenth-century prosody may appear today, but both systems will have been thoroughly suitable if they have been honest, even though unconscious, expressions of their respective ages' commitments (or lack of them) in areas of metaphysics, ethics, and aesthetics.

The eighteenth century was, in the main, an empirical age, and one therefore does not expect to see much done towards seeking a sanction for the conservative prosody in a very transcendent metaphysic. A few of the bolder spirits, especially early in the century, did make an attempt to connect the order and pure regularity of conservative verse structure with a metaphysical theory of universal order, an order which transcended the material universe; but the prevailing naturalism of the age seems to have been too overpowering to permit the production of many theories of prosody which soared very far above the empirical and the publicly perceivable. It should not be anticipated that the eighteenth century contribute to prosodic theory an Augustine or a Boethius; we must be satisfied to behold a multitude of efforts to ground the conservative theory of prosody in what were conceived to be the truths of a universal morality and a universal psychology.

Alfred North Whitehead has emphasized the fact that the contribution of the later seventeenth century to pure science was mainly one involving theories of recurrence. The naturalistic bent of the new science impelled a re-examination of the bases of knowledge, and many thinkers of the seventeenth century came to realize that "Apart from recurrence, knowledge would be impossible; for nothing could be referred to our past experience."[2] It should be kept in mind during any discussion of the ethical and aesthetic bases of the conservative prosody in the eighteenth century that the prevailing scientism of the age, with its quest for a valid theory of periodicity, was one influence on the desire of many of the prosodists to extract from the *materia* of versification a theory of recurrence which might prove useful in larger areas of human engagement. These efforts may seem at times more than a trifle ridiculous and overdone, but the fact that they were confidently and seriously undertaken indicates that some new conceptions of empirical order were felt to be necessary; many seemed to believe that the analysis of verse structure might possibly lead to the discovery of principles of universal harmony which could supply the age with the stability and fixity which it sought.

It seems apparent that many of the late seventeenth-century prosodists were attracted to the conservative system of stress regularity mainly because it seemed to offer, when fused with the matter of poetry, a means of restoring

---

[2] *Science and the Modern World* (New York, 1925), pp. 47-48.

to that matter the order and purposive regularity of which the naturalistic current in philosophy during the seventeenth century had helped deprive it. The great popularity of the "blind atoms" of Lucretius and Ovid as subject-matter among seventeenth-century versifiers reveals the somewhat morbid thrill of fascination these poets and their readers achieved from the contemplation of "blind chance," "the confused heap of things," and "atoms casually together hurled." The idea of a world left running by itself and gradually slipping into a state of disorder was being received by many with a boldness which was shocking to the divines.[3] It was also shocking to the majority of the prosodists, and their efforts to impose some order on all this potential irregularity may be compared with those of Hobbes in ordering the commonwealth and Locke in ordering the methods of human perception. It has been suggested, in fact, that Dryden's extraordinary concern with the ordering function of verse was mainly the result of his acute apprehension of (and at times, actual fascination with) the apparent incursion of the forces of universal disorder and chaos.[4]

In the midst of this search for stable principles, Charles Gildon was one of the few who gravitated towards what might be called the theological extension; he sought once, in 1718, to give to the conservative prosody a universal validity by associating elements of it with the traditional concept of the Creation: " . . . the Particles and Seeds of Light in the Primocal Chaos strugled in vain to exert their true Lustre, till Matter was by *Art Divine* brought into order, and this *noble Poem* of the *Universe* compleated in *Number* and *Figures,* by the Almighty *Poet* or *Maker*."[5] But Gildon seems somewhat embarrassed in presenting this High-Renaissance analogy about a century too late, and he quickly drops his *quasi*-theological theorizing, never to return to it again. James Harris, in 1744, tries to associate metrical phenomena which recur in a "certain order" with a more mundane set of regularly ordered occurrences; Harris points to such unvaried and regularly recurring events as years and seasons, months and days, and even offers the example of a single human life, "a *Compound of various and multiform Actions,* which succeed each other in a certain Order. . . . "[6]

Joshua Steele, although not one of the conservatives, attempts much the same thing in 1779, and with more success: "In the time of the world, a

[3] Mark Van Doren, *John Dryden: A Study of his Poetry* (3rd ed.; New York, 1946), p. 15.

[4] *Ibid.,* p. 17.

[5] *Complete Art of Poetry,* I, 95.

[6] *Three Treatises,* p. 32.

natural day (night included) is a single *cadence;* the setting and rising of the Sun are the *thesis* and *arsis;* seasons and years are rhythmical clauses: the real beginning and ending of this melody are out of our sight; but to human apprehension, the apparent are birth and death, and life is our part in the song."[7] One will perhaps be reminded of Sir John Davies' *Orchestra.* Naturalistic and positivistic as Steele's statement is, it does represent the attempt on the part of the prosodists to extend the significance of the regularity of conservative verse structures to larger areas, and, conversely, to utilize certain regularities perceivable by all as analogies for bolstering the conservative theory.[8]

With the gradual narrowing of the empirical boundaries and with the loss of the apparent validity of abstract metaphysical systems, however, most of the prosodists came to seek primarily an ethical sanction for regularity in verse structure. Sir John Beaumont had, in the mid-seventeenth century, seized the occasion of paying tribute to his sovereign's memory to inculcate a little lesson about the alliance of moderation in ethics with "smooth" cadences; praising James I's work in prosody,[9] Beaumont writes,

> He leads the lawless poets of our times
> To smoother cadence, to exacter rhymes:
> He knew it was the proper work of kings
> To keep proportion, eu'n in smallest things.[10]

And Samuel Wesley, writing in 1700, praises the verse of Nahum Tate in these terms:

> For *smooth* and *well-turn'd Lines* we *T*——— admire,
> Who has in *Justness* what he wants in *Fire:*
> Each *Rhime,* each *Syllable* well-weighed and fair,
> His *Life* and *Manners* scarce more *regular.*[11]

The association of prosodic with moral regularity was sometimes assisted by the prevalence of the rather flattering notion that the English were, as a people, naturally given more than other races to "irregularity," and conse-

---

[7] *Prosodia Rationalis: or, an Essay towards Establishing the Melody and Measure of Speech, to be Expressed and Perpetuated by Peculiar Symbols* (2nd ed.; London, 1779), pp. 117-118.

[8] Cf. Santayana: "Although a poem be not made by counting of syllables upon the fingers, yet 'numbers' is the most poetical synonym we have for verse, and 'measure' the most significant equivalent for beauty, for goodness, and perhaps even for truth." (*Interpretations of Poetry and Religion* [New York, 1905], p. 251).

[9] See *Ane schort Treatise, conteining some revlis and cautelis to be obseruit and eschewit in Scottis Poesie* (Edinburgh, 1584).

[10] "To the Glorious Memory of our Late Sovereign Lord, King James," lines 121-124.

[11] *An Epistle to a Friend Concerning Poetry,* p. 19.

quently were in continual need of very strong devices for

The *Regulation* of our *Native Fire*.[12]

William Coward makes a scornful connection between "Poetic Liberty" and "Licentious Roving of the Mind,"[13] and Gildon, in 1721, goes so far as to explain the contemporary distaste for poetry by the fact that the verse is not regular enough to appeal to the natural craving for regularity which exists in people of every time and place.[14] Assuming that Greek poetry was both regular and popular, Gildon believes that certain irregular works among the moderns will never reach their intended readers at all, for "confusion," he says, "can never produce a strong and lively pleasure,"[15] and works which produce no natural pleasure will never be read.

2. *Johnson and the Ethical Implications of Stress Regularity*

As would be expected, the most perceptive moralist of prosody in the eighteenth century, and probably of all modern times, was Samuel Johnson, who almost always approaches problems of verse structure as if mindful of his own adage, "we are perpetually moralists, but we are geometricians only by chance."[16] If "geometricians" is replaced by "prosodists" (and such a substitution would have struck Edward Manwaring and many others as perfectly rational), one has a critical *dictum* which can shed a good deal of light not only on Johnson's critical practice but on the whole subject of the ethical significance of prosody in the eighteenth century.

One of Johnson's prosodic *loci classici* is this statement from *Rambler* 88: " . . . however minute the employment may appear, of analysing lines into syllables, and whatever ridicule may be incurred by a solemn deliberation upon accents and pauses, it is certain that without this petty knowledge no man can be a poet; and that from the proper disposition of single sounds

---

[12] *Ibid.*, p. 27.

[13] *Licentia Poetica discuss'd*, p. 82.

[14] Few theorists during this period would have admitted that stress regularity was an ideal peculiar to the Restoration and eighteenth century and limited to the British Isles and the Continent. The more general neo-classic tenet of universality became connected with the verse theorizing; regular rhythm was naturally regarded as universally satisfying, for mankind was presumed to be, in essentials, everywhere and at all times the same. See, *e.g.*, William Congreve, *A Pindarique Ode, Humbly Offer'd to the Queen, on the Vigorous Progress of Her MAJESTY'S Arms, under the Conduct of the Duke of Marlborough* (London, 1706), sig. A2 ("A Discourse on the Pindarique Ode"); Sir John Hawkins, *General History of the Science and Practice of Music*, I, sig. [a]ᵛ, iii-iv, xii, lxv, and lxxxii; and Walter Young, "An Essay on Rythmical [*sic*] Measures," *Transactions of the Royal Society of Edinburgh*, II (1790), Part II, Sect. ii, 56, 99. For an example of the sort of relativistic utterance which finally banished the idea of universality in favor of a kind of pre-romantic localism, see William Shenstone's remarks "On Taste," *The Works in Verse and Prose, of William Shenstone, Esq.* (London, 1764-1769), II, 327.

[15] *The Laws of Poetry*, pp. 25-26.

[16] Hill, ed., *Lives*, I, 100.

results that harmony that adds force to reason, and gives grace to sublimity; that shackles attention, and governs passions."[17] It will be remembered that "harmony" to Johnson means regularity of stress; that the mere "proper disposition of single sounds" could have the power to regulate the passions must seem to many modern readers totally incredible, but this assumption, firmly based as it was in ancient criticism and sanctified by associationist psychology, was simply self-evident to Johnson, and helps explain many of his more extreme critical pronouncements.

That some direct connection existed between the nature of perceived phenomena and the condition of the mind perceiving them was, of course, a notion almost automatically held after the speculations of such associationists as Locke, Hartley, Priestley, Burke, and others.[18] The reiterated emphasis by the associationists on the ability of empirical events, through the various mechanisms of association, to alter the temper and almost the "shape" or structure of the mind quite naturally tended to encourage ethical theories of prosody; and these ethical theories will be found to assume, to a large extent, the associationists' purely naturalistic premises. Once some direct empirical relationship is established between the characteristics of observed phenomena and the characteristics which the mind will exhibit as the specific result of the perception, such concepts as "regulating the affections" and "ordering the passions" (let alone "shackling the attention") will appear to be more than metaphors. Thus, when Thomas Sheridan (a great admirer of Locke, incidentally) writes in 1775 that "poetic numbers keep the mind in a constant state of gentle agitation,"[19] one can be fairly certain that Sheridan is thinking of "agitation" not entirely in a figurative sense.

To Johnson, learning and intelligence were moral matters, and when he says that there is no "irregularity of numbers which credulous admiration cannot discover to be eminently beautiful,"[20] he is naturally assuming that this admiration for irregularity confesses some moral want in the reader. "Fixed principles" appeared the very essence of morality to Johnson (one even

---

[17] *Rambler*, II, 195. (Sat., Jan. 19, 1751). Cf. Daniel Webb: " . . . the movements of music being in a continual opposition to all those impressions which tend either to disorder or disgrace our nature, may we not reasonably presume, that they were destined to act in aid of the moral sense, to regulate the measures and proportions of our affections; and, by counteracting the passions in their extremes, to render them the instruments of virtue, and the embellishments of character." (*Observations*, p. 37).

[18] See Samuel H. Monk, *The Sublime: A Study of Critical Theories in XVIII-Century England* (New York, 1935), pp. 84-133; and Walter J. Bate, *From Classic to Romantic: Premises of Taste in Eighteenth-Century England* (Cambridge, Mass., 1946), pp. 93-128; 153-156.

[19] *Lectures on the Art of Reading*, p. 309.

[20] *Rambler*, II, 237. (No. 94, Sat., Feb. 9, 1751).

suspects occasionally that the fact that the principles were "fixed" counted as much with him as the nature of the principles themselves), and for a poet to "fix" or "settle" his prosodic principles early in his career was a great virtue; we have already heard Johnson remarking approvingly that Waller's prosodic principles were properly fixed during his whole life,[21] and he repeats the sentiment when he says, "According to the opinion of Harte, [Dryden] settled his principles of versification in 1676. . . . "[22] Johnson would simply not have understood a technique of versification which drew the prosodic structure of each poem from the nature of the matter of that particular poetic occasion; to Johnson, as to most of the conservative metrical theorists, it was the poet's duty to settle his prosodic principles early, to triumph by an effort of the will over his adolescent taste for irregularity and inequality in rhythmical effects, and to apply his fixed prosodic principles to whatever subject-matter might present itself: it was the nature and the office of the subject-matter to yield, not the prosody.

Johnson believes that regular stresses aid the poetic inculcation of morality in the same way that regular habits of ethical conduct help lead to the final belief in the supernatural stay for the ethical system. Consider, for example, this comment on Gilbert Walmesley: "He had mingled with the gay world without exemption from its vices or its follies, but had never neglected the cultivation of his mind; his belief of Revelation was unshaken; his learning preserved his principles; he grew first regular, and then pious."[23] Prosodic regularity forces the ordering of the perceiver's mind so that it may be in a condition to receive the ordered moral matter of the poem, just as, in ethics and religion, a conscious regularizing of principles and even of daily habits is the necessary condition for the growth of piety. The regularizing, whether prosodic or ethical, serves an attention-calling function; it hammers into the consciousness of the perceiver the recognition that a formal process is at work, a process comprising certain elements of ceremony, self-awareness, artifice, and control. The moral office of all poetry, the ethical function of a regularistic prosody, and the concept of regularity and fixity of ethical habits and religious commitment are thus seen to be indissolubly fused. Once it is understood that to Johnson matters of verse structure are in one sense religious matters, it is possible to read even his brutal condemnation of certain lines in *Lycidas* with, if not sympathy, at least understanding. Since harmony is one manifestation of truth, and since harmony and irregular prosody cannot

[21] See above, Chap. I, n. 7.
[22] Hill, ed., *Lives,* I, 436.
[23] *Ibid.,* II, 21.

sort together, "rugged numbers" can hardly, to Johnson, embody anything but worthless or vicious ideas. As he writes of Dryden, "the rectitude of [his] mind" is evidenced by his "rejection of unnatural thoughts and rugged numbers."[24]

Johnson's morality of prosody is probably the most complete and coherent expression one can find in any post-Renaissance criticism of the ancient belief, essentially humanistic, that the mechanics of poetry, trivial perhaps as they may appear to the uninitiated, are at once a regulation and a revelation of man's ethical and religious state. It may be added that those currently engaged in an effort to re-establish a stable hierarchy of values in the arts and in conduct might well direct a portion of their attention to this matter of the philosophy of verse structure which has been strikingly neglected during the first half of the twentieth century.

3. *Regularistic Aesthetics*

In addition to being equipped with a fairly comprehensive empirical ethic based essentially on associationism, the theory of stress regularity will appear to issue from and depend on many of the aesthetic commonplaces of its age. One of the most important aesthetic principles lying behind the theory of stress regularity is that which can be observed to influence most neo-classic art, the principle of distinctness and clarity. The Augustan impulse which rejected the metaphysical conceit, early seventeenth-century specialized diction in poetry, and works in which immediate certainty of intention and clarity of method were not almost instantly apparent was to a large degree responsible for the general eighteenth-century insistence on distinctness of stress in prosody. The wide familiarity with classical principles had a great deal to do with the conservatives' assumption that a given syllable must be either accented or unaccented, for the classical quantitative prosodists had adhered to the invariable rule that, prosodically, only two types of syllables exist, the long and the short, with the long being precisely equal to two of the short. It was left for prosodists of a later day, a day in which classical studies were beginning to lose their traditional position as the core of the humane curriculum, to discover such a novel concept as that of "secondary" stress, or to assume that as many as five or six degrees of accent exist. To the classically educated eighteenth-century conservatives, a given syllable in poetry was either distinctly stressed or clearly unstressed, and they found absolutely no necessity for any secondary or partial stresses. William Mitford is probably

---

[24] *Ibid.*, III, 220. And see Jean H. Hagstrum, *Samuel Johnson's Literary Criticism* (Minneapolis, 1952), p. 177.

the first (1774) to conceive of an intermediate degree of stress between the purely plus and minus poles: Mitford employs three degrees in his scansions, a strong stress, a secondary stress, and what he terms an "unstress."[25]

This attention to aesthetic distinctness and clarity of effect in general impinges in many ways on the conservative prosodic theory. James Harris, in 1744, confounds accent in English with quantity in Greek and Latin, and is thus able to reject the possibility of varied degrees of stress in English verse: "Music has no less than *five different lengths of Notes in ordinary use,* reckoning from the Semi-brief to the Semi-quaver; all which may be infinitely compounded, even in any *one* Time, or Measure———Poetry, on the other hand, has but two *Lengths* or *Quantities,* a *long* Syllable and a *short,* (which is its Half) and *all the Variety of Verse* arises from such Feet and Metres, as these *two Species* of Syllables, *by being compounded,* can be made [to] produce."[26] In this either-or view of the nature of accents, then, classical authority blends with the contemporary preference for clear, well-defined, and immediately apprehensible aesthetic effects. As Harris comments a little later in the same work, "the *Definite* and *Certain* is ever preferable to the *Indefinite* and *Uncertain.*"[27] It is easy to understand why the conservatives were determined to limit to two the types of syllables used in the construction of the line, and why one of these units was held to be totally different from the other: had Mitford and others like him succeeded somewhat earlier and more forcefully in proclaiming the existence of varying degrees of stress, the way could have been open for an early disruption of the stress-regularists' "strict alternation of stressed and unstressed syllables."

Lord Kames reveals this same desire for clarity, fixity, and certainty when he says, speaking of the poetic necessity for "fixed" pronunciations, that "though custom may render familiar, both a long and a short pronunciation of the same word; yet the mind wavering between the two sounds, cannot be so much affected as where every syllable has one fixed sound."[28] This feeling of Kames's is implicit in much eighteenth-century prosodic theorizing: the mind, which, when "wavering," is unable to perceive immediately the aesthetic (and moral) effect intended, must not be confused by such levities as variations of stress, varying degrees of accent, lines of differing lengths, complex stanza patterns, and other such instabilities; the aesthetic

[25] *Inquiry into the Principles of Harmony,* p. 89.
[26] *Three Treatises,* pp. 73-74. Cf. Lord Kames: " . . . the quantities employed in verse are but two, the one double of the other; . . . every syllable is reducible to one or other of these standards." (*Elements of Criticism,* II, 271).
[27] *Three Treatises,* p. 80.
[28] *Elements of Criticism,* II, 272.

effect must be hard, clear, immediate, and capable of being anticipated in advance. The mind, too much inclined to waver by nature, must receive from its perception of art in poetic structure an ordering, a tightening, and a regularizing: to achieve this required effect, clear, direct, and even, indeed, somewhat blunt rhythmic devices are necessary.

The general conservative antipathy to rhythmic effects of any great subtlety is expressed by Johnson; he is here discussing the necessity of clear and direct denotations in diction, but his remark is perfectly expressive of his views on prosodic clarity: "Whatever professes to benefit by pleasing must please at once. . . . What is perceived by slow degrees may gratify us with the consciousness of improvement, but will never strike us with the sense of pleasure."[29] This desire for immediate clarity of aesthetic effect underlies Johnson's criticism that the rhymes of *Lycidas* are "uncertain,"[30] and that the meaning of the lines

> We drove a field, and both together heard
> What time the Gray-fly winds her sultry horn,
> Batt'ning our flocks with the fresh dews of night,
>
> (27-29)

is "uncertain and remote."[31] The poet who employs variations which the reader does not expect, and who seems to be proceeding according to no clear, distinct, and stable principles of prosodic structure, is in danger of lapsing into confusion, and "in mere confusion, there is neither grace nor greatness."[32]

Associated with this desire for distinctness and clarity was the premise of simplicity. Richard Hurd was expressing many of the aesthetic assumptions implicit in the theory of stress regularity when he said in 1766, "true taste requires chaste, severe, and simple pleasures; and true genius will only be concerned in administering such."[33] Thomas Jefferson specifically associates regularity with simplicity: all verse is the better the less it departs "from that simplicity and regularity of which the ear is most sensible."[34] The desire for simplicity in prosodic construction did not, however, imply the abandonment

[29] Hill, ed., *Lives,* I, 59. Cf. Walter Young's Lockeian comment, "Nothing but what is distinctly felt can communicate real pleasure." ("Essay on Rythmical Measures," p. 87).
[30] Hill, ed., *Lives,* I, 163.
[31] *Ibid.,* I, 164.
[32] *Ibid.,* II, 234. Cf. Robert Nares: "Needless irregularity is the worst of all deformities." (*Elements of Orthoepy: Containing a Distinct View of the Whole Analogy of the English Language; so far as it relates to Pronunciation, Accent, and Quantity* [London, 1784], p. iv).
[33] *The Works of Richard Hurd, D. D., Lord Bishop of Worcester* (London, 1811), II, 20-21. ("On the Idea of Universal Poetry").
[34] Lipscomb, ed., *Writings,* XVIII, 451.

of the principle of obvious artifice; just the opposite, in fact, for artifice is best perceived where it is bold and simple. Poetry had to be plainly differentiated from prose, and the rhythmical devices which secured it from confusion with prose had to be clearly "artificial." As Daniel Webb says, "there cannot be a beauty without a manifestation of art";[35] to have hinted to Webb that such a concept as that of unpremeditated art was in the offing would surely have confused him sorely, for the very *sine qua non* of art was of course presumed to be the element of human premeditation. The notion of a poetry without obvious indications of artifice decently in evidence would also have shocked Erasmus Darwin, who sums up a great deal of Augustan aesthetic theory in his well-known remark, "The Muses are young ladies, we expect to see them dressed."[36] John Walker is another who associates the theory of artifice with the regular, alternate disposition of accented and unaccented syllables. To be "harmonious," Walker holds, the "return" of the accent in verse must be "constant, regular, and artificial."[37] It will seem only fitting that Walker dedicated the work in which this passage occurs to Samuel Johnson.

It may seem somewhat odd that William Mitford, one of the "inventors" of secondary stress in English prosody, should align himself with the more conservative proponents of obvious artificiality of stress; nevertheless, one discovers Mitford saying, "The order of sounds in prose, like the order of forms in a beautiful landscape, not to be decided by rule and line, requires that art should never show itself. But, on the contrary, the order of sounds in poetry, like the forms of a beautiful building, must be so decidedly regular as to be obviously artificial."[38] Here we come upon the highly meaningful architectural analogy in eighteenth-century prosodic criticism. Mitford carries on the analogy: " . . . offensive . . . in architecture is the irregular line of a clumsy workman, which may approach in some degree the picturesk, and in poetry the irregular measure of the ill-eared versifier, of which the common censure is expressed by the word prosaic. In verse and in architecture, art must be evident; and, to satisfy, it must show itself exquisite. Roughness, indeed, well-introduced, may please; as, in a building, rusticated stonework; yet any disproportion, any perceptible inexactness, in uprights, parallels, [etc.] . . . will surely offend the eye. So, in poetry, tho there are admired

---

[35] *Observations*, p. 150.

[36] *The Botanic Garden, Part II. Containing the Loves of the Plants, A Poem. With Philosophical Notes. Volume the Second* (Lichfield, 1789), p. 43.

[37] *Elements of Elocution*, II, 148.

[38] *Inquiry into the Principles of Harmony*, p. 84.

examples of rough sound, yet any obvious deficiency in that order, that fitness of parts, which characterizes poetical harmony, will surely offend the ear."[39] And he adds that "in verse . . . cadences must be disposed with obvious regularity, a regularity that cannot escape the ear."[40] Dryden had been one of the first to employ the figure of architecture to illustrate principles of poetics and prosody;[41] it is significant that this comparison suggested itself to the syllabist and regularist school, and that the proponents of the new accentual prosody in the late eighteenth century found in musical and biological or organic analogies the most suitable illustration of the principles they advocated for the making of the poetic line.[42] To the conservatives, the process was genuinely one of construction, of fitting existing materials into a preconceived plan; to the liberals, the process was one of organic "creation," in which the plan gradually evolved as the created work took shape.[43] One analogy emphasizes the static and fixed nature of the materials and of the finished construction; the other focuses on the dynamic, kinetic, continually changing condition both of the elements of the work and of the finished (more often, unfinished) work itself. The system of conservative prosody thus acts as a "fixer" of the poetic material by confining and stabilizing it within a clear and hard form, like an insect preserved in amber, while the liberal prosody conceives of itself as a "releaser" of the poetic material by allowing it to escape into a more readily perceivable "reality" through electing, as it were, its own form, and by allowing the material to shape the form until its essence and the form become one.[44]

Generalizations such as these are not intended to represent the last word on this matter of the archetypal analogies employed by the two different schools of prosodic theorists; they are merely intended to suggest that the transition from eighteenth-century to nineteenth-century prosody is not a simple matter of a sudden influx of "freedom" due to a weariness with the "monotonous" beat of the heroic couplet. It can hardly be overemphasized that each of these two systems, regarded in its essence, takes its own distinct view of reality and of the relationship in which art should stand to reality.

---

[39] *Ibid.*, p. 85.
[40] *Ibid.*, p. 86.
[41] Ker, ed., *Essays*, I, 107.
[42] See Prosser Hall Frye, *Literary Reviews and Criticisms* (New York, 1908), p. 171.
[43] Cf. Wordsworth's "Forest-tree," which attains grandeur
    . . . not by casting in a formal mould,
    But from its *own* divine vitality.
                    (*"A Poet!"*—He hath put his Heart to School," lines 13-14).
[44] See Morse Peckham, "Toward a Theory of Romanticism," *PMLA*, LXVI (1951), 5-23, esp. 10-11.

The two views, although they can be shown to share certain common assumptions, are basically distinct and finally irreconcilable; each view of reality and art must have its own unique prosody, which will not necessarily resemble the prosody capable of handling a different concept of reality and art. Modern metrists and prosodic historians who choose to neglect the distinct moral and aesthetic theory behind each distinct historical prosody are, whether knowingly or not, obliterating vital distinctions which can illuminate historical aesthetics in general, and distinctions which are absolutely indispensable if work in metrics is to have any usefulness above that involved in teaching weary undergraduates to scan.

The antipathy felt by most of the conservative prosodists towards variation of stress positions from the expected pattern is also allied with the preference, in more general contemporary aesthetic theory, for the principle of the gratification of the sense of expectation, rather than the experience of surprise. In prosody, Johnson will always be found one of the champions of expectation. "The greatest pleasure of verse," he says, "arises from the known measure of the lines and uniform structure of the stanzas. . . . "[45] A measure which was not known to the reader when he began the poem could only frustrate, astonish, and annoy him. It is probably Johnson's embarrassment at being prosodically surprised which moves him to say that Cowley's "combination of different measures is sometimes dissonant and unpleasing; he joins verses together, of which the former does not slide easily into the latter."[46] That is, Cowley will employ lines of slightly different lengths, or lines containing some slight variation of feet, for which the reader naturally cannot be prepared, and these variations will surprise the reader who is expecting instead the temperate gratification of his regularistic expectations. As Johnson says elsewhere, one of the greatest beauties of verse-writing is "to relieve the ear without disappointing it."[47] Severe disappointment would of course ensue if the reader, hopefully expecting a stress in a certain position, were to discover that, like the fancied extra step at the bottom of an unfamiliar stairway, the expected stress suddenly proved to be absent. It is no wonder that many of the conservative prosodists took their revenge on the offending poet by simply supplying the expected stress themselves.

This same desire to be forewarned manifests itself in Johnson's attitude towards the use of the triplet. Johnson believes that the reader must somehow

[45] Hill, ed., *Lives,* I, 47. See also Hawkins, *History,* I, lxxxii.
[46] Hill, ed., *Lives,* I, 60.
[47] *Ibid.,* I, 467.

be prepared for the approach of triplets, and he considers the customary
marginal bracket the only device available for this office. The bracket, however, is an eyesore on the page, and even preferable to its use would be
"some stated mode of admitting" triplets.[48] To surprise the reader by the
sudden appearance of a triplet in the midst of couplets, unsignaled by the
warning marginal bracket and governed by no "stated mode," would be to
violate some of the most sacrosanct conservative prosodic principles.

Walter Young, in 1786, uses a musical analogy to lend authority to his
distaste for effects of surprise: "The frequent and sudden changes of the
arrangement of strong and feeble sounds, require an uneasy effort of attention
in the [musical] performer, and give an unpleasing surprise and disappointment to the hearer."[49] Here again is the Johnsonian emphasis on disappointment. Despite this implied opposition to variety in stress positions, Young
is to be found a few pages later unaccountably saying that "We are often
pleased by a bold variation from what is strictly regular."[50] We can only
assume that, by this comparatively late date, Young was seeking by this statement to propitiate the rapidly growing number of prosodic liberals by casting
a small sop in their direction. Young is, for the most part, a strikingly conservative metrist, and though fond of exercising himself in the fashionable
poetry-music analogies, never permits such comparisons to lead him where
they led many others, straight towards the overthrow of syllabism and stress
regularity, and the establishment, in their stead, of accentual and equal-time
systems.

Very little of moment is said about alliteration in eighteenth-century
prosodic writing, and when anything is said which rises above the merely
automatic citation of particular beauties, it will generally be found to be in
disparagement of the device. Coventry Patmore points out the fairly obvious
fact that while rhyme is a device appealing to the memory and the sense of
expectation, alliteration, at least in post-Old-English verse, is a device of pure
surprise.[51] It seems very likely that the customary eighteenth-century neglect
of or outright scorn for alliteration as a prosodic device was partly due to this
fact that the appearance of alliteration cannot be anticipated according to any
stated system; it seemed too purely accidental to please the conservatives, too
liable to please by surprising, and too devoid of the obvious display of temporal artifice necessary to make it a satisfactory effect. Bysshe is one of many
conservatives who say that alliteration is to be avoided, and he instances

48 *Ibid.*, I, 468.
49 "An Essay on Rythmical Measures," p. 83; cf. p. 95.
50 *Ibid.*, p. 90.

Davenant and Dryden (in the *Aeneid* translation) as horrible examples.[52] Bysshe will permit it to be a beauty only on those extremely rare occasions when it actually succeeds in heightening the sense through onomatopoeic means.[53]

The concepts of "energy" and the "march" also seem to be allied with the regularistic delight in gratified expectation. In the *Epistle to Augustus,* Pope combines these two ways of describing the regular line:

> Waller was smooth; but Dryden taught to join
> The varying verse, the full-resounding line,
> The long majestic march, and energy divine.
> (267-269)

Sir John Hawkins speaks of "that force and energy which it is observed to derive from the regular commixture and interchange of long and short quantities,"[54] and John Walker writes that "all verse requires a stated regular march of the syllables, and it is in this *march* the grandeur and beauty of the verse consists."[55] This idea of marching, in its purest form, was inseparable from strict regularity of stress and from a "stated" system, one, that is, which pleases not by surprising, but, like a familiar march rhythm, by gratifying the reader's expectations. To look for the effects of "energy" and "marching" in verse in which the stresses fall on unexpected syllables would be, to most of the conservative prosodists, like expecting a body of troops to march with dignity and precision to the freely varied rhythm of plainsong. As I have attempted to show, one of the accepted functions of stress regularity was to seize the mind, to compel it to an unaccustomed effort of attention, to organize it, and, finally, to help regularize it. The mind had to be definitely aware of the act of reading verse as an activity very different from the relaxed method of reading prose. The march-like regular beat of the pure iambic heroic line was best fitted to perform this function of impressing on the mind the requisite effect of organization and control.

4. *Philosophic Idealism and Conservative Prosody*

One speaks of general philosophic concepts in the eighteenth century at great risk of oversimplification and even of entire falsification. Nevertheless, I believe that the term "neo-Platonic" (or better yet *"quasi*-neo-Platonic") can be useful in suggesting certain emphases of the conservative prosodic

---

[51] "English Metrical Criticism," p. 147.
[52] *Art of English Poetry,* p. 10.
[53] *Ibid.,* p. 11. Cf. Newbery, *Art of Poetry on a New Plan,* I, 17, and Shenstone, *Works,* II, 179. ("On Writing and Books").
[54] *History,* I, liv.
[55] *A Rhetorical Grammar, or Course of Lessons in Elocution* (London, 1785), p. 343.

theory. I should make it clear that I am aware of the dangers involved in discovering neo-Platonisms where they do not really exist; what I will be doing here will be simply to suggest that the whole aesthetic of the stress regularists can be rewardingly approached through the idea of pre-existent, universal, and ideal form which has become associated with neo-Platonic aesthetics.

It will perhaps have become clear by now that the conservative and the liberal theoretical prosodic traditions in the eighteenth century differ fundamentally and even, as I have held, irreconcilably. For the conservative theory in its essence chooses to begin with a "pure" and unalterable aesthetic form which is always the same, and to lay this ideal form over the poetic matter, which must then adapt itself to the archetypal form. The process is one of idealizing the real, of "improving" and "regularizing" phonetic materials which are by nature unimproved and devoid of the element of art. The liberal theory, on the other hand, rejects this concept of pre-existent form, and insists that each poetic act be the occasion for the creation of a unique form which can express only that one poetic occasion. In the one theory, the phonetic matter adapts itself to the pre-existing, ideal pattern, and in the other, the materials either change the pattern until it loses its initial essence, or provide a unique pattern which is unlike any other, and which will even be a different one each time the same materials are reorganized.[56] This will, I believe, be found to be the fundamental theoretical difference between the syllabic, or predominantly eighteenth-century theory, and the accentual, or predominantly nineteenth-century theory. No matter how many superficial resemblances each theory may pick up from the other, and no matter how similar the net results appear to the hasty reader, the two different theories on which the two different methods of poetic composition and construction ultimately rely cannot, and should not, be merged into one;[57] to attempt to blend them is to fail to discriminate between two different methods of composing verse, or of writing a novel, or of building a house. The difference between the two ways of working is finally a fundamental difference of sen-

---

[56] See Stewart, *Modern Metrical Technique*, p. 117.

[57] Robert Bridges has perceived that accentual verse is not simply "loose" or free syllabic verse, but is an entirely different prosodic system, requiring a different method of composition and a different mode of reception, whether read silently or aloud. (*Milton's Prosody*, pp. 111-112). S. Ernest Sprott emphasizes the differences in compositional technique: he points out that, in the accentual pentameter, "the poet is moulding his prosody to his rhythms," while, in the syllabic pentameter, "the poet is moulding his rhythms by his prosody." (*Milton's Art of Prosody*, p. 106). Cf. Coleridge: "Since Dryden, the metre of our poets leads to the sense: in our elder and more genuine poets, the sense, including the passion, leads to the metre." (Thomas M. Raysor, ed., *Coleridge's Miscellaneous Criticism* [Cambridge, Mass., 1936], p. 67).

sibility, and implies a distinction between two ways of regarding reality itself.[58]

This neo-Platonic tendency in the conservative aesthetic of prosody will thus be seen to be related to the conception of ideal and universal art advanced by Sir Joshua Reynolds in his earlier *Discourses*.[59] To the conservative prosodists and to Reynolds, the function of the artist is to improve, to present the materials of nature in ideal shape, to purge away the deformities and irregularities and appearances of accident inherent in the natural condition of things, and to present the object ennobled by all the devices of purposive and conscious art.[60] It was very widely held during the century that the function of regularistic prosodic devices was to "improve" the ordinary appearance of linguistic elements, and the reading of verse aloud was assumed to be an act entirely differing from the act of delivering prose. William Cockin, for example, says in 1775 that "reading [aloud] is an art *improving* and not *imitating* nature."[61] In music, dancing, and gardening, as well as in poetry, "the pleasure received flows principally from a *beautiful* arrangement, and *artful* improvement of the simple natural elements, of which these articles respectively consist."[62] Poetry is and should always sound "as much different from the language of ordinary discourse . . . as the movements of the dance are from common walking."[63] John Walker presents the theory in terms similar to Reynolds': " . . . the pronunciation of verse is a species of elocution very distinct from the pronunciation of prose; both of them have nature for their basis, but one is common, familiar, and practical nature; the other beautiful, elevated, and ideal nature; the latter as different from the former as the elegant step of a minuet is from the common motions of walking."[64] And Johnson phrases the theory of the ideal in this way: "Poetry pleases by exhibiting an idea more grateful to the mind than things themselves afford. This effect proceeds from the display of those parts of nature which

---

[58] Cf. T. S. Eliot: " . . . a different meter is a different mode of thought." ("A Talk on Dante," *Kenyon Review*, XIV [1952], 182).

[59] See Louis I. Bredvold, "The Tendency toward Platonism in Neo-classical Esthetics," *ELH*, I (1934), 91-119.

[60] Samuel Rogers, for example, describes Reynolds' portrait of Gibbon as "that wonderful portrait, in which, while the oddness and vulgarity of the features are refined away, the likeness is perfectly preserved." (J. B. Bury, ed., *Autobiography of Edward Gibbon, as Originally Edited by Lord Sheffield* [World's Classics ed.; Oxford, 1907], p. xiii).

[61] *The Art of Delivering Written Language; or, an Essay on Reading. In Which the Subject is Treated Philosophically as well as with a view to Practice* (London, 1775), pp. 84-85.

[62] *Ibid.*, pp. 111-112.

[63] *Ibid.*, p. 135.

[64] *Elements of Elocution*, II, 176.

attract, and the concealment of those which repel, the imagination."[65] That is, both poetic structure and the elocutionary delivery of poetry idealize the natural, unimproved phenomena of speech; they order what is naturally disorderly by fitting and cutting and trimming natural linguistic material until it coincides as exactly as possible with a form previously agreed upon as beautiful.

The term "melody" is often employed by the conservative prosodists in a way which illuminates these tendencies of the conservative prosodic theory to express itself in terms of an ideal theory of art. "Melody" is similar to "harmony," which I have shown used as a general description of the condition of the purely iambic line, but "melody" actually seems to be suggestive of the notion of ideal harmony. Harmony, that is, is a description of the regu-laristic metrical manifestations of a given actual line, "considered by itself." Melody is the ideal and completely abstract archetype of which harmony is the specific, almost material, prosodic representation. Melody is thus wholly ideal, and a line never really achieves perfect melody; the most perfect harmony, or regularity, which a line exhibits can merely make an approach to ideal melody, just as material objects never attain the perfection of their Platonic forms. This notion of ideal melody became so widespread that even some of the liberal prosodists came to use it as a handy means of sanctioning variety: a prosodist who was in favor of bold variations of stress could always point out that, although a certain line might indeed be freely varied for the sake of "expression," its abstract "melody" was still purely regular. This transparent device seems to have functioned quite well at times in quieting conservative objections to bold substitution.

The words of a few of the prosodists themselves will perhaps clarify some of these uses of "melody." Lord Kames, for example, is one of those who regard melody as the abstract scansion pattern of a perfectly regular line; it is what results if, after one marks the scansion of a regular iambic pentameter line, one erases the words and leaves the marks of scansion. What remains is the abstract pattern of rhythmical perfection, or melody; what one has if the words are replaced under the scansion marks is an example of harmony, for there is no possible way in which ten syllables can be arranged so as to produce genuine melody. That would be a work for the Creator of the pattern Himself; the mortal poet can only approach melody through as perfect a harmony (*i.e.*, stress regularity) as possible. Proper accent in reading verse is thus, to Kames, partly a matter of "humoring the sense"

---

[65] Hill, ed., *Lives*, I, 292.

(that is, reading verse as if it were printed as prose) and partly an affair of paying attention to "melody" (that is, indicating in the reading that the reader is aware of the existence of the abstract stress pattern by stressing regularly each alternate syllable, whether it receives a sense stress or not).[66] Kames prefers, then, in the reading of verse, a compromise between the abstract melodic pattern and the ordinary sense stresses.

John Scott finds the term "melody" convenient in commenting on a line from Dyer's *The Ruins of Rome:*

Tumbling all precipitate down-dash'd.

(41)

This line, to Scott, "has not the structure of any English verse," and consequently makes no approach to melody.[67] Peter Walkden Fogg, in his *Elementa Anglicana* (1792-1796), makes melody equal to the impression of the pattern of the verse left behind on the reader's consciousness after the verse has been read. Melody depends on "the exactness and nature of the feet. A mixture of feet is prejudicial to . . . melody."[68] Fogg wishes, however, to authorize occasional departures from strict regularity of stress, and he goes about the task this way: some variety is necessary, he says, to set off and call attention to harmony when it occurs; "for the sake of this," he goes on, "some things are admitted inconsistent with the finest melody, although nothing absolutely harsh or dissonant."[69] In this position of Fogg's, we have a fine example of the use of "harmony" and "melody" to mean different things. Harmony is, to Fogg, the utmost actual regularity which the stress pattern can approach without sacrifice of the requisite element of variety; melody is the abstract ideal towards which the harmony of the line always tends. By paying the conventional attention to the requirements of melody here, Fogg manages to soften his plea for greater variety of stresses, and to make his position appear much more conservative than it really is.

As late as 1795 the conception of melody as the abstract ideal of absolute stress regularity is still in currency. Lindley Murray speaks with deference of melody while seeking, like Fogg, to advance the cause of variety; Murray gives to each varied line a purely automatic and totally nonexistent melody to keep conservative objectors satisfied, and then, once this has been taken care of, proceeds to advocate very free stress variations.[70] The melody, Murray

---

[66] *Elements of Criticism,* II, 255.
[67] *Critical Essays,* p. 121.
[68] *Elementa Anglicana: or, The Principles of English Grammar Displayed and Exemplified, In a Method Entirely New* (Stockport, 1792-1796), II, 195.
[69] *Ibid.,* II, 196.
[70] *English Grammar,* p. 209.

could point out to the incredulous, was still "there" in each line, but searchers for it would look in vain, since melody was, by this time, purely theoretical. Hence, by the 1790's, the theory of melody is serving no purpose except the rather deceptive one of offering a respectable theoretical justification for varied stresses. Melody had been earlier, however, an idea which had had a very powerful and widespread influence on both the scansion and the public delivery of poetry, and the nature and results of this influence we must now consider.

5. *The Fruits of Idealism: Artificial Scansion and Elocution*

The use of a rather special terminology here requires some explanation. The term "artificial scansion" is already in currency to indicate a system of verse notation which tends to neglect the natural speech stresses in favor of the theoretical "melodic" stress pattern;[71] it is a useful term to denote that sort of scansion which became widespread among the conservative prosodic theorists of the eighteenth century who came under the influence of the notion of melody. In dealing with the elocutionary delivery of verse according to this "melodic" artificial scansion, I shall have recourse to the term "artificial elocution." On the other hand, the two phrases "sense scansion" and "sense elocution," clumsy as they may be, I must use to refer to scansion and delivery of poetic lines according to the true speech stresses of the words, with little or no attention being paid to the "proper" melody, or abstract pattern of accents in the lines.

The ideal or *quasi*-neo-Platonic theory of prosody was being daily put into practice during the century by perfectly well-intentioned gentlemen of letters, and the results, both in artificial scansion and artificial elocution, are difficult indeed to face with objectivity. Bentley's cavalier treatment of Milton's prosody can hardly be viewed without irritation, and it is not the intention of these remarks to palliate Bentley's offense against the prerogatives of genius and against simple open-mindedness. It will become apparent, however, that the Bentleys of the century were not simply indulging their spleen or their envy of their betters when they deliberately scanned artificially; they were for the most part attempting to apply in practice, the best way they knew, the theory of ideal art, which, with its dual emphases on universality and ideality, bears a close resemblance to the humanistic aesthetics of Johnson and Reynolds. The results are indeed not often happy, but they are one fumbling manifestation of an imposing and consistent aesthetic, and they are

---

[71] George R. Stewart, "The Iambic-Trochaic Theory in Relation to Musical Notation of Verse," *JEGP*, XXIV (1925), 70.

a great deal less haphazard and accidental than they may seem. They thus deserve to be inspected with all available tolerance.

William Benson, in 1739, applies artificial scansion to the verse of *Paradise Lost*, and, by laying a strong stress on each alternate syllable, finds that "audibly," in

. . . Thus to his Son audibly spake

must be pronounced "audíbly." Benson declares that Milton surely intended this "Varying of the common pronunciation," and in fact believes such unusual stresses to be one of Milton's conscious beauties. "For so it must be read," Benson says of the line, "and not after the common manner."[72] The "common manner" would be, of course, a reading of the line according to a system of sense scansion, with the natural speech stresses furnishing the rhythmical pattern. Such a method of reading would seem to Benson, because of its neglect of the concept of art and melody, totally unsuitable for rendering Milton's grandiose style. In the same way, Milton's phrase

. . . Thro' th'infinite Host

is to be read "Thró' th'infínite Hóst," in such a way as to "fit" the words into the melodic stress pattern.[73] This technique of artificial scansion, very well developed in Benson, permits him to believe without the necessity of further investigation that "all *English* Verses are *Iambick.*"[74]

Again, the interests of harmony impel Edward Manwaring to scan this way:

Swĕar | thát nŏne ‖ ére hăd | súch ă | grácefŭl | Árt.

Manwaring goes on to explain, "If in reading this Verse we acute or circumflex [*i.e.,* stress] . . . had or a, which all that read it are apt to do, the Harmony of the Verse is utterly lost."[75]

Lord Kames expresses the very essence of the conservative prosodists' tendency towards the ideal theory when he says in 1762, speaking of classical verse, that the feet must "regulate the arrangement [of words], for they serve no other purpose."[76] The notion of the words themselves furnishing the stress pattern of a line would of course seem visionary and preposterous to Kames; words are the static, inert material, and they must be regulated by a pattern which has independent existence, and by which they are transformed from nature into art. In a situation in which the words seem to adjust themselves imperfectly to the ideal melodic archetype, "false quantity" exists, and

---

[72] *Letters Concerning Poetical Translations,* p. 50.
[73] *Ibid.*
[74] *Ibid.*, p. 69.
[75] *Of Harmony and Numbers,* p. 52.
[76] *Elements of Criticism,* II, 257-258.

false quantity can only be "uncouth." As an instance of this imperfect adjustment of the phonetic matter to the melodic pattern Kames offers this line
from *The Rape of the Lock:*

Th'ad*vent'*rous *ba*ron the bright *lo*cks ad*mir'*d.

(II, 29)

Kames italicizes to mark the "seats" of the accents, and says of the stress on
"the," "Let it be pronounced short [*i.e.,* without a strong accent] and it
reduces the melody almost to nothing."[77] These theories of ideality and
artificial scansion have thus deprived Kames of the ability to read even Pope's
poetry in the way it was intended, for melody must now be served at the
expense of every other consideration. As Richard Hurd complained in 1766,
the original "natural ear" for both poetic production and reception has become
rare, and the whole art is now being "conducted by artificial rules."[78]

William Kenrick is another who favors a method of artificial elocution
which will adapt "the oratorical accent, or the natural stress of voice in
declamation, to the artificial mechanism of the verse."[79] Lord Monboddo
likewise sees the necessity of the scansion

Bĕfŏre Pórtŏ Béllŏ lýĭng,

"in order to make the verse run,"[80] he explains. Whether the abstract
melodic pattern is pure iambic pentameter or pure trochaic tetrameter, the
natural speech materials fitted into it must be boldly adjusted, trimmed, and,
in general, "improved."[81] Artificial scansion of the first line of *Paradise
Lost* became almost a rite among the conservative prosodists; Monboddo scans,
of course,

Ŏf Mán's fĭrst dĭsŏbédĭence, ánd thĕ Frúit.[82]

Elsewhere, he defends this scansion by saying, "It is a beauty in our versification, when the emphasis, which the sense requires, and the *fortè* [stress],
which is necessary to the verse, coincide. . . . if in reading the first line of the
Paradise Lost, you were to lay an emphasis upon the word *first,* which by no
means is necessary [!], the verse would plainly halt. . . . "[83]

I have largely been concerned with the influence of the theory of ideality

[77] *Ibid.,* II, 273-274.

[78] *Works,* II, 12. ("On the Idea of Universal Poetry").

[79] *New Dictionary of the English Language,* p. 51; see also pp. 49-50.

[80] *Of the Origin and Progress of Language,* II, 392.

[81] See also James Beattie, *Dissertations Moral and Critical* (London, 1783), p. 289.
("The Theory of Language"); Hugh Blair, *Lectures on Rhetoric and Belles Lettres,* III,
104; and Jefferson, *Writings,* XVIII, 419-421.

[82] *Of the Origin and Progress of Language,* II, 326. For another of the many appearances of the same scansion, see Anselm Bayly, *The Alliance of Musick, Poetry, and
Oratory* (London, 1789), p. 297.

[83] Steele, *Prosodia Rationalis,* p. 109.

on the prosodists; Allan Ramsay the Younger provides a glimpse into its influence on the poet himself. This is Ramsay's conception of the way poetry is, and should be, composed: "There is nothing more certain than that a poet before he writes a word, has already formed in his mind the tune, measure, or cadence to which his words are to be adapted [!]. If the words he chuses are of themselves composed of such syllables as fit the places he had allotted to them; so much the better. If not, he must, in the pronunciation, shorten or lengthen them . . . till they become fit: for the measure must be preferred, *coute qui coute*, otherwise it is no longer poetry, but prose."[84] Ramsay seems unaware of the possibilities of the logical extension of this view, for all one would have to do to produce "poetry" as differentiated from prose would be to decide first on a "measure" (say, trochaic tetrameter), and then boldly "shorten" or "lengthen" the words in a prose sentence as required to make them "fit the places," thus:

> Thé prŏsódĭc sýstĕm héld bў
> Á. Rămsáy thĕ Yóungĕr ínvĭtes
> Ábŭsés ŏf thé grŏssést kĭnd.

Ramsay's phrase "the measure must be preferred" is an excellent statement of the essential and unique quality of syllabic and stress-regularist prosody, as differentiated from accentual prosody, in which natural speech stresses are "preferred."

Johnson's confession of an inability to read Cowley's lines is another indication that the art of sense scansion was fast becoming lost, even among professional men of letters. Johnson says that "if what [Cowley] thinks be true, that his numbers are unmusical only when they are ill read, the art of reading them is at present lost."[85] Johnson is, in general, a sort of hybrid scansionist; he generally holds to the mid-point between artificial and sense scansion advocated, but not always practiced, by Lord Kames. Sometimes Johnson will appear to be entirely under the influence of the artificial scansion system, as when he says of Gay's *Fables* that "the versification is smooth, and the diction, though now and then a little constrained by the measure or the rhyme, is generally happy";[86] and sometimes, as when he discovers Milton's "dissonances," he reveals himself perfectly capable of reading verse according to a system of natural speech stresses.

William Mason, around 1780, delivers the artificial scansionists' credo when he says, while discussing psalmody, that every line in common meter

---

[84] "An Enquiry into the Principles of English Versification," fol. 7. But see below, Chap. V, Sect. 1.
[85] Hill, ed., *Lives,* I, 59.
[86] *Ibid.,* II, 283.

"is usually of the Iambic species, that is, the first syllable, whether long or short in actual quantity, is always pronounced short, and the next syllable long, and so alternately to the end of every line."[87] The implications here as to Mason's reception of the favorite Augustan device of the initial trochee are interesting, for if Mason reads all verse as he does poems in common meter, effects of stress variety to which Dryden and Pope devoted intense effort he would completely miss.

Walter Young supplies a remark which indicates that the practice of artificial elocution was intended to help guard the listener from unwelcome surprises. Predictability of recurrence is what is wanted. A rhythm that is to be perfectly satisfactory and agreeable "must be constructed according to some measure"; the hearer must be made aware of this measure at the very beginning of the poem; "he must be instantly led to adopt" the measure "and retain it to the end of the [rhythmical] succession."[88] It was apparently often felt that artificial elocution, if not an absolutely perfect method of reading verse, at least helped avoid the sudden surprises which might strike and "disorder" the hearer, surprises which the poet's use of substitution might produce. The art of reading thus becomes, like the art of constructing verse, an additional act of ordering matter, and a given poem, if regularly composed in the first place, will reach the hearer two removes away from "nature"; the poet will do all the ordering he can, and the reader will then complete the process of regularization, so that the finished aesthetic product, the poem as read aloud, will not want ample evidence of artifice.

Samuel Horsley lays it down as a rule for reading verse aloud that "we give the sharp stroke of the voice upon the syllable which, by its place in the verse, ought to be long."[89] Had Pope been able to anticipate what the late-century artificial scansionists would be doing to all his delicately contrived effects arising from skillful and controlled dissyllabic substitution, he would no doubt have left some specific instructions for the reading of his verse; as it was, the artificial elocutionists were reading Milton, Pope, and Glover in exactly the same way, and in a way which might have drawn from Pope something stronger than his ironic comment on fashionable love poetry,

Nature must give way to Art.[90]

Joseph Robertson confesses in 1799 that he likes, in reading verse, to "favour the measure," and he scans,

---

[87] *The Works of William Mason, M. A.* (London, 1811), III, 389-390. ("On Parochial Psalmody").
[88] "An Essay on Rythmical Measures," pp. 84-85.
[89] *On the Prosodies of the Greek and Latin Languages* (London, 1796), p. 5.
[90] "Song by a Person of Quality," line 4.

Whose límbs unbúryed, ón the náked shóre.[91]

Robertson's artificial scansion seems to proceed from an obsession with the principle that the line of distinction between poetry and prose must be well marked and absolutely rigid. "Let it always be remembered," he warns, "that, in reading, as well as in writing and printing, the different characteristics of prose and verse should be inviolably preserved"; verse, after all, "should be read as verse, and prose as prose."[92] Robertson advances his conception of form as something distinct from the matter poured into it when he declares that "When the accented syllable happens to be an insignificant particle, or a syllable, on which the voice cannot properly rest, the verse is lame and inharmonious."[93] There is no suspicion here that the relative sense significance of a given syllable determines the amount of stress the syllable automatically receives; the "accented syllable" which Robertson speaks of is a segment of the familiar melodic archetype, and the actual syllables which the line contains must, like formless atoms being organized out of chaos, range themselves in the appropriate manner. The true poet is a "maker," and it is his prime function to bring order out of confusion by arranging matter until it resembles the plan he has in mind; like the Creator, he transforms chaos into order by command, and makes thereby a garden of due proportion, harmony, and delight.

To Robertson, "the structure of the verse is irregular, when the poetical [i.e., melodic] and the oratorial [sic] accent do not perfectly coincide,"[94] and if the poet has been careless of this principle, the reader must "favour the measure" to produce the requisite harmony. Robertson's favoring of the measure of Paradise Lost produces such unique and engaging pronunciations as "nevér," "undér," "latér," and "shadíng."[95]

Even with the appearance, around the beginning of the nineteenth century, of a prosody based on the totally different principle of accentualism, the theory of ideality and the ghost of artificial scansion were never wholly dissipated. Although Wordsworth generally shares Coleridge's accentualistic theories, we come upon a remaining faint shadow of the theory and practice we have been investigating in Wordsworth's statement that the 1798 Lyrical Ballads was produced " . . . as an experiment, which, I hoped, might be of some use to ascertain, how far, by fitting to metrical arrangement a selection

---

[91] Essay on the Nature of the English Verse, p. 3.
[92] Ibid., p. 9.
[93] Ibid., p. 25.
[94] Ibid., p. 27.
[95] Ibid., p. 59.

of the real language of men in a state of vivid sensation,"[96] poetic pleasure might be imparted. Even Coleridge himself occasionally seems to intend an artificial stress in the purportedly accentual *Christabel;* although the poem was professedly composed on "a new principle; namely, that of counting in each line the accents, not the syllables,"[97] and although Coleridge imagined that he had preserved an accentual skeleton of four stresses per line, many of the lines can become accentually regular only by the reader's laying an accent on unimportant articles, conjunctions, and prepositions.[98] Lines such as

> From her kennel beneath the rock
> Maketh answer to the clock
>
> (9-10)

we must suppose Coleridge thought accentually regular, although according to the method of pure sense scansion which is indispensable in accentual prosody, each contains at most three stresses. Coleridge's prosodic sensibility, it would seem, was strongly influenced by the artificial scansionist tradition which flourished in the time of his youth; the young Coleridge must have heard many performances of artificial elocution and, although he was determined to write verse according to a new system, the traditional method of "favouring the measure" made too strong an impression on him to be entirely effaced. It may illuminate Coleridge's prosodic sensibility and help emphasize that eighteenth-century modes of feeling did not depart as if on signal in 1798 to remember that Coleridge once said of the young Tennyson, "I can scarcely scan his verses."[99] A thoroughgoing accentualist, who would necessarily scan and read strictly according to sense, would have no trouble at all with the meter of Tennyson's early poems.

The system of eighteenth-century artificial elocution was still attracting adherents in the late nineteenth century, at least in connection with *Paradise Lost,* a work which seems to draw to it prosodic eccentrics with a power almost occult. Robert Bridges notes that the same sort of artificial elocution which I have shown functioning in the eighteenth century was very commonly the method of reading the poem around 1887. "It was generally thought necessary and correct," Bridges reports, "to mispronounce words so as to make them scan with a regular alternate accent." It was mainly to

---

[96] A. B. Grosart, ed., *The Prose Works of William Wordsworth* (London, 1876), II, 79. (My italics).

[97] James Dykes Campbell, ed., *The Poetical Works of Samuel Taylor Coleridge* (London, 1938), p. 601.

[98] See Bridges, *Milton's Prosody,* p. 88.

[99] Raysor, ed., *Coleridge's Miscellaneous Criticism,* p. 419.

correct this widely practiced mode of reading Milton, in fact, that Bridges published the first edition of *Milton's Prosody* in 1893.[100]

In 1913, T. B. Rudmose-Brown is to be observed taking M. Verrier, the French metrist, severely to task for assuming that the sense scansion of a line and the actual oral delivery of the same line should coincide. Rudmose-Brown holds the very eighteenth-century view that "the phonetic liquid" is somehow altered in its natural accents by being "poured into metrical bottles."[101] Thus the same theory of ideality and the same practice of artificial scansion which flourished in the mid-eighteenth century thrust themselves anomalously into the world of Ezra Pound and E. E. Cummings, where they remain to this very day, visiting occasionally the brains of the most learned and sensitive critics. In fact, there is no better way to appreciate the power of eighteenth-century prosodic conventions to perpetuate themselves almost indefinitely than to contemplate the prescriptive "scansions" and regularistic exhortations which now and then offer themselves to the public view in various modern critical works and in the scholarly quarterlies.[102] For historical reasons, verse composed syllabically should be so scanned, and verse composed accentually should be scanned according to true speech stress. Nothing is gained by reading into eighteenth-century verse the modes of nineteenth-century verse construction, and a very great deal is lost by laying over modern accentual verse a prosodic "explanation" which is suited to dealing only with certain poems composed syllabically.

That artificial scansion and elocution were extremely popular practices in the middle of the eighteenth century will appear from the immense number of complaints against them; these criticisms of the contemporary methods of elocution reveal that artificial elocution, or something very much like it, had invaded the schools, the universities, the stage, and the pulpit. The majority of readers and speakers were delivering poetry with strict attention to alternating stresses, whether supplied by the sense of the verse or not, and they were even delivering prose with as close an approximation to pure iambic cadences as possible. Artificial elocution had become the fashion, and a reading of verse according to natural sense emphases was regarded as an inharmonious or "low" delivery.

Isaac Watts furnishes evidence that artificial elocution was in fashion

---

[100] *Milton's Prosody*, p. 113.

[101] "English and French Metric," *MLR*, VIII (1913), 105.

[102] See, *e.g.*, Scholl, "English Metre Once More"; Brander Matthews, *A Study of Versification* (New York, 1911); and Yvor Winters, "The Audible Reading of Poetry," *Hudson Review*, IV (1951), 433-447.

as early as 1721, but was mainly being practiced, at that first stage of its development, by "ignorant Persons," who, imagining that English verse should always manifest alternating stresses, automatically "lay a Stress upon every second Syllable."[103] A few lines later, however, "ignorant Persons" becomes "most People."[104] In 1762, Thomas Sheridan complains of the widespread practice of stressing naturally unaccented syllables in declamation; this affectation, he says, is particularly prevalent in the reading of the church service.[105] Sheridan makes the same observation over twenty years later and supplies the information that this habit of laying a stress on every alternate syllable is generally acquired in the elementary schools (many of them taught, of course, by the very grammarians whose hack textbooks helped perpetuate Bysshian syllabism and stress regularity), from which institutions it is carried abroad to corrupt the whole world of readers.[106] As a result of this sort of training in the schools, arising from a concern with "elegance" at the expense of meaning, "few are found whose reading or recitation can be endured."[107]

John Rice in 1765 terms artificial elocution a "vicious Custom,"[108] and says that it is the "common Method" of reading aloud. Most readers, Rice asserts, would read the line

Tow'rds four fair Nymphs, ran four tall men full speed

as if it consisted of five iambic feet, when it should be read with a precisely equal stress on each word.[109] Rice calls the fashionable elocution "artificial Modulation," and says that it "breaks in upon that natural Modulation [*i.e.,* sense elocution] which is essential to Expression."[110]

This neglect of natural emphasis in favor of a predetermined system of "melodic" stresses came to infect even the lowly ballad-singers on the London streets, who were merely, in all probability, innocently attempting to imitate the method of reading verse which they occasionally heard from the lips of their more genteel betters. Allan Ramsay the Younger, discoursing very wittily[111] on the technique used by the balladmongers to vend "certain dismal

---

[103] *Art of Reading and Writing English,* pp. 69-70.

[104] *Ibid.,* p. 70.

[105] *A Course of Lectures on Elocution: Together with Two Dissertations on Language: and Some Other Tracts Relating to those Subjects* (London, 1762), pp. 53-55.

[106] *A General Dictionary of the English Language. One main Object of which, is, to establish a plain and permanent Standard of Pronunciation. To which is prefixed a Rhetorical Grammar* (London, 1780), I, 43 ff.

[107] *Lectures on the Art of Reading,* pp. 385-386.

[108] *Introduction to the Art of Reading,* p. 109.

[109] *Ibid.,* pp. 144-145.

[110] *Ibid.,* p. 145. See also pp. 158-159 and 196-235.

[111] Of a man who finds diversion in setting (and singing) the Twenty-third Ode of Catullus to the tune of "Sally in our Alley," some wit may be expected. See "Enquiry into the Principles of English Versification," fol. 30ᵛ.

ditties," writes in 1775 that "these rhapsodists sing their ditties as if they were all pure Iambics, not regarding the quantity of the words of which they happen to be composed"; most of the ballad-singers, behaving exactly like their more learned brethren in pulpits, universities, and drawing-rooms, make "long short and short long, as the five cadences of their time require."[112] Ramsay is merely reporting the obvious when he says, "the generality of people, and among these some of the most learned, do not admit that verses are to be pronounced as they are scann'd."[113]

William Cockin states in the same year, however, that artificial elocution, although once highly fashionable, is now showing signs of waning. The "cant" of artificial elocution is "disgustful now to all but mere rustics, on account of its being out of fashion." This method of delivery was once "the favourite modulation, in which heroic verses were recited by our ancestors." Cockin concludes with a moral not entirely irrelevant to modern prosodic study: "So fluctuating are the tastes and practices of mankind!"[114]

Despite Cockin's perhaps wishful consignment of artificial elocution to the past, Joshua Steele, writing four years later, still finds the practice current enough to require correction: "Poetry is often read in a certain formal manner, supposing the ten syllables of *our heroics* must be cut exactly into five cadences of two syllables each"; and those who make this division of the poetic line in their minds, Steele declares, "frequently misplace the *light* and the *heavy* [accents]."[115] In 1781, John Walker criticizes "most readers" of poetry for not possessing "a sufficient delicacy of ear to keep the harmonious smoothness of verse from sliding into a whining cant; nay, so agreeable is this cant to many readers that a simple and natural delivery of verse seems tame and insipid, and much too familiar for the dignity of the language."[116] Walker, unlike most of those who simply denounce artificial elocution, offers a specific remedy: let those "whose ears are not just" read verse "exactly as if it were prose: for though this may be said to be an error, it is certainly an error on the safer side."[117] Walker also furnishes evidence that the artificial mode of delivering verse on the stage "very generally prevailed" before the time of Garrick, and he adds that it even "now [1798] prevails among some classes of speakers," although it is rapidly becoming "despised."[118]

[112] *Ibid.*, fols. 23-23ᵛ.
[113] *Ibid.*, fol. 38ᵛ.
[114] *Art of Delivering Written Language*, pp. 72-73, n.
[115] *Prosodia Rationalis*, pp. 76-77.
[116] *Elements of Elocution*, II, 173-174.
[117] *Ibid.*
[118] *A Key to the Classical Pronunciation of Greek, Latin, and Scripture Proper Names* (5th ed.; London, 1815), p. 281.

Hugh Blair holds that the desire to lend "gravity and force to their Discourse" prompts many to use the techniques of artificial elocution even in their everyday conversation.[119] And Joseph Robertson, who was not always successful in resisting temptations of this sort himself, says that many initial trochees are lost and wasted simply because readers are so anxious to "read properly" that they always stress the second syllable in an iambic line, even if it happens to be a minor and completely unemphasized part of speech.[120]

All these comments on the fashionable practice of stressing lines of verse artificially point to some interesting speculations. It may be inferred, for one thing, that the rise of this artificial elocution (which seems to have been the conventional way of reading verse from about 1720 to the 1790's) may partly represent the impact of an enormous group of new readers, drawn mainly from the middle class, who, deficient in some areas of formal education but possessing an overpowering compulsion to read verse as a mark of gentility, began to interest themselves in poetry early in the eighteenth century. The level of their understanding of the verse they avidly declaimed aloud in their drawing rooms may be deduced from these testimonies of the way they customarily read it. How much the decline of the heroic couplet as a popular form around the end of the century was a result of the simple inability of most of its readers to make sense of its prosodic mechanisms (and thus, to a large degree, its total meaning) it would be hazardous to estimate. It may be said, however, that a verse form depends a great deal for its usefulness on the ability of its readers to appreciate not merely what the words express, but also the subtle technical devices through which a form expresses a large part of the meaning. To a young man embarking on a poetic career in the 1780's or 1790's, a form which through no inherent deficiency of its own had largely lost the power to communicate would be a form obviously to be avoided. When one sees Wordsworth and Coleridge returning to ballad measure and superficially simple little stanzas, one may profitably recall what had happened during the eighteenth century to the heroic line's ability to carry meaning. Part of the couplet's decline as a form is attributable, I believe, to influences which are primarily elocutionary.

In this chapter I have sought to present some of the ethical and aesthetic implications of a prosody of regularity. I hope that these theories with which the conservative prosodists hoped to defend their syllabic and regularistic metric help illuminate the true nature of that system of versification which

---

[119] *Lectures on Rhetoric and Belles Lettres*, II, 436.
[120] *Essay on the Nature of the English Verse*, p. 12.

has come to be known as neo-classic. One would not care to justify everything the conservative prosodists advanced as a theoretical support for the system of versification which their ears told them was a suitable one for fixing and stabilizing the reality which presented itself to them. One would, however, wish to suggest that condemnations of the "monotony" of the conservative prosody are quite idle unless the wider ethical, aesthetic, and finally metaphysical and religious correlatives of that prosody are taken into consideration. The aesthetic speculations of the neo-classic period comprise, I think, a body of theory which is remarkably unified and singularly logical. The versification of some of the lesser poets of the period and the prosodic theorizing of the more lightweight critics and metrists are not always inspiring exhibits, but the ethical and aesthetic tenets of which the conservative prosodic theory is but a single expression compel our respect for their coherence and solidity. Perhaps the prosody may some day gain our respect for its uncompromising assertion of the power of the mind to control experience, and for its humane conviction of the dignity of that power.

CHAPTER III

THE THEORY OF POETIC CONTRACTIONS

Most modern readers of poetry, presented with the following line and asked to ascertain its number of syllables,

> Wandering in many a shade becheckered grot,

would no doubt consider the question of its date of composition entirely irrelevant. And yet, an historical approach to post-Renaissance prosodic theory and practice reminds us that had the line been composed during the early eighteenth century, it would consist of ten syllables only, while if it had been written yesterday, it would consist plainly of twelve. This elementary example is sufficient to show that historical and linguistic foundations are quite indispensable to metrical study: once we detach the study of metrics from what can be gained of a relevant historical perspective, we are immediately cast adrift to float about in mere frivolity or, at worst, total confusion.

In this chapter, then, I should like to approach historically four major topics: first, the influence upon eighteenth-century contraction theory of various classical interdictions of hiatus; second, syllabic theories of poetic contraction and the question of the degree of actual contraction in elocution; third, the reaction of the accentualists to the contraction tradition; and finally, the influence on poetic contractions of the prevailing syncopations in early eighteenth-century colloquial speech.

1. *The Debt to Classical Precepts*

It is important to remember, at the very outset of an investigation of eighteenth-century poetic contractions, the immense debt of this practice to classical precepts and examples. Cicero and Quintilian especially had devoted a great deal of attention to the ugliness of hiatus, or the open conjunction of initial or terminal vowels in adjacent words in verse, and most eighteenth-century sanctions of the use of apocope (*e.g.,* "th'unwieldy") to overcome this sort of "botch" are generally indebted, ultimately, to the rhetorics of these two ancients.[1] It seems clear that classical prohibitions of hiatus also influenced the opinion held by most of the eighteenth-century conservative prosodic theorists that contiguous vowels, even within words, must be con-

---

[1] Walter J. Bate, *The Stylistic Development of Keats* (New York, 1945), p. 24.

tracted through synaeresis (*e.g.,* "happ-yer"), although this sort of contraction is, of course, practically demanded by a syllabic and stress-regularist prosody.[2]

Whatever the effect of contiguous vowels may have been to the Greek and Roman ear, there certainly seems nothing inherently offensive to moderns in a phrase like "the oboe on the edge," or even in Pope's line from the *Essay on Criticism*

> Though oft the ear the open vowels tire.
> (II, 345)

In fact, one may be safe in assuming that many modern students have found themselves rather puzzled by just what Pope was imitating in this line. The interdiction of contiguous vowels almost never makes an appearance in nineteenth-century and later prosodic theorizing, and it is difficult to put oneself into a position where one can perceive their "ugly" effect in the same way that it struck the classically trained theorists of the eighteenth century.

The influence of classical criticism and practice here is apparent from the very beginning. Dryden, for example, goes to Virgil for authority against gaping vowels. In his "Dedication of the Aeneis," Dryden points out with some pride that "there is not, to the best of my remembrance, one vowel gaping on another for want of a *caesura* [meaning here contraction by apocope], in this whole poem,"[3] and he indicates that Virgil has been his master in this avoidance of hiatus.[4] Of course, Dryden is writing a syllabic poem. We know that he does not permit trisyllabic feet, and it will thus be a central tenet of his prosodic theory that apocope may be freely employed to smooth out and regularize lines which otherwise would contain trisyllabic stress groups.

The syllabist Bysshe likewise maintains that "concourse of vowels" is to be avoided; it has not been sufficiently eschewed by Chaucer and "Spencer," but was carefully avoided by "the Latins."[5] "E" must always be elided in phrases like "the open," and Waller's "Thy Iambicks" contains a "fault," since two vowels of similar sound must never coincide.[6] Bysshe lays down the general rule that because hiatus is "very disagreeable," "whenever . . . a Vowel ends a Word, the next ought to begin with a Consonant."[7]

Bentley, for all his deep concern with the "certain number of syllables"

---

[2] See Sprott, *Milton's Art of Prosody,* p. 74.
[3] Ker, ed., *Essays,* II, 216-217.
[4] *Ibid.,* II, 215.
[5] *Art of English Poetry,* p. 9.
[6] *Ibid.,* p. 10.
[7] *Ibid.,* p. 17.

which a line must contain, occasionally considers the device of apocope so mandatory that he gives it precedence over even the syllabic regularity of the line. In his haste to eliminate hiatus in this line from *Paradise Lost*,

> Glory of him that made them, to transform,
> (I, 370)

Bentley marks an apostrophe between "Glory'of," and thus reduces the line to a very un-Miltonic nine syllables. A perception that something or other was vaguely amiss here may have prompted his comment on the passage in which this line occurs: "All this Passage is negligently done, as if the Poet was then tired or sleepy."[8]

Du Bos, whose rules for the construction of French verse were translated into English by Thomas Nugent in 1748, considers gaping vowels a very great fault, and, speaking of French practice, says, " . . . the combination of such words [as occasion hiatus] are [*sic*] expressly forbidden in the rules of our poetry."[9] By 1796, however, the prejudice against hiatus is beginning to disappear; Peter Fogg in that year is able to find nothing whatever objectionable in the collocation of vowels in the phrase "He also against."[10] However, in 1816, John Carey is again going to classical authority to prove the desirability of elisions and contractions in English poetry: "Although some instances of synaeresis and syncope . . . may, to the English reader appear harsh and portentous, I feel confident that the classical scholar, accustomed to the much bolder licences of Homer, will account these English licences, perfectly moderate and warrantable."[11] Here we have one genuine instance of pure neo-classicism influencing English prosodic theory.

William Crowe, writing as late at 1827, furnishes additional evidence that the classical prejudice against hiatus was one reason for the conservatives' ready acceptance of synaeresis and syncope (as in "happ-yer" and "trem'lous") when such mechanisms were required to keep the line within the syllabic limitation. Crowe feels that the dissyllabic pronunciation of "heaven" and "tower" and the trisyllabic pronunciation of "violet" and "evening" produce an effect of ugliness and awkwardness very like that resulting from hiatus.[12] It is certainly true that words such as "glorious" and "earlier," if the last two syllables are given a full and distinct pronunciation, are bound to appear

---

[8] *Milton's Paradise Lost*, p. 18.
[9] *Critical Reflections*, I, 258. See also Newbery, *Art of Poetry on a New Plan*, I, 16-17.
[10] *Elementa Anglicana*, II, 189.
[11] *Practical English Prosody*, p. 56, n.
[12] *Treatise on English Versification*, p. 267.

inharmonious to an ear trained to recognize, and automatically to consider objectionable, vowel gaping between words.

2. *Theory of Contractions in Syllabic Poetry*

This association of Crowe's between strict hiatus, or vowel gaping occurring between two words, and the internal contractions demanded by the syllabic system leads us to a consideration of synaeresis and syncope in eighteenth-century prosodic theory, and with it, the troublesome question of whether these contractions were merely fictions or whether they were actually read by contemporary readers as printed.

It is essential here to remind oneself that the nineteenth and twentieth centuries have no exclusive lien on prosodic beauty; the beautiful in verse structure is a quality always dependent on the expressiveness of the prosody in heightening the total meaning and effect of a poem, and what makes a prosody beautiful is largely a consummate suitability and fidelity to the unique tendencies of poetic expression in its age. The eighteenth century's attitude towards poetic contractions is dependent on the larger aesthetic presuppositions of the age, and the modern reader should not be outraged when he learns that the early eighteenth century's commitment to poetic contractions was total.

Unpleasant as it may be to recognize the fact, contemporary evidence leads to the conclusion that almost all readers in the early eighteenth century both scanned and pronounced "am'rous," "om'nous," and "del'cate" when such words confronted them in poetry.[13] The normal way of reading an apparently hypermetrical line during this period would be, then, something like this:

> Wándrĭng ĭn mán yă sháde běchéckĕred grót.

Not only would readers of taste, education, and intelligence deliver the line in this way, but they would consider such a delivery the only possible one, and they would furthermore believe it to be an eminently lovely and effective way of reading verse, for it would at once make apparent to all auditors the line's "harmony" and its syllabic justness. A certain respect for what is imagined to be the dignity of Restoration and eighteenth-century poets often breeds the modern notion that they could not have intended their verse to be thus read, since such a reading erases much of the prosodic variety of the

---

[13] See George Saintsbury, *Historical Manual of English Prosody* (2nd ed.; London, 1914), p. 180; George R. Stewart, *The Technique of English Verse* (New York, 1930), pp. 52-53, and *Modern Metrical Technique*, p. 30; Culler, "Edward Bysshe and the Poet's Handbook," p. 884; Bridges, *Milton's Prosody*, p. 18; and Sprott, *Milton's Art of Prosody*, p. 73.

lines. The supposition that prosodic variety of the nineteenth-century type is the goal of earlier poetries often sends modern scholars and critics into ambiguities on this matter, and some have sought to defend eighteenth-century poetry by explaining that the apostrophe was intended to be merely a "fiction," and by scanning as if the syllables so elided were read anyhow.[14] But there is an overwhelming amount of contemporary evidence to the contrary.

Syllabic prosody is not a mere theoretical convention without basis in the contemporary poetry: it represents, in general, a codification of eighteenth-century prosodic practice, and the use of elisions and contractions is vital to a syllabic prosody. If the line was felt in almost all respectable quarters during the early part of the century to require strict decasyllabic limitation, it seems rather naive for some modern metrists to suppose that the effect of such decasyllabic limitation was not intended to reach the reader, and that the reading of verse was somehow supposed to obliterate all evidence of the poet's careful attention to syllabic limit and to regularity of stress. Precisely the opposite was the more usual practice, as researches into the prevalence of artificial elocution will amply demonstrate. Poet and reader alike during the early decades of the century definitely elided, and not merely "theoretically," those syllables which, if pronounced, would swell the line to a total of more than the "certain number of syllables" appropriate to it.

One should not forget that elisions are directly connected with the syllabic criterion.[15] Bysshe himself writes, "Our Verses consisting only [!] of a certain Number of Syllables, nothing can be of more ease, or greater use to our Poets, than the retaining or cutting off a Syllable from a Verse, according as the measure of it requires."[16] With the number of syllables the essence of the poetic line (or the quintessence, as in Bysshe), devices for normalizing the number of syllables become not mere "poetic licences" but part of the very structural mechanism of the line; "ne'er" and "e'er" may appear in nineteenth-century non-syllabic verse as poetic diction, so-called, but in the eighteenth century such contractions were essential and were not regarded merely as embellishment or as infrequently permitted indulgences. A glance at the opinions of a few of the Restoration and eighteenth-century prosodists will perhaps clarify some of these points.

---

[14] See, e.g., Donald A. Stauffer, *The Nature of Poetry* (New York, 1946), p. 198; Wallace C. Brown, *The Triumph of Form: A Study of the Later Masters of the Heroic Couplet* (Chapel Hill, 1948), p. 71; and Matthews, *A Study of Versification*, p. 239.

[15] See Culler, "Edward Bysshe and the Poet's Handbook," p. 874; and Saintsbury, *Historical Manual*, p. 16.

[16] *Art of English Poetry*, p. 14.

Dryden points out in his Dedication of *Examen Poeticum* that the reduction of hiatus by apocope is "an inviolable precept" not only in ancient prosody, but also in the practice of the French and the Italians, and he considers the "reform" of English prosody closely connected with the modern poet's absolute avoidance of vowel gaping.[17] Dryden perceives, however, that a strongly consonantal tongue such as English must admit contractions only with great caution, lest the resulting loss of vowels create an increased "roughness."[18] It is interesting that Dryden's comments on elision and contraction are all concerned with roughness or smoothness of sound; Dryden evidently feels that the principle of syllabic limitation is so well understood and so universally apparent that it is not necessary to explain that the devices of elision and contraction primarily serve to keep the line within its strict syllabic limitation, and serve only secondarily the purpose of eliminating "ugly" collocations of vowels.

To most of the prosodists of the Restoration and early eighteenth century, the contraction of the preterit and passive-participial suffix "-ed" was felt to be one of the visible signs of prosodic progress, and was assumed to be an immense advance over the barbaric usages of Chaucer and Spenser. The following snippet of dialogue from Dennis' *Impartial Critick* will show that Dennis, like Bentley, sometimes even forgot for a moment that a line had to consist of "a certain number of syllables," so anxious was he to avoid barbarisms by employing the proper contractions:

> *Beaumont* reads: *But we, most happy, who need fear no*
> *Force,*
>   *But winged Troops, or Pegasean Horse.*
> *Freem*[an:] That *winged* should have been *wing'd;* but that
> was the fault of the age, and not of Mr. *Waller,* who, to do him
> justice, was the first who began to contract our Participles which
> ended in *ed,* which, being not contracted, exceedingly weaken a
> Verse.[19]

Bysshe agrees with Dennis that the "e" in "preterperfect" endings must not be pronounced. "Amazed" is thus dissyllabic, and "loved" is always to be considered monosyllabic. The phrase "Thou lovest" must be contracted

[17] Ker, ed., *Essays,* II, 11.

[18] *Ibid.,* II, 215. See also Poole, *English Parnassus,* sig. A6ᵛ.

[19] Spingarn, ed., *Critical Essays,* III, 173; and see p. 175. One reason why the uncontracted "-ed" termination was held in low regard by most of the conservative prosodists of the century was that it bore inevitable associations of the medieval and the Gothic. It is significant that the author of "The Eve of St. Agnes," together with Blake and Burns, was one of the pioneers in bringing the uncontracted "-ed's" back into fashion.

[20] *Art of English Poetry,* p. 10.

to "Thou lov'st," even at the cost of incurring a certain "roughness."[20] Syncope is to be used wherever possible: "beauteous" is thus a word of two syllables, and "victorious" of three.[21] The phrase "many a" is to be pronounced, according to Bysshe, "man ya,"[22] and the terminations "-ism," "-asm," and "-osm" are to be used in verse as if monosyllabic.[23] Bysshe offers a specific rule for the practice of syncope: words of more than two syllables accented on the antepenult, in which "r" occurs between two vowels, may be contracted by eliminating the vowel which precedes the "r," as in "temp'rance," "pref'rence," "diff'rence," "flatt'rer," "am'rous," and "vict'ry." The same rule holds for the elision of a post-consonantal vowel preceding "l," "m," "n," and "v," and "c" when pronounced as "s." Thus one achieves such forms as "pris'ner," "med'cine," and "cov'nant."[24] Even though he permits all these opportunities for contraction, for the dual purpose of ease in syllabic construction and the avoidance of an effect suggestive of classical hiatus, Bysshe, like most of the prosodists, draws the line at contractions which, no matter how successful they may be in reducing the line to its proper syllabic number, cause excessive groupings of consonants. Bysshe thus accuses Cowley of taking "too great a Liberty in his Contractions," and warns that "we must be cautious of following his example."[25]

William Coward, in 1709, is particularly offended by the attempts of some poets to "cheat" in their elisions, and to elide a consonant before another consonant (e.g., "o'the") in a hasty effort to keep their line within the due syllabic confines.[26] The idea of progress is a strong influence on Coward's approbation of contractions such as "o'er," and on his delight in a monosyllabic pronunciation of "seeing" and "being." "For since our Language is refin'd," he says, " . . . such *Contraction* of Words gives the Verse Elegance and Grace."[27] Here we see that a typical early eighteenth-century prosodist finds nothing whatever unfortunate about the necessity of contractions: they are, to Coward, one of the specific beauties of poetry, and even though he realizes that they are required by the fact that English verse admits no trisyllabic substitution, Coward sees nothing inherently objectionable in such pronunciations as "murm'ring" and "trem'lous." It should be

---

[21] *Ibid.*, p. 12.
[22] *Ibid.*, p. 13.
[23] *Ibid.*
[24] *Ibid.*, pp. 14-15.
[25] *Ibid.*, p. 17.
[26] *Licentia Poetica discuss'd*, sig. B2ᵛ. Coward also makes it plain by scanning "Furious with an Invincible Desire" in two different ways that he was pronouncing "Furious" strictly as a trochee. (Sig. B4).
[27] *Ibid.*, sig. B3ᵛ.

kept in mind here that one of the basic aesthetic principles of conservative metric in the eighteenth century is that the poet has not only the right but the duty to improve natural phonetic materials until they become fit for elevated uses. The trochaïzing of dactylic or semi-dactylic words[28] is regarded as a definite improvement of them for poetic purposes, since it enables them to fit into the harmonic (*i.e.*, purely accentual-syllabic) pattern which the poet has in mind.

Addison emphasizes that elisions and contractions are most appropriate and beautiful in epic verse, since they help set the verse apart from prose by giving it the requisite heightening.[29] Addison accepts the necessity of smoothing out the "-ed" terminations, but regrets that this usage "has very much disfigured the Tongue, and turned the tenth part of our smoothest Words into so many Clusters of Consonants." Excessive reduction of the "-ed's" is all the more remarkable to Addison because "our Politest Authors" are continually complaining about "the want of Vowels in our Language."[30]

Charles Gildon holds that, although contractions are properly employed in epic verse, elegy and the lesser *genres* should admit them more sparingly, presumably because these lower forms approach nearer to the everyday idiom.[31] Gildon also supplies an interesting scansion which can illustrate the fact that synaeresis was no mere fiction but was actually practiced by the reader. He scans a line from *Alexander's Feast* thus:

Sóftlў swéet, ĭn *Lўdĭan* méasŭres,
(97)

and almost certainly Gildon pronounced "Lydian" as "Lyd-yan" to prevent the latter half of the line from assuming a dactylic movement.[32] Almost every modern reader would, I presume, read the line as if scanned

Sóftlў swéet, ĭn *Lўdĭăn* méasŭres,

and as if the third foot were a "dactylic substitution." In relation to Gildon's reading of this line, I would suggest that any professedly historical approach to English poetry will be incomplete without a knowledge that eighteenth-century prosodic practice and theory require this line to be read as Gildon reads it; if we transform "Lydian" into a pleasant nineteenth-century dactyl, the resulting line is not the one that Dryden wrote or Gildon read.

Syllabism has seemed to many to have had its disadvantages as a prosodic

---

[28] See below, n. 177.
[29] G. Gregory Smith, ed., *The Spectator* (New York, 1897-1898), IV, 131. (No. 285, Sat., Jan. 26, 1712).
[30] *Ibid.*, II, 192. (No. 135, Sat., Aug. 4, 1711).
[31] *Complete Art of Poetry*, I, 169.
[32] *Ibid.*, I, 301. See also Watts, *Art of Reading and Writing English*, p. 72.

system, but it at least enabled certain of the conservative prosodists to read Milton's elisions properly long before Robert Bridges was forced to present modern readers with a reminder of the prosodic system under which Milton was composing. Henry Pemberton, for example, although one would not care to agree with him in some of his attitudes towards *Leonidas,* is at least able to perceive that Milton's "annual" and "Syrian" are intended to be read dissyllabically, and not as dactyls.[33] Edward Manwaring also receives certain advantages from his commitment to the syllabic system; he sees that each half of this line,

> About his Chariot ‖ numberless were pour'd,
> (*P.L.,* VII, 197)

contains five syllables, and his pronunciation of "Chariot" as a trochee would, we may be fairly certain, agree with that which Milton intended.[34] Johnson is another who has none of the trouble that modern readers occasionally experience with Milton's elisions, for he brings to *Paradise Lost* the expectation that he will find a fairly strict decasyllabism.[35] Most twentieth-century readers, accustomed to reading poetry of all periods very much the way they read Eliot and Auden, would probably read the line

> Whose annual wound in *Lebanon* allur'd,
> (*P.L.,* I, 447)

with an anapest in the second position, and would erroneously assume that the resulting syllabic irregularity stems from one of Milton's intentional variations. Johnson, however, accustomed to making the required elisions and contractions automatically, instinctively practices synaeresis, and is thus enabled to read Milton in a way that would not have offended the poet. Johnson's reading of this line would resemble

> Whŏse ánn-yăl wóund ĭn *Lébănón* ăllúr'd,

and such a reading would be, in Johnson's own words, a legitimate "compliance with the [ideal] measure."[36] It will thus be evident that poetic contractions are inseparably linked with the central tenet of the syllabic aesthetic, which requires that the phonetic materials arrange themselves in accordance with the immutable melodic pattern. Poetic contractions within such an aesthetic will seem not ugly and distorting but ideal and harmonious, an improvement of the irregularities of words in their state of nature. This unique aesthetic of syllabic and stress-regularist prosody must be thoughtfully

---

[33] *Observations on Poetry,* p. 133.
[34] *Of Harmony and Numbers,* p. 48.
[35] See *Rambler,* II, 194-200, esp. p. 199. (No. 88, Sat., Jan. 19, 1751).
[36] *Ibid.,* II, 199. For other contraction remarks by Johnson see *Dictionary* (6th ed.), sig. h6; and Hill, ed., *Lives,* I, 294, and III, 341.

considered before the poetic contractions are damned as affectedly genteel or as attempts at poetic embellishment which have lamentably failed.

John Newbery's *Art of Poetry on a New Plan* (1762) provides further evidence that the poetic contractions were meant to be read exactly as printed, without the reader's "filling in" the elided vowels. In poetry, Newbery states, *"two* syllables are contracted into *one*, and are so pronounced. . . . the words being written or printed *temp'rance, diff'rence, flatt'rer, vict'ry, am'rous,* [are] pronounced accordingly."[37] Instead of complaining that such contractions are unfortunately necessary in a syllabic prosody, and that one must simply make the best of an uncomfortable situation, Newbery finds them all "agreeable enough" for their own sake, together with such examples as "fab'lous," "pris'ner," "bell'wing," and "pow'r" (pronounced as a strict monosyllable, probably something very much like "par").[38]

Lord Monboddo is also, not surprisingly, a conservative contractionist: he refers specifically and pointedly to the "-dience" of the first line of *Paradise Lost* as one unaccented syllable,[39] and there can be little doubt that he read the line as follows:

Ŏf Mán's fírst dís-ŏ-béd-yĕnce ánd thĕ Frúit.

In fact, if Monboddo possessed a good stout walking stick, it is not hard to imagine him pounding it on the floor to reinforce the "harmony" here, and to accompany his accomplished Scots y-glide.

The problem of poetic contractions apparently gave Thomas Gray, however, a great deal of trouble; he finally is forced into a position of prosodic ambiguity which one frequently meets during the third quarter of the century. In fact, Gray's attitude towards most prosodic matters must be called somewhat schizophrenic. He generally is a hearty champion of all possible prosodic variety in poetry produced before his own time, and is so pleased to "find" variations of stress and of number of syllables in *Paradise Lost* that he continually fails to regard Milton's designed contractions, scanning

With ĭmpétŭŏus rĕcóil ănd járrĭng sóund,[40]
(*P.L.,* II, 880)

whereas more conservative metrists would actually have been closer to Milton's own rhythmic conception of the line by scanning "With ĭmpétŭous," and pronouncing something like "With im-pet-chus." Despite this desire to read as much rhythmical variety as possible into the earlier classics, even to the

[37] *Art of Poetry on a New Plan,* I, 14.
[38] *Ibid.,* I, 14-16.
[39] *Of the Origin and Progress of Language,* II, 327.
[40] Gosse, ed., *Works,* I, 340.

extent of seriously misreading them, Gray's reaction to the contraction practice of his contemporaries is one of timid acceptance. Gray's own verse ventures none of the prosodic variety which its author enjoys in pre-eighteenth-century poetry. For example, Gray, revising the text of *The Bard*, wishes to replace the line

> Youthful Knights & Barons bold,

with one of an equal number of syllables. He consequently produces the line

> Girt with many a Baron bold,[41]

and presumably thinks of it as syllabically equal to his original line, which it is, of course, only by the customary device of the pronunciation "man ya."[42]

Gray displays the same conservative commitment to contractions in a reworking of another line of *The Bard*. He writes first,

> Descending slow their golden skirts unroll!

and then replaces "golden" with "glitt'ring."[43] The syllabic limitation is not felt to have been violated, and we are thus to assume that Gray considered both "golden" and "glitt'ring" equal trochees, and that he was easily able to pronounce the latter with the same stress-pattern as the former. Gray also advises Mason that "mould'ring" might replace "clay-cold" in a line of one of Mason's Elegies.[44] It should be noted that Gray displays no tendency to consider "mould'ring" as any sort of dactyl; it is precisely the syllabic equal of "clay-cold," and the facts give us no other warrant than to assume that Gray read the word exactly as printed. It seems highly characteristic of Gray's temper that he should seek the rhythmical variety he desired in an age earlier than his own, and at the same time find it possible to comply decently with contemporary conservative practice.[45] Gray freely accepted, and even came to relish, rhythmical variations in the older poets, but he evidently had too great a fear of criticism (or simply too strong a desire for tranquillity and privacy) to risk drawing its strictures down upon himself by using any such variety in his own verse.[46]

In 1775, Allan Ramsay the Younger, sporting with Ambrose Philips' "Namby-Pamby" verses, cites the following two lines as perfectly regular examples of trochaic tetrameter catalectics:

[41] Toynbee and Whibley, edd., *Correspondence,* I, 436.

[42] This line occurs at the beginning of the third antistrophe, and each of the other antistrophes begins with a seven-syllable line, followed by one of eight: it seems extremely unlikely that Gray would permit a syllabic irregularity here, where the proper number of syllables in each line would be especially noted.

[43] Toynbee and Whibley, edd., *Correspondence,* I, 436.

[44] *Ibid.,* II, 714.

[45] See Herbert W. Starr, *Gray as a Literary Critic* (Philadelphia, 1941), pp. 112, 116.

[46] *Ibid.,* p. 140.

Little thing of placid mien,
Miniature of Beauty's Queen.[47]

To almost any modern reader, the second line would be a perfect example
of an initial dactylic substitution in a truncated trochaic tetrameter line, but
it is a perfectly regular line to Ramsay's ear, as indeed it would be to anyone's
if one read, as Ramsay surely does, "min-ya-ture."

Thomas Jefferson's fidelity to the syllabic and stress-regularity tradition
keeps him safely within the conservative camp on the question of elisions
and contractions. To Jefferson, contiguous vowels may, in poetry, become
single syllables if necessary for the maintenance of the syllabic limit.[48]
Jefferson, like a true Augustan, is even able to pronounce "original" as
"orig'nal" with no suggestion of difficulty or distortion.[49]

Prosodic anti-progressives like Joseph Robertson continued to cling to
the Augustan modes of contraction until very late. Speaking of Milton's line

In heav'n by many a tow'red structure high,
(P.L., I, 733)

Robertson says, "if *many* be made a dissyllable in this line, the measure will
be entirely destroyed."[50] Robertson undoubtedly read the line like this:

In héavn bў mán yă tówĕr'd strúctŭre hígh.

Robertson complains that the dissyllabic pronunciation of "heaven" which
he is now apparently hearing frequently in the reading of poetry should be
avoided: such a pronunciation "has a bad effect in poetry."[51]

Just as eighteenth-century syllabism and stress regularity continued to
exact support from certain conservatives during the greater part of the nineteenth century, so the allied doctrine of poetic contractions continued to
appeal to certain prosodic reactionaries long after most prosodists had laid
it aside. John Carey, writing in 1816, still prefers the Augustan reading of
"virtuous" and "happier" as strict trochees,[52] and he is delighted with a
reading of a line from *Romeo and Juliet* (II, ii, 33) which, by bold employment of the y-glide, keeps it within the hendecasyllabic limit thought even
by the conservatives to be permissible in dramatic verse; Carey wishes the line
to sound like this:

O Rom yo! Rom yo! wherefore art thou Rom yo?[53]

---

[47] "Enquiry into the Principles of English Versification," fol. 16.
[48] Lipscomb, ed., *Writings*, XVIII, 429.
[49] *Ibid.*
[50] *Essay on the Nature of the English Verse*, p. 64.
[51] *Ibid.*, p. 65.
[52] *Practical English Prosody*, p. xv; cf. pp. 9, 53-55, 73-76.
[53] *Ibid.*, p. 114, n.

Ludicrous as this reading may appear to moderns, one should keep in mind that the suggestion of the effect of hiatus in the twentieth-century pronunciation "Rom-e-o" might be disagreeable to an Augustan alert to anything resembling, even within words, the sort of hiatus avoided by Virgil.

Finally, William Crowe, in 1827, prefers Monboddo's pronunciation "disobed-yence" in the first line of *Paradise Lost* to the more modern reading,[54] and, extreme as this contraction seems to be, it is again more correct when Milton's syllabic intention is recalled than a pronunciation which turns the word into one of five syllables and in addition creates an effect of hiatus through the conjunction of the "i" and the "e."

3. *The Contractions in Transition*

During the 1740's, the first effective attacks began on the system of syllabism and stress regularity, and many of the prosodic liberals perceived that an assault on the whole convention of poetic contractions was as good a way as any to weaken the syllabic principle, for, if they could succeed in spreading abroad dactylic pronunciations of words intended to be read as trochees, the liberals felt that they could demonstrate the attractions of a non-syllabic system which admitted trisyllabic substitution. Samuel Say, for example, one of the first really acute anti-syllabists, deliberately scans Milton in 1745 as if Milton were not composing syllabically:

> Whŏse ánnŭăl wóund ĭn *Lĕbănŏn* ăllúr'd.

Say's contempt for the syllabic limitation similarly impels him to read "Syrian" and "amorous" as dactyls,[55] and he even gives a trisyllabic pronunciation to "fiery."[56] Say seems to revert to earlier modes occasionally, as when he scans "furious" as a dissyllable,[57] but this word was probably still being pronounced "fur-yus" in colloquial idiom.[58] John Mason, who in certain modern histories of prosodic theory has received much of the credit really due Samuel Say for merely repeating Say's earlier anti-regularist positions,[59] affects the pronunciation "slávĕrў" in 1749, and even offers the word as an example of a

---

[54] *Treatise on English Versification*, p. 247.

[55] *Poems on Several Occasions: and Two Critical Essays, viz. The First, on the Harmony, Variety, and Power of Numbers, whether in Prose or Verse. The Second, On the Numbers of Paradise Lost* (London, 1745), p. 128.

[56] *Ibid.*, p. 129.

[57] *Ibid.*, p. 170.

[58] See below, section 4.

[59] See Saintsbury, *History*, II, 561; *Historical Manual*, p. 247; and Omond, *English Metrists*, p. 50. It seems doubtful that either of these historians of metric and metrical theory really read Say's work with care: one need spend only a brief time on Say's *Poems on Several Occasions* to perceive that John Mason is a mere popularizer of Say's vigorous opinions.

perfect dactyl.[60] Twenty years earlier there would have been little question of its being a perfect trochee.

An interesting document in the history of the rise and decline of poetic contractions in English is the Preface to James Fortescue's *Pomery-Hill, a Poem* (1754). Fortescue is a liberal or emancipated prosodist who favors the free admission of trisyllabic feet in the iambic pentameter line.[61] But Fortescue prefers to advance his argument against contractions not as an open avowal of trisyllabic substitution, but simply on the grounds that contractions are eliminating too many vowels. As Fortescue rather archly puts it, "Vowels to the consonants, are of the same use, as the ladies among men; to soften, to refine the conversation. . . . surely these fair ones cannot be too familiar with our English consonants."[62] Fortescue's coyness throughout this preface makes it difficult to ascertain just what he does favor, but it at least appears that he is receptive to greater variety in stresses and number of syllables than he discovers in most contemporary poems, and he finds that the least offensive way to go about an oblique plea for trisyllabic substitution is to suggest that excessive contraction tends to cut so many vowels out of the line that little but hissings and breathings is left. It is significant that by 1754 the classical prejudice against hiatus in English verse is beginning to weaken: Fortescue is willing to allow all the vowel gaping necessary, so long as it is not "too strong" and too distracting.[63]

During the 1760's and 1770's, one finds a great many complaints against poetic contractions, mainly on the liberal grounds that they inhibit trisyllabic substitution. John Rice, for example, writing in 1765, announces his approval of John Mason's dactylic scansions of "fluttering," "humorous," "wavering," and "impious."[64] William Kenrick very characteristically involves himself in difficulties of logic and consistency by preferring the full pronunciation of every syllable with no contraction whatever, and at the same time favoring strict alternation of stressed and unstressed syllables.[65] It would seem that Kenrick actually did prefer trisyllabic substitution, but felt bound, in his self-consciously Johnsonian role of lexicographer, to retain a sort of outer shell of the conventionally respectable stress-regularist dogmas.

---

[60] *Essays on Poetical and Prosaic Numbers, and Elocution* (2nd ed.; London, 1761), p. 16.

[61] *Pomery-Hill, a Poem . . . With Other Poems, English and Latin* (London, 1754), p. xii.

[62] *Ibid.*, p. v.

[63] *Ibid.*, pp. iii-iv.

[64] *Introduction to the Art of Reading*, pp. 126, 129.

[65] *New Dictionary*, p. 54.

James Beattie, in the seventies and eighties, is willing to allow such relatively harmless contractions as "e'er," and "o'er,"[66] but he firmly draws the line at the reduction of trisyllabic feet by contraction, saying, "It has indeed been thought by some criticks, that in our heroick verse, when the syllables exceed ten in number, there must be redundant vowels, which in reading are suppressed or cut off, and instead of which, in printed books, the apostrophe is often inserted. But, whatever be the case in printing, and writing, this is contrary to the practice of all good readers; who pronounce every syllable distinctly, and by so doing gratify our ear much more than if they had made the supposed elisions."[67] Beattie's comment helps indicate roughly what was happening to the poetic contractions. Many readers late in the century, instinctively seeking a rhythmical variety which the Augustan poets had never intended, were simply filling in the carefully placed apostrophes, and were beginning to read the poetry in the way most twentieth-century readers, accustomed to the same sort of variety, habitually read the same verse. The ideal form of the heroic line was intentionally being obscured and lost by a method of reading which disguised the line's intended approach to melody. The syllabic limitation of the line naturally began to weaken under the influence of these liberal methods of reading: when Beattie insists that "thundering" is always a dactyl in verse,[68] it is obvious that existing decasyllabic lines which use "thundering" as a trochee will no longer display harmony, nor will the fact that they are no longer harmonious, in the old sense, be regarded as a great failing.

Joshua Steele, in *Prosodia Rationalis* (1779), advances the new equal-time theory of prosodic construction which was to flower into romantic accentualism a few years later. Such an equal-time theory has plainly no use for contractions, since the syllabic limitation no longer exists as one of the primary structural criteria. Steele scans

Tŏ all ĭnférĭŏr ánĭmáls 'tĭs gívĕn,[69]

and thus changes a line intended to consist of ten syllables into one of twelve. The line would of course have been read earlier in the century,

Tŏ all ĭn-fér-yŏr ánĭmáls 'tĭs gívn,[70]

---

[66] *Essays: On Poetry and Music as they Affect the Mind; on Laughter, and Ludicrous Compositon; on the Utility of Classical Learning* (Edinburgh, 1778), p. 239.

[67] *Dissertations Moral and Critical*, p. 280. In the Harvard College copy, a pencilled marginal notation in an early nineteenth-century hand disagrees with Beattie here and suggests the following pronunciation as a perfectly satisfactory one:
Full manyan amrous manya querlous ditty.

[68] *Essays*, p. 315; cf. *Dissertations*, p. 284.

[69] *Prosodia Rationalis*, p. 26.

[70] *Ibid.*, pp. 75-76.

and both the syllabic limitation and the regularity of stress would have been preserved. Steele still allows contractions, however, as a purely optional mechanism, if not overworked: such words as "various" and "curious" may be either trochees (Steele says "spondees") or dactyls.[71] Steele's new prosody allows him to read *Paradise Lost* with a total neglect of the syllabic equality intended by Milton: "disobedience" in the first line now becomes a word of five syllables, and the line becomes hendecasyllabic.[72]

John Walker, however, takes a typically late-century schizophrenic view of contractions. Walker feels impelled in 1781 to retain the conservative syllabic limitation, but he also wishes to permit a more informal pronunciation of indicated contractions. He thus rationalizes, "The vowel *e*, which is often cut off by an apostrophe in the word *the*, and in syllables before *r*, as *dang'rous, gen'rous*, etc. ought to be preserved in the pronunciation, because the syllable it forms is so short as to admit of being sounded with the preceding syllable, so as not to increase the number of syllables to the ear, or at all hurt the harmony."[73] This is an interesting position for a prosodist to find himself in, and it was a position that many of the late eighteenth-century metrists, trying to give their loyalty to two opposed prosodic traditions at once, were forced to take. Harmony is still conservatively felt to be the end of poetical measures, and harmony cannot be achieved without a definite syllabic limitation of the line, but a sort of half-way pronunciation of the "e" in "dangerous" will supply what Walker desires of a suggestion of trisyllabic substitution without materially altering the number of syllables. This equivocal position apparently rather troubled Walker, as is plain from his treatment of the contraction problem in later years. In 1791, Walker explains that his ambiguous attitude towards contractions does not depend on "uniting two vocal sounds into one simple sound, which is impossible, but pronouncing two vocal sounds in succession so closely as to go for only one syllable in poetry."[74] Walker obviously feels the need of explaining his desire to give a full pronunciation to poetic contractions, but to say that two sounds can "go for" only one for poetical purposes is to shed more light on Walker's own embarrassment than on the matter of contractions itself. Walker is finally reduced to the position that "a poetic syllable and a prosaic one are sometimes very different quantities."[75] Walker's performance here simply

[71] *Ibid.*, p. 146.
[72] *Ibid.*, p. 77.
[73] *Elements of Elocution*, II, 197.
[74] *A Critical Pronouncing Dictionary and Expositor of the English Language, to which are prefixed Principles of English Pronunciation* (Dublin, 1794), p. 27.
[75] *Ibid.*, pp. 76-77.

reveals the immense power of the Bysshian theory of syllabic limitation even in an age in which most prosodists were so eager to discover rhythmical variety that they continually misread Milton and the Augustans to achieve it.

Hugh Blair is also worried about the conflict between the official syllabism and the rising practice of filling in the poetic contractions. He admits that "instances occur" of lines appearing to contain more than their due number of syllables; "But in such cases," he goes on, "I apprehend it will be found, that some of the liquid syllables are so slurred in pronouncing, as to bring the Verse . . . within the usual bounds."[76] It is indicative of the condition of prosodic theorizing in the eighties that Blair is not certain just what he should do about poetic contractions; he is caught between two prosodic complexes: the syllabic, now moribund or at least so inoperative as to be a mere genteel mannerism, and the accentual, not yet really lively but certainly in the offing. Phrases such as "I apprehend" suggest that Blair's predicament is an uncomfortable one. Reactionaries like William Jackson, however, were not willing to admit that any change in the syllabic system of contractions was required; Jackson feels no confusion about the matter: "The poetical language admits of elisions . . . we cannot have in prose."[77]

Robert Nares, in his *Elements of Orthoepy* (1784), is manifestly disturbed over the prosodic uncertainty which the partial disuse of the correct Augustan reading of poetic contractions has spread abroad. The whole problem of whether syllables marked for elision by apostrophes are genuinely elided in verse bothers Nares greatly. The question would never have occurred during the earlier years of the century, so accustomed had readers become to making the indicated elisions automatically, but later readers whose ears sought more variety than the decasyllabic line was capable of furnishing were themselves supplying the variety which the poets had intentionally avoided. The question of the proper treatment of indicated contractions now began to assume the proportions of a national embarrassment.

Nares says, for example, that "filial" in poetry is "made a dissyllable" and pronounced "fil-yal" when it appears in verse;[78] later on, however, he begins to wonder, and asks in a footnote whether perhaps "filial" in verse is not pronounced somewhere between a dissyllable and a trisyllable.[79] "Power" and "shower" are used in poetry as monosyllables, Nares believes.[80] The "eo"

---

[76] *Lectures on Rhetoric and Belles Lettres*, III, 105.
[77] *Thirty Letters*, II, 23.
[78] *Elements of Orthoepy*, pp. 41-42.
[79] *Ibid.*, p. 65, n.
[80] *Ibid.*, p. 81.

diphthong is to become a y-glide for poetic purposes, as in the pronunciations "hid-yus," "pit-yus," and "plent-yus."[81] "Barrier" is a "poetic" dissyllable,[82] and "odorous" "stands in the place of" a dissyllable in verse.[83] Nares's uncertain attitude is summed up in his assertion that if poetic contractions are necessary (an assumption that his conservatism causes him to incline to), the "deforming" typographical apostrophe should at least be omitted.[84]

Walter Young neatly evades the real issue when he tells the Royal Society of Edinburgh in 1786 that "The time in which a short syllable is expressed in reciting verses, is often too small to be regularly counted and parcelled."[85] Anselm Bayly, on the other hand, takes an extreme anti-contractionist position; he writes, in 1789, "The expulsion of a vowel or consonant, with an apostrophe, is not only a deformity to the eye, but it oftentimes embarrasses the sense, and spoils the melody of the verse."[86] Employing the term "melody" with no remnant of its former suggestion of the ideal regularistic pattern but almost as a synonym for "variety," Bayly takes no notice whatever of the syllabic limitation of the line, and reads all the variety possible into purely syllabic poetry. That the liberal British ear in the eighties no longer feels obliged to affect a classical disgust at the appearance of hiatus appears from some of Bayly's scansions; he scans, for example,

Bĕfóre áll témplĕs, thĕ úprĭght héart ănd púre,[87]
(*P.L.*, I, 18)

deliberately neglecting the elision of "e" before "upright" which was intended both to reduce the line to the decasyllabic norm and to avoid the gaping of the two vowels.[88] "Even" and "heaven" are plainly dissyllables to Bayly,[89] and "wandering" and "various" are always to be treated, in poetry, as dactyls.[90] Having occasion to quote from Chaucer, Bayly foresees that many readers nurtured in the Augustan poetic tradition will instinctively read "Christopher" as "Christ'pher" to keep the line within its decasyllabic limit; Bayly consequently marks the line,

A Christŏphĕr on his brest of silver shene.[91]

---

[81] *Ibid.,* p. 61.
[82] *Ibid.,* p. 159.
[83] *Ibid.,* p. 353.
[84] *Ibid.,* p. 251.
[85] "Essay on Rythmical Measures," p. 100.
[86] *Alliance of Musick, Poetry, and Oratory,* p. 94.
[87] *Ibid.,* pp. 91-93.
[88] Cf. Darwin's approval in 1789 of the phrase "the inchanted grove" with no elision of the "e." (*The Botanic Garden,* pp. 124-125).
[89] *Alliance of Musick, Poetry, and Oratory,* p. 93.
[90] *Ibid.,* p. 100.
[91] *Ibid.,* p. 118.

The fact that this reading increases the number of syllables to eleven troubles Bayly not at all; it is exactly for the purpose of breaking down the syllabic criterion that Bayly insists on the full pronunciation of every syllable, whether purposely contracted or not.

Peter Fogg writes, as we move towards the close of the century, that most readers are now simply ignoring the poets' apostrophes, and are thus producing "real beauties in reading, which yet the poet never meant."[92] Fogg has read Southey's early poems with great delight,[93] and he is desirous of finding the same sort of trisyllabic substitution in the verse of Dryden and Pope that he discovers with infinite pleasure in *Joan of Arc*.

But even Southey himself strangely takes the same equivocal position about contractions which many poets and metrists of the late eighteenth century held. Southey approves of trisyllabic substitution and a full pronunciation of every syllable, but his regard for at least a "theoretical" syllabism leads him to assert that the syllabic number of the line is really not destroyed by these liberties. Of an un-Miltonic dissyllabic pronunciation of "spirit" in *Paradise Lost,* Southey explains that it really does not increase the number of syllables in the line (which it patently does), since "the rapid pronunciation of the two syllables" is exactly equal to "the dilated sound of one."[94] Thus theoretical equality of line lengths, whether expressed in the terms of conventional syllabism or not, was still considered necessary even by one of the early practitioners of the new prosody of the nineteenth century.

William Mitford's opinions on poetic contractions reveal the new historical and relativistic temper at work in advancing the cause of prosodic liberalism. Mitford is aware, despite the classical precedents for the practice, that elision and contraction are not universal and invariable poetic devices: he goes to sixteenth and seventeenth-century prosodic practice to demonstrate that the suffixes "-ion" and "-ious" may be used either monosyllabically or dissyllabically.[95] Mitford deplores the practice of smoothing out the "-ed" termination, and has recourse to Spenser for illustrations of the "melodic" effect of an uncontracted use of this suffix.[96]

John Thelwall, one of Joshua Steele's admirers and one of the high priests of romantic metric, vigorously opposes, in 1812, any sort of contrac-

92 *Elementa Anglicana*, II, 189-190.
93 *Ibid.*
94 J. W. Warter, ed., *Selections from the Letters of Robert Southey* (London, 1856), I, 69.
95 *Inquiry into the Principles of Harmony in Language*, p. 134.
96 *Ibid.*, pp. 361-364.

tion, "either in typography or utterance."[97] Thelwall's vehemently anti-syllabic reading of Dryden and Pope indicates the way accentual prosody tends, exactly like syllabic, to impose its own prescriptive standards on all previous poetry; in his desire to destroy any remaining shreds of the syllabic system, Thelwall is led to deny syllabism even to its most illustrious and successful practitioners.

*   *   *   *   *

From this presentation of some of the conservative and liberal attitudes towards poetic contractions, two important facts emerge: first, from the Restoration until about 1740, the contractions indicated by apostrophes in the poetic texts were actually read in oral delivery, and were intended by the poets themselves to be so read; this practice of reading the contractions exactly as printed, although it began to wane around the middle of the century, continued sporadically until early in the nineteenth century; second, from the middle to the end of the eighteenth century, there was a great deal of confusion, in the minds of poets, readers, and prosodists alike, about the way the contractions should be dealt with. Partly responsible for this confusion in the latter half of the century was the rise of a strong current of accentualism, which, in the interest of introducing trisyllabic substitution, encouraged a reading of Restoration and Augustan verse which supplied the poetry with a great deal more rhythmical variety than the poets had intended. The arrival on the critical scene of many prosodists with only the bare rudiments of an education in classical prosodic principles helped overcome the conservative prejudice against hiatus or effects which resembled it, a prejudice which for a century had served as one authoritative sanction for the contractions demanded by the syllabic system.

4. Contractions in Colloquial Idiom

It will be necessary now to determine just how far these poetic contractions differed, or were felt to differ, from those prevailing in the common speech of the period. There is, fortunately, a very great deal of evidence available of the general modes of pronunciation in the eighteenth century: the contemporary desire to "fix" the language and to bring pronunciation into conformity with the sort of standard which a tongue recently emerged from barbarism should possess was responsible for the production of many pronouncing dictionaries such as Kenrick's and Sheridan's; we also have a great

---

[97] Selections for the Illustration of a Course of Instructions on the Rhythmus and Utterance of the English Language: with an Introductory Essay on the Application of Rhythmical Science to the Treatment of Impediments, and the Improvement of our National Oratory (London, 1812), p. xlviii.

many documents phonetically spelled, and certain occasional spellings in the writing and printing of prose can furnish valuable hints of some unique eighteenth-century pronunciations. In addition, the period's general self-consciousness in linguistic matters produces many specific remarks about diction and pronunciation which can be of use in determining how far poetic and prose contractions were related.

During the first quarter of the eighteenth century, for example, we have many occasional spellings of "usual" as "yousall,"[98] and this pronunciation would approximate the standard contraction employed in syllabic verse, which would probably sound more like "use-zhull." "Venison" is frequently found spelled "venson," "medicine" as "medson," and "diamond" as "dimond" or even "dimon."[99] Like "usual," "punctual" is found habitually contracted to a dissyllable, and its sound is often represented by contemporary writers as "puntall."[100] "Partiality" occurs in colloquial speech and writing as "parshallity,"[101] which seems an almost perfect representation of the way it would have been contracted by a conservative reader of a syllabic poetic line. During the second and third quarters of the century, "spaniel" was commonly being pronounced "spanel," "ingenious" appears as "ingenus," and "natural" as "natrel," although by this time such pronunciations were generally considered vulgar by orthoepists.[102] Phonetic shorthand systems preserved from the late seventeenth and early eighteenth centuries show that during these years there was a distinct tendency in ordinary speech to drop the vowels of unstressed syllables before "l," "n," and "r," as in "trem'lous," "dang'rous," and "murm'ring."[103] The similarity of this colloquial tendency to the specific rules governing poetic contractions advanced by Bysshe and others will not go unobserved.

Specific examples are also to be found in the writings of certain poets and critics of the period, as well as in less distinguished documents containing phonetic or occasional spellings. Sir William Davenant, in his Preface to *Gondibert* (1651), spells "rendering" in prose exactly as he would had he

---

[98] William Matthews, "Some Eighteenth-Century Phonetic Spellings," *RES*, XII (1936), 181. On this whole matter of the extent of colloquial contractions in the early eighteenth century, see Eilert Ekwall, ed., *Dr. John Jones's Practical Phonography* [1701] (Halle, 1907), *passim*.

[99] Matthews, "Some Eighteenth-Century Phonetic Spellings," p. 181.

[100] *Ibid.*, p. 184.

[101] *Ibid.*, p. 187.

[102] William Matthews, "Some Eighteenth-Century Vulgarisms," *RES*, XIII (1937), 319.

[103] Helge Kökeritz, "English Pronunciation as Described in Shorthand Systems of the Seventeenth and Eighteenth Centuries," *Studia Neophilologia*, VII (1935), 130-131.

been composing syllabic verse, that is, "rendring."[104] He does the same with "remembring."[105] It has been surmised that the word "idolatry" during the Restoration was often pronounced as if spelled "idoltry."[106] Perhaps it is indicative of the rise of the Augustan contracted colloquial pronunciation that Milton generally uses the word as uncontracted in *Paradise Lost* but employs it as if contracted in *Samson Agonistes*.[107] One also finds such spellings as "lingring" in *Samson*.[108] Although Milton uses the word "power" as a dissyllable in *Il Penseroso* (line 95), it is always a monosyllable in *Paradise Lost*.[109] Might this altered usage perhaps indicate the gradual rise of the tendency towards colloquial contractions which becomes marked a few decades later? The pronunciation "obed-yence," in fact, beloved, as we have seen, by the conservative prosodists of the eighteenth century, seems to have been the normal one, both in poetry and ordinary discourse, from around 1600 on.[110]

Atterbury, in his Preface to Waller's *Poems* (1690), prints "mouldring,"[111] which we may assume was the normal conversational pronunciation of "mouldering." And Lady Wentworth writes in her letters (1705) "unusyell" for "unusual," and "Isbell" for "Isabel."[112] In the letters of Ann Cecil (1708), "general" appears as "genrall" and "natural" as "natrell."[113]

Addison declares in 1711 that the inborn British love of rapidity and dispatch is responsible for such commonly heard pronunciations as "lib'ty," "conspir'cy," "the'tre," and "or'tor,"[114] and Addison himself writes, to cite only one of hundreds of examples in the *Spectator*, "entring" for "entering."[115]

It is amusing that Swift, in his *Proposal for Correcting the English*

[104] *Gondibert*, p. 23. Cf. Abraham Cowley, *Pindarique Odes, Written in Imitation of the Stile and Maner [sic] of the Odes of Pindar* (London, 1656), sig. Aaa2ᵛ.

[105] *Gondibert*, p. 34.

[106] Bridges, *Milton's Prosody*, p. 47.

[107] *Ibid.*, p. 65. It is significant that Coleridge scans *SA* 1670 as follows:
Drŭnk with Ĭ---dōlătr̆y---drŭnk with Wīne
(See Ada L. F. Snell, "The Meter of 'Christabel'," *Fred Newton Scott Anniversary Papers* [Chicago, 1929], p. 112, n. 1). Milton almost certainly intended the line to be octosyllabic, with "idolatry" receiving a trisyllabic treatment. (See Sprott, *Milton's Art of Prosody*, p. 96). Coleridge is instinctively seeking a rhythmical movement different from the one Milton provides; he thus quite naturally expands "idolatry" to a word of four syllables.

[108] Bridges, *Milton's Prosody*, p. 54.

[109] *Ibid.*, p. 20.

[110] *Ibid.*, p. 19.

[111] *The Second Part of Mr. Waller's Poems* (London, 1690), sig. A5ᵛ.

[112] Constance Davies, *English Pronunciation from the Fifteenth to the Eighteenth Century: A Handbook to the Study of Historical Grammar* (London, 1934), p. 140.

[113] *Ibid.*, p. 142.

[114] Smith, ed., *Spectator*, II, 191-192. (No. 135, Sat., Aug. 4, 1711).

[115] *Ibid.*, I, 215. (No. 60, Mon., May 7, 1711).

Tongue (1712), vigorously opposes any contractions, whether in verse, prose, or conversation, and speaks with some show of heat about "that Barbarous Custom," and yet himself writes "rendring" in the same essay.[116]

Isaac Watts's *Art of Reading* (1721) sheds more light on the colloquial contractions which prevailed until about the middle of the century. "Diamond" is continually heard as a dissyllable, Watts says;[117] the "i" is mute in "venison";[118] "atheist" is to be pronounced "athist";[119] and "conscientious" has in ordinary speech its poetic pronunciation, "conshenshus."[120] Trisyllables such as "carrion," "chariot," and "conduit" are to be sounded "carren," "charrut," and "cundet."[121] The trisyllable "nauseous" is to be found universally as "nawshus" in ordinary speech,[122] and "medicine" becomes "mets'n."[123] Watts also gives the standard pronunciation of "hierarchy" as the trisyllabic "hirarky."[124] And Nathan Bailey, making his translation of Erasmus' *Colloquia Familiaria* around 1724, writes, in a prose passage, "upon tendring my Present."[125]

Evidence of the extent of colloquial contractions is very deficient for the second quarter of the century, and when we come upon the next indications of the existence of common speech contractions, we begin to feel that the peak of such linguistic usage has been passed. That the contractions were generally becoming less frequently used near the middle of the century seems to be indicated by Mather Flint's work on orthoepy. Flint does list these words as contracted: "venison,"[126] "eucharist,"[127] and "ingratiate";[128] but he reveals that the following are, in 1740, generally receiving now the full trisyllabic pronunciation: "desperate,"[129] "favourite," "violence,"[130] "piteous,"

---

[116] *A Proposal for Correcting, Improving, and Ascertaining the English Tongue; in a Letter to the Most Honourable Robert Earl of Oxford and Mortimer, Lord High Treasurer of Great Britain* (London, 1712), pp. 21, 38.

[117] *Art of Reading and Writing English*, p. 15.

[118] *Ibid.*, pp. 16, 123.

[119] *Ibid.*, p. 119.

[120] *Ibid.*, p. 120.

[121] *Ibid.*

[122] *Ibid.*, p. 121.

[123] *Ibid.*

[124] *Ibid.*

[125] E. Johnson, ed., *The Colloquies of Desiderius Erasmus, Concerning Men, Manners, and Things* (London, 1900), II, 209.

[126] Helge Kökeritz, ed., *Mather Flint on Early Eighteenth-Century Pronunciation* (Uppsala, 1944), p. 15.

[127] *Ibid.*, p. 28.

[128] *Ibid.*, p. 43.

[129] *Ibid.*, p. 14.

[130] *Ibid.*, p. 16.

and "beauteous."[131] From about 1740 or 1750 on, there is none of the wide agreement on colloquial contractions which had marked the first decades of the century; this may indicate that the fixity which the language had attained for the Augustans is now breaking down, and that colloquial contractions are to be pronounced 'or not, depending on the individual preference of the speaker, and on whether he wishes to appear somewhat old-fashioned or more up-to-date.

Gray is still certain in 1755 that some trisyllables are heard in ordinary speech contracted the way they were during the earlier part of the century, and he offers the examples of the dissyllabic pronunciation of "memory," "heavenly," and "every." "We are uniform in this," he adds, "and pronounce such words always alike in prose and verse."[132] "Heaven," according to Gray, is monosyllabic in colloquial idiom as well as in verse[133] (one wonders whether Gray, in his literary researches, ever came across Spenser's remark, made in a letter to Gabriel Harvey, that "Heauen, being used . . . as one syllable, . . . is like a lame Dogge that holds vp one Legge").[134]

By 1762, the fashion of colloquial contractions seems definitely to have passed. John Foster, driven to a state of annoyance by the equivocating that has gone on about the matter, announces that "temperance" is now pronounced trisyllabically not only by all the English, but by Scots, Irish, and Welsh besides.[135] To be sure, Lord Kames, always alert like most of the conservatives for any prop which will support the collapsing edifice of syllabic prosody, finds in the same year that contraction is still "the prevailing taste" in common speech;[136] but John Rice, in 1765, agrees with Foster that trisyllables are now pronounced without contraction, and he gives as examples certain words which surely would have been contracted before 1740: "ominous," "magazine," "negative," "eminent," "amity," "dedicate," and so on.[137]

Certain ghosts of the old pronunciation persisted, but they tended to appear mainly in the speech of the vulgar from the 1760's to the end of the century. Granville Sharp, in his *Short Treatise on the English Tongue* (1767), inveighs against the pronunciation of "atheist" as "athist" by the

[131] *Ibid.*, p. 28.
[132] Gosse, ed., *Works*, I, 393-394, n. 1.
[133] *Ibid.*, I, 396.
[134] G. Gregory Smith, ed., *Elizabethan Critical Essays* (Oxford, 1904), I, 99.
[135] *An Essay on the Different Nature of Accent and Quantity, with their Use and Application in the Pronunciation of the English, Latin, and Greek Languages* (Eton, 1762), p. 54.
[136] *Elements of Criticism*, II, 164.
[137] *Introduction to the Art of Reading*, p. 96.

London lower orders, and considers a dissyllabic pronunciation of "carrion" a distinct mark of low breeding.[138]

Thomas Chatterton's Rowley poems provide evidence of the persistence of the Augustan contracted pronunciations in areas somewhat removed from London. It will be found, I believe, that many of Chatterton's invented "medieval" spellings are virtually phonetic representations of the colloquial pronunciation current in Bristol during the seventies. Chatterton, in using these contracted spellings, must have believed that poetic contractions did not differ from those customarily heard in common speech, for he surely would not have used contractions in the Rowley poems if he had been conscious that the contractions of poetry were specifically and uniquely poetic contractions: such a blunder would have marked the poems as obviously contemporary. The fact that Chatterton not only employs contracted spellings, but presumably thought them in no danger of branding his verses as modern, tends to support the conclusion that, at least in relatively provincial areas, Augustan colloquial contractions persisted until quite late. For example, Chatterton spells "champion" both "champyon" and "champyonn."[139] "Encountering" appears as "encontrynge";[140] "forweltering" ("blasting") as "forweltrynge";[141] "laboring" as "labrynge";[142] "murmuring" as "mormrynge";[143] "muttering" as "mottring";[144] and "shimmering" as "shemrynge."[145] Had Chatterton continually heard "muttering" and "shimmering" as trisyllables from the lips of the Bristol burghers, it would have been very evident to him that "mottring" and "shemrynge" were obviously based on modern poetical contractions, and were thus dangerous to use in the Rowley poems. It is my belief that Chatterton used them without thinking of them as contractions at all, since he heard them daily in ordinary conversation. In the same way, Chatterton produces "javlynne" for "javelin,"[146] and even allows the current prejudice against the uncontracted final "-ed" to influence "arraung'd."[147] The picture of the cowled Thomas Rowley, seated before a Chippendale escritoire with a bit of lace protruding from the cuff of his habit, writing,

---

[138] Matthews, "Some Eighteenth-Century Vulgarisms," p. 308.
[139] "Goddwyn: a Tragedie," Prologue, line 12; "The Tournament," line 149.
[140] "The Tournament," line 36.
[141] "Aella: a Tragycal Enterlude," line 681.
[142] "The Storie of William Canynge," line 77.
[143] "Aella," line 753.
[144] "The Storie of William Canynge," line 4.
[145] "Aella," line 739.
[146] *Ibid.*, line 459.
[147] "Songe to Aella," line 7.

. . . and wondrynge at mie myghte,[148]
is an entertaining one, but it can provide, in addition to mere amusement, fairly good evidence that such contractions were still actually to be heard in the Bristol colloquial idiom in 1770. Thomas Warton seems to be saying as much when he declares in his *History of English Poetry* that, in the Rowley poems, "sometimes the antiquated diction is most inartificially misapplied, by an improper contexture with the present modes of speech."[149]

In 1775, Allan Ramsay the Younger, in the act of denigrating double rhymes, spells "doggerel" as "doggrel,"[150] which may be assumed still to have been, in some circles at least, its customary pronunciation. But in 1781, the older forms have receded so far into the background that Thomas Sheridan, who probably had an alert and accurate ear for current modes of speech, says that "amorous" and "humorous" are now always pronounced as trisyllables.[151] Even Sheridan, however, still gives a trisyllabic pronunciation of "laborious" in his *Dictionary*, although he also records the more modern pronunciation of "powdery" and "watery," words which would have been strict dissyllables during the first quarter of the century.

Robert Nares also documents some survivals of colloquial contractions in 1784: "arsenic," he says, is generally heard without the "e";[152] "medicine" is still pronounced "med'cine";[153] the vulgar are persisting in such pronunciations as "amlet" for "omelet" and "ornary" for "ordinary," and these forms are, to Nares, "corruptions . . . established by custom."[154] And in 1791, John Walker reports that "geography" and "geometry" are still heard occasionally as "joggraphy" and "jommetry," "but this gross pronunciation seems daily wearing away, and giving place to that which separates the vowels into two distinct syllables."[155] It may be noted that contiguous vowels, even in the conversational idiom, are coming to seem less and less objectionable as we move farther away from the period of the high-water mark of classical studies in England: pronunciations once affected by the learned and the genteel partly to avoid the "ugliness" of hiatus on the strict classical model are rapidly being abandoned to the use of the London vulgar. Many of the contracted pronunciations which, during the first quarter of the century,

---

[148] "Aella," line 480.
[149] *The History of English Poetry, From the Close of the Eleventh to the Commencement of the Eighteenth Century* (London, 1774-1781), II, 155.
[150] "Enquiry into the Principles of English Versification," fol. 32ᵛ.
[151] *Lectures on the Art of Reading*, p. 221.
[152] *Elements of Orthoepy*, p. 19.
[153] *Ibid.*, p. 28.
[154] *Ibid.*, pp. 262-267.
[155] *Critical Pronouncing Dictionary*, p. 33.

were current among the educated and the elegant are being used by Dickens a little over a century later as comic speech tags for his Cockneys.[156] Despite the loss of the old pronunciation in "geography" and such words, Walker declares that the diphthong "ia" is, in 1791, still turning into a sort of y-glide, sufficient to make a dissyllable of "filial" and a trisyllable of "conciliate."[157] Both the lower and the more elevated orders still say "o-jus" and "tee-jus" for "odius" and "tedious,"[158] according to Walker, and "miniature" is often to be heard as "mineture."[159] Yet "dangerous" has become definitely a tri-syllable, and so has "various."[160]

The transition from the generally contracted pronunciations of the early eighteenth century to the newer pronunciation of the early nineteenth century was plainly causing a great deal of confusion, not only among readers of poetry who encountered and had somehow to deal with the poetic contractions, but even among the professional grammarians and lexicographers. Walker has before him both Kenrick's and Sheridan's pronouncing dictionaries, and he finds them disagreeing on the most basic colloquial contractions: "Mr. Sheridan divides *diamond* and *deviate* into *di-mund* and *de-vyate*, making them but two syllables; while Dr. Kenrick, in my opinion, much more correctly, divides them into *di-a-mond* and *de-vi-ate*. The same incorrectness runs through almost every word of the same kind in Mr. Sheridan, who divides *partiality* and *satiate* into *par-shal-i-ty* and *sa-shet*, which, if my ear does not grossly mislead me, ought always to be pronounced with a syllable more than he has bestowed on them."[161] One explanation for this sharp disagreement between Walker and Kenrick on the one hand, and Sheridan on the other, might be that Sheridan frequented the sort of conservative company (Johnson's circle, for example[162]) which clung to the Augustan contractions long after most literary persons had adopted the new pro-nunciation.

Peter Fogg in 1796 deplores this confusion which the decline of the Augustan pronunciations has spread abroad: "Many and loud," he writes, "have been the complaints of the difficulty and incertitude of pronuncia-tion."[163] Fogg gives the following pronunciations: "deity" as three syllables;

---

[156] See Matthews, "Some Eighteenth-Century Vulgarisms."
[157] *Critical Pronouncing Dictionary*, p. 34.
[158] *Ibid.*, pp. 34-36.
[159] *Ibid.*, p. 35.
[160] *Ibid.*, pp. 76-77. See also *Key to Classical Pronunciation*, pp. 182, n., and 203, n.
[161] *Critical Pronouncing Dictionary*, pp. 76-77. But notice the liberal scansion of "murmuring" and "many a" in Sheridan's *Art of Reading*, p. 216.
[162] See also Ramsay, above.
[163] *Elementa Anglicana*, II, 164.

"Leopold" as two ("Leppuld") ;[164] "enthusiast" and "various" after the earlier manner, "en-thus-yast" and "var-yus."[165] Fogg regards the old pronunciation "glor-yus" as correct, and censures the newer "glor-ee-us" as a "modish" affectation native to the London area.[166] Fogg also does what one wishes more of the eighteenth-century grammarians and linguists had seen fit to do: he essays a phonetic transcription of a few stanzas of Gray's *Elegy* and reproduces the lines exactly as they were read. Fogg proves to be one of those who are still reading the contractions called for by the syllabic theory of the line, and he thus reads "misery" as "mizri" and "heaven" as a monosyllabic "hevn."[167] There could be no better single item of proof that the indicated contractions in syllabic verse were so read than this phonetic transcription of Fogg's. In another place, Fogg instances "ling'ring" as the same sort of trochee as "flying" and "hoping."[168] Fogg's work thus shows that the Augustan colloquial and poetic contractions both were still to be heard even as late as the 1790's.

John Carey also prefers the older modes, and reveals that the classical prejudice against hiatus is behind many of his suggested contractions; he says, for example, of the pronunciation of "Orpheus," "This word contains only two syllables. . . . and let me further observe, that Milton, Dryden, Pope———in short, every English poet who had any pretensions at all to classical knowledge, has paid due regard to classic propriety in these cases, by making the *EU* a diphthong."[169] Carey's general concern with what ought to be rather than with what is must make one rather suspicious, however, of such "findings" as, " . . . our English *Beauteous*, . . . though in reality a word of three syllables, is usually pronounced as two. . . . "[170]

This is some of the evidence, then, of the existence of colloquial contractions during the eighteenth century. It may be repeated that such contractions seem to have been the standard in pronunciation from the Restoration until about 1730 or 1740, after which time they began to become vulgar, and were then gradually disused by the literate and literary classes. Very few traces of these colloquial contractions are to be found by 1815 or 1820, except in the speech of the London lower classes.

[164] *Ibid.*, I, 16.
[165] *Ibid.*, I, 19.
[166] *Ibid.*, II, 168.
[167] *Ibid.*, II, 178.
[168] *Ibid.*, II, 188.
[169] *Practical English Prosody*, p. 112, n. Cf. "Theseus," p. 159, n.
[170] *Ibid.*, p. 113, n.

5. *The Relationship of Poetic and Colloquial Contractions*

Some modern scholars have been aware of the extent of early eighteenth-century colloquial contractions, and have not been hesitant with interpretations of their impact upon the contractions of the syllabic poetry. A. Dwight Culler, for example, believes that the poetic contractions of the early century are simply reproductions of the ubiquitous colloquial contractions; as he says, "The important thing to understand about these elisions—and even scholars like Saintsbury fail to realize it—is that none of them was originally a 'poetic' form. By Bysshe's day, some very few had become slightly archaic, and hence were usually restricted to poetry; others existed side by side, in both prose and poetic speech, with the longer forms that at last superseded them; but the great majority represent the regular colloquial idiom of the late seventeenth and early eighteenth century."[171] This interpretation seems to me not to take full account of certain Augustan statements that poetic contractions are useful in elevating verse above mere prose.[172] We must bear in mind, too, the element of art in eighteenth-century verse construction; it is important to remember that the process of versification was generally held to be an idealizing of the natural phonetic materials, an improvement, not an imitation of them. To believe with Culler that the majority of the poetic contractions were simply imported without any improvement from the prevailing colloquial idiom is, I think, to assume that the poets were proceeding along some very nineteenth and twentieth-century naturalistic lines in their concept of what the act of creating verse entailed. It is Culler's neglect of the pervasive ideal aesthetic of the syllabic theory of prosody that weakens his interpretation and renders it too simple, perhaps, to contain the whole truth.

Again, a linguist has spoken of the poetic contractions as being intended to represent "a natural everyday pronunciation."[173] But surely we have seen enough of the importance of devices of art and artifice in both the construction and the oral delivery of eighteenth-century verse to perceive that the natural and the everyday were two things specifically to be avoided. I find it difficult to believe that an age which developed a special poetic vocabulary to help set poetry apart from common speech, and which even evolved unique artificial modes of reading the verse to keep it distinct from everyday prose, would admit contractions *because* they were to be heard in everyone's daily

---

[171] "Edward Bysshe and the Poet's Handbook," p. 875.

[172] See below, n. 174.

[173] Otto Jesperson, *Linguistica: Selected Papers in English, French, and German* (Copenhagen and London, 1933), pp. 273-274.

conversation.[174] This is certainly to ignore some of the essential distinctions between eighteenth-century and modern poetic and prosodic theory.

I should like to offer the following suggestion as a partial explanation of the significance of the appearance of these contractions in both poetry and the colloquial idiom. The specific conscious avoidance by the poets of that which might appear merely colloquial and "low" seems to suggest that the direction of influence here was, on occasion, as much from the poetry to the colloquial idiom as it was from the colloquial idiom to the poetry. Although many of the contractions were undoubtedly imbedded in colloquial speech long before much of the New Poetry of the later seventeenth century was produced,[175] many of the contractions would appear to have come down into common speech after having proved elegant in the poetry. The custom of reading verse aloud, and reading it, as we have seen, in such a way as to preserve its full syllabic and artificial character, would have been, it seems to me, a strong stimulus towards the adoption of certain "poetic" genteelisms in conversation which aspired to elevation and elegance. A man who customarily, because of the syllabic rule, read "tend'ring" in poetry (and few would have read it "tendering" much before 1740) would, I think, be tempted to say "tend'ring" in his conversation, and the temptation would be stronger as the conversation approached nearer an ideal of elegance. The influence between the dictional forms of poetry and those of conversational speech was, I would hold, reciprocal, and each furnished certain contractions to the other. To assume that the course of the contractions was one wholly from the colloquial toward the poetic is to forget the importance of some of the most basic predispositions of eighteenth-century poetics and aesthetics.

It is sometimes difficult for moderns to realize the full extent of the custom of declaiming verse aloud during the century: the poetry was primarily public poetry, and part of its public character consisted in the fact that its final form was to be that of spoken language heightened and polished by all the devices of elocution and declamation. The last century's output of subjective and meditative lyrics has caused some modern readers, until the most recent years, to think of all poetry as a sort of private communication

---

[174] Addison states specifically that Milton uses contractions as a deliberate means of "raising his Language": the implication is surely that the poetic contractions were by no means simply reproductions of contractions found in colloquial idiom. (See Smith, ed., *Spectator*, IV, 131. [No. 285, Sat., Jan. 26, 1712]). William Coward's remark that contractions in poetry give to the verse "Elegance and Grace" also seems to suggest that a mere imitation of colloquial forms is not what is being aimed at. (*Licentia Poetica discuss'd*, sig. B2ᵛ). See also Gildon, *Complete Art of Poetry*, I, 169.

[175] See Kökeritz, *Shakespeare's Pronunciation*, pp. 29, 283, 371-391; and Sprott, *Milton's Art of Prosody*, pp. 63, 69.

between the whispering poet and the silent and solitary reader. But the verse of the eighteenth century was, in the main, intended to be a public performance, and certain specifically poetic modes of speech, required by the syllabic theory of prosody under which the verse was constructed, would attain a wide currency very quickly and very easily from the custom of formal declamation. I would suggest, then, that the poetic contractions cannot be fully explained by finding a multitude of similar forms existing in the normal colloquial idiom, and by then assuming that the language of verse was somehow deliberately modelled after that which was to be heard from all lips. The uniqueness of the syllabic prosody with its necessary contraction and improvement of natural speech materials; the prevalence of the classical prejudice against contiguous vowels; the strong position of concepts of the artificial and the ideal in theories governing both the construction and the delivery of the poetry: surely these can hardly be considered results or mere rationalizations of the abundance of contractions in the everyday idiom. I think that any explanation of the poetic contractions which neglects this possibility that colloquial speech occasionally adopted certain poetic forms for the purpose of elegance will be in danger of oversimplifying the problem. In an age in which "art" and even "artifice" bear no opprobrious connotations, there can be little objection to the language of daily use itself displaying occasionally a little artifice. The consummately artistic conversational periods of Johnson will come to mind immediately.

In this chapter, an attempt has been made to show that the poetic contractions of the eighteenth century are an integral element of the system of syllabic prosody, and that they may be approached by means of the same theory of the ideal on which the syllabic prosody depends; that the contractions were intended to be read precisely as printed, and that they were thus read until about 1740; that an "unauthorized" filling in of the contractions in reading around the middle of the century was at once a manifestation and an encouragement of the growth of a new prosodic system which, in the nineteenth century, was to become that of accentualism; that, although many contracted forms can be shown to have been simultaneously fashionable in both poetical and colloquial usage, contraction took place to a much greater degree in poetry than in ordinary speech, especially in poetry which aspired to elevation and so to an ideal regularizing of the materials of colloquial speech. I have also suggested that perhaps some of the colloquial contractions owe their popularity to their proven success in the syllabic poetry.

One is now and then surprised to find modern critics and scholars, in their zeal for the continued vitality of eighteenth-century poetry, rather equivocating on the subject of poetic contractions and intimating darkly that the contractions were really mere "prosodial fictions"[176] not intended to be pronounced as written and simply serving as a "theoretical" regularization of the line under the syllabic principle. It is even hinted occasionally that it is physically impossible to pronounce a word like "watery" as a pure trochee, and that most of the poets and readers were aware of this fact.[177] It would seem, however, that if moderns can sound "bawdry" as a pure trochee, with no suggestion of such a pronunciation as "bawdery," then the eighteenth-century reader's phonetic equipment was perfectly capable of pronouncing "wat'ry" with no suggestion of the form "watery."

Perhaps some of the modern enthusiasts of eighteenth-century verse believe that to admit frankly that the apostrophized contractions were so read will only lend support to modern allegations that the verse is "unnatural" and "artificial." But the verse is indeed quite shamelessly artificial, if that term implies that the poetry is so constructed as to display obvious artifice. To attempt to justify and defend eighteenth-century poetry by asserting that it and nineteenth-century poetry are both seeking the same rhythmical effects is, first, to falsify, and second, to degrade eighteenth-century verse to a much lower position than it need occupy. It seems the wiser course to admit freely that a poetry of art will display its strict mechanisms of art, or even of artifice, and then to seek in the eighteenth-century temper the reasons why the poetry was not intended to be read as we should, perhaps, prefer it to have been. Those intent on disparaging Augustan poetry will not, I think, be won over simply by being permitted to believe, erroneously, that the verse of this period is rich in the same devices of rhythmical variety (trisyllabic substitution, for example) and a naturalistic approximation of the rhythm and tone of informal speech which have come to please in later poetry. Those who prefer trisyllabic substitution may find it in great abundance in nineteenth-century verse, but no amount of defensive equivocating can obscure the fact that a trisyllabic foot in iambic verse, unnormalized by the customary contracted mode of oral delivery, is rare in the Restoration and early eighteenth century to the point of being virtually nonexistent.

Those habituated to the New Critical concept of expressive organic form

---

[176] The phrase is Robert Bridges'.

[177] See, e.g., Saintsbury, History, II, 552-553. Much has been made of a statement of Shenstone's that "watry" has more of the dactylic in it than the strictly trochaic word "liquid." (Works, II, 180). I believe that this statement merely indicates that Shenstone, like many others in the 1760's, was filling in the elided syllable in "watry" and was thus producing a trisyllabic substitution wholly unintended by the Augustan poets, but one which the mid-century ear was beginning to crave.

need hardly be reminded that the prosody of a given poem is part of its meaning:[178] if the prosodic principles according to which the poem has been constructed are obscured or altered, the meaning of the poem will suffer a correspondent obscurity or alteration. It has been said that "we can today recapture only with great difficulty the authentic esthetic experience of the Neo-Classical age."[179] The task is assuredly not made any easier by ignoring the basic prosodic principles which were felt to govern the poetry of the age, and by casting over the poetry of the early eighteenth century prosodic pre-suppositions and expectations which belong properly only to later periods. A sympathetic comprehension of the nature, function, and contemporary theoretical justification of the poetic contractions can help modern readers to read each early eighteenth-century

> . . . work of Wit
> With the same spirit that its author writ.

---

[178] See Karl Shapiro, "Prosody as the Meaning," *Poetry*, LXXIII (1949), 336-351.
[179] Bredvold, "The Tendency toward Platonism in Neo-Classical Esthetics," p. 91.

CHAPTER IV

REACTIONS TO THE CONSERVATIVE PROSODY: TO 1770

I have been concerned hitherto mainly with certain characteristics of the prosody of syllabism and stress regularity, the system of prosody which may be considered the expression of unique conservative rhythmical predispositions during the eighteenth century. I should here like to begin a survey of some of the most significant reactions against this prevailing theory of prosody. The reactions began weakly and tentatively early in the century, but soon enlisted the support of some very penetrating minds indeed, and by the late century had established a firm theoretical foundation for the support of a new metric capable of expressing new poetic modes of thought and feeling which rose to an ascendant position early in the nineteenth century. The transition one witnesses is a change from a predominantly syllabic theory of prosody to a system primarily accentual, and the theoretical background of this transition is, in its major emphases, almost an exact parallel of similar contemporary tendencies in such areas of thought as philosophy, political theory, and aesthetics.

The rise of the accentual prosody mainly took the form of a new appreciation of triple cadences and of trisyllabic substitution in lines composed primarily of dissyllabic feet. Also to be observed is a new admission of trochaic substitution, especially in medial positions, and a revived interest in the sort of abrupt reversal of a flowing regular rhythm which such substitution imparts. The return of the principle of trisyllabic substitution to English prosody during the later eighteenth century has been designated "the revival of equivalence"[1] (that is, the revival of the assumption that, under certain conditions, a trisyllabic foot is "equivalent" to a dissyllabic one) : the prosodic mutation which was taking place was one from a structure such as

    Thĕ príde | ŏf Brít | ăin, sáil | ĭng óut | tŏ séa, |

to one like this:

    Bў thĕ síde | ŏf fáir | ў fóun | tăins, flów | ĭng ănd frée. |

In the latter line, an anapest is felt to be equal to an initial iambic foot, and an anapest also substitutes for the normal iamb in the fifth position.

We have seen that the conservative theorists' position on the subject of

---

[1] Saintsbury, *Historical Manual,* p. 92.

trisyllabic feet is either that they do not exist or that their occasional introduction into lines composed predominantly of dissyllabic feet spoils the
measure (as indeed it must, if "measure" is equated with syllabic regularity)
and reduces the line almost to the level of prose. To a conservative, the only
true equivalent of an iambic foot is either another iamb or a pyrrhic or
spondee. To a liberal prosodist, an anapest is close enough to an iamb in
structure to replace it quite freely, and to a radical prosodist (if the political
analogy may be pressed here), even a dactyl can substitute for an iamb.
What one observes, then, is the reaction to the conservative prosody shaping
up around the principle of the validity of free trisyllabic (and trochaic)
substitution in iambic lines, and the allied principle of free dissyllabic substitution in poems composed in triple cadences.[2] In the process of the transition
from syllabism to accentualism, it was first necessary to break down the traditional principles of syllabic limitation and regularity of stress, and a reintro-
duction of the concept of equivalence into English prosodic theorizing seemed
to most of the liberal prosodists to be the readiest way to attain this initial
victory.

In addition to the aesthetic reasons for the opposition to trisyllabic substitution which I have examined above, a little more should be said of the
reason why opposition to the new prosodists with their doctrines of equivalence and free substitution was so intense and, on occasion, so violent. There
was among certain conservatives a strong belief, for example, that any
trisyllabic substitution produced "a light-horseman sort of stanza" (as Sir
Walter Scott put it), and thus tended to dissipate the requisite dignity and
seriousness of public poetry.[3] It should also be noted that since, in colloquial
English, unstressed syllables are in a slight numerical majority over stressed
ones, verse in which a precisely equal number of each type occurs will always
seem slightly removed from common speech, and will tend to appear, consequently, elevated and uniquely poetic.[4] By increasing the number of unstressed syllables, the free admission of trisyllabic substitution will tend, if
ever so slightly, to impart a colloquial suggestion to verse, and, as we have
seen, the colloquial suggestion, whether in prosody, syntax, or diction, was
precisely one of the tendencies to be shunned by an art postulated on an
aesthetic of ideality and the improvement of nature. Only by keeping alive
and operative the rule of strict alternation of stressed and unstressed syllables

---

[2] See Culler, "Edward Bysshe and the Poet's Handbook," pp. 884-885; Stewart,
Modern Metrical Technique, p. 43; and Bate, *Stylistic Development of Keats*, p. 200.
[3] Stewart, *Technique of English Verse*, p. 58.
[4] *Ibid.*, p. 59.

could the conservative theorists make certain that poetry would not approach too near prose: every unstressed syllable admitted which was not compensated by an extra accented syllable (*e.g.,* a pyrrhic substitution uncompensated by a contiguous spondee) brought the verse that much nearer the level of prose. The aesthetic of ideality is here again one of the keys to an understanding and appreciation of the conservative opposition to trisyllabic substitution.

The transition from the conservative to the new prosody is paralleled by a decline in popularity of periodic sentence structure, and this decline accompanied the disuse of the closed heroic couplet as the dominant form: it is primarily because of the ubiquity of periodic structure that the Augustan poets were always supplied with the necessarily strong rhyme-word when they were in need of it, at the end of a sentence or clause.[5] As in most of these matters, it is impossible to assign definite priority to either of these two phenomena, the decline of the closed couplet or the loss of the technique of the periodic style: each may have "caused" the other, or, more probably, each may have been but a single manifestation of some *tertium quid* which it is impossible to encumber with any specific nomenclature.

We have observed enough of the fantastic persistence of syllabism, even into our own age, to make it perhaps unnecessary to point out that, for well over a century, syllabism and accentualism were being practiced and defended in theory simultaneously: their juncture was of the nature of a wide overlap, and not of a death and subsequent birth at some specific date. It may, however, be generalized that the transition from the one dominant prosodic system to the other breaks conveniently into three main periods: the years from 1660 to 1740 appear to be the years of syllabism's real reign; the thirty years from 1740 to about 1770 may be regarded as a period of experimentation and tentative exploration in the new theory of prosody; and finally, the period from 1770 to the end of the century is generally one characterized by consolidation and dogmatic formulation on the part of the accentualist liberals. As in most movements of this sort, the central period is the one of most interest, for in this period one finds the old and the new functioning concurrently, and one comes upon many examples, fascinating to the metrist and the literary pathologist alike, of what I have termed prosodic schizophrenia, resulting from confusion and indecision. In this engaging central period, most theorists are really deprived, for the most part, of the old facile rationalizations, and the need for revision of the syllabic theory is too apparent to be longer ignored. And yet, the specific direction in which theorizing should

[5] See Stewart, *Modern Metrical Technique,* pp. 32-35.

next move is not clear: one thus finds many of the prosodic theorists of the middle period in rather that state of mind which informs Arnold's "Stanzas from the Grande Chartreuse," caught embarrassedly between two worlds, one dead and the other not yet born. A chronological survey of these three periods can illustrate certain currents which mark this reaction to the conservative prosody.

1. *The Beginnings of Dissent: 1660 - 1740*

The first period, that comprising the years from 1660 to about 1740, need not detain us long. Opposition to the dominant syllabism was during these years weak, disorganized, and almost totally ineffectual, displaying all the characteristics of extreme minority opinion everywhere. The first real indication that the satisfaction with syllabism is not unanimous is Samuel Woodford's plea for trisyllabic substitution in 1679. Woodford's definition of "verse" is strikingly different from the definitions of Bysshe and his followers; verse is, to Woodford, "a Number and Movement metrical, with enterchang'd variety, according to the kind of our Verse, of diverse sorts of Feet."[6] Woodford goes to the ancients for authority in his argument that feet of three (and even four) syllables may be often pleasingly "intermixt" with dissyllabic feet. His position is somewhat weakened, however, by his assumption that French, Spanish, Latin, and English verses are at present "correctly" composed of dissyllabic feet alone.[7] It is plain that Woodford's suggestion that perhaps trisyllabic feet might now and then substitute for the customary dissyllabic ones is timid and half-hearted; yet he is the earliest of the Augustans to announce in print his slight dissatisfaction with the prevailing prosody, and for that he deserves whatever credit one thinks fitting to assign to a mild rebel.

All was now quiet on the anti-conservative front for a period of nine-

---

[6] *A Paraphrase Upon the Canticles,* sig. C2ᵛ.

[7] *Ibid.,* sig. B5. Woodford's poems in this work are composed in a significant variety of meters: heroic couplets, Spenserian stanzas, iambic tetrameter couplets, dactylic tetrameter stanzas, rhyme-royal stanzas (both with and without final alexandrines), Cowleyan Pindarics, elegiac quatrains, and Petrarchan sonnets. Woodford's rather equivocal position on the question of substitution produces such lines as these, which occur in a poem written presumably in iambic tetrameter couplets:

> But look how our Fields do smile,
> And in the Villas lodg a while. . . .
> I my BELOVED'S am alone,
> And beside me has he none;
> None beside me does he love,
> Equal none, and none above. . . . (p. 46).

Whether the triple cadences here are the result of conscious effort or simply the heat of zeal it is, unfortunately, impossible to tell. Whatever the cause, Woodford is one of the very few poets of this period who would dare mix triple with duple movements in the same poem.

teen long years following Woodford's very minor disturbance. But in 1698, the anonymous author of *Pendragon* (an iambic tetrameter burlesque on the model of *Hudibras*) lays down some rules for the composition of verse in this *genre*, and admits that the syllabic limitation may be broken, if only such a violation justifies itself by being sufficiently comic: "[Burlesque verse] stands indeed upon Four Feet; but its Liberties and Privileges are unbounded; and those Four Feet are, I think, by no means oblig'd to be but Eight Syllables; for in place of the Last, it is part of its Excellency sometimes to have Two, Three, or Four Syllables (like so many Claws) crowded into the Time of One Foot."[8] Two things seem especially noteworthy here: the first is that, to this author, trisyllabic substitution is a mechanism comic by its very nature, and one which he is confident can be the agent of risibility by its mere appearance in a duple cadence; the second is that the phrase "the Time of One Foot" is a striking anticipation of the equal-time theory which was not to be developed fully for a good many decades. This author perceives the customary sanction for trisyllabic substitution (that is, the principle of equal-time equivalence), but his assumption that there is something jocose about the very fact of trisyllabic substitution (no doubt encouraged by its extreme rarity in the serious poetry of the age) prevents him from going further. This is an attitude one encounters many times in the prosodic writing of the eighteenth century. Many theorists believed that there was something rather inexplicably comic about the attempt to present three syllables where only two had traditionally stood.

In 1690, Sir William Temple is already beginning to think of poetry and music in the same terms, and is thus preparing the ground for later prosodists who found in the bar-foot analogy the best theoretical defense of the principle of trisyllabic substitution. Such a notion, however, is far from Temple's mind at this date; he merely suggests that there must be some sort of an alliance between these two temporal arts, and he helps establish the fashion of bewailing their modern separation from each other.[9] There is even a certain element of latent primitivism in Temple's longing backward glance towards ancient history when the two arts had been brought to a linked perfection, and when the strength of one depended upon the health of the other.[10]

An early defense of prosodic variety in general comes from the anony-

---

[8] *Pendragon; or, the Carpet Knight his Kalendar* (London, 1698), sigs. A2v-A3.
[9] Spingarn, ed., *Critical Essays*, III, 108-109. ("Of Poetry").
[10] See J. W. Draper, "Poetry and Music in Eighteenth-Century Aesthetics," *Englische Studien*, LXVII (1932), 83-84.

mous editor of *Poems on Affairs of State* (1697). Incidentally, it should be noticed that many of the early pleas for prosodic freedom appeared anonymously, as if their authors were in fear of direct personal ridicule for their temerity in opposing the reigning prosodic system. This writer has obviously appeared about forty years before his time; some critics and theorists, he writes, "will exclude all Variety of Numbers from *English* Poetry, when they allow none but *Iambics*, which must by an identity of sound bring a very unpleasing satiety upon the Reader. I must own that a great many rough Cadences that are to be found . . . in the admirable *Paradise Lost*, are so far from Faults that they are beauties, and contribute by their variety to the prolonging the pleasure of the Readers."[11] Who this bold liberal was, we shall probably never discover. It is significant that his approbation of the stress variety of *Paradise Lost* takes almost the form of a guilt-ridden confession: he "must own" that he finds varied numbers pleasing. It is also apparent that this reader still possessed the knack of reading Milton according to a system of sense scansion; the artificial scansionists had not yet made the stylized reading of *Paradise Lost* into practically a British folk ritual from which only the most hardy individualists ventured to depart.

The first decade of the new century offers two prosodic liberals whose performance indicates that the opposition movement is now beginning to gather some slight strength. These two are William Coward and the poet Isaac Watts. Coward speaks very contemptuously in 1709 of "those who esteem a *right number of Measures sufficient to make a true* Verse" (Bysshe is obviously in his mind), and of *"Those who will have all Verse to consist in Dissyllables*, viz. *Spondees, Troches*, or *pure Iambics."*[12] All those he is opposing are, to Coward, "bigots,"[13] and he is bent on searching into "the Defects of our English Poetry,"[14] a matter which he believes has not been sufficiently noticed.

It is interesting that Coward, in his opposition to a prosody generally considered "neo-classic," goes directly to the classics for authority against it. He argues that since English verse is derived "unquestionably" from Latin poetry, the English poets are not only free but are even obliged to make use of all the feet (including the trisyllabic) which appear in Latin lyric measures:

[11] *Poems on Affairs of State: From the Time of Oliver Cromwell, to the Abdication of K. James the Second. Written by the Greatest Wits of the Age* (London, 1697), I, sig. A3ᵛ.

[12] *Licentia Poetica discuss'd*, sig. B3.

[13] *Ibid.*, sig. B2.

[14] *Ibid.*, sigs. A2ᵛ-A3.

" . . . we have no *Authority* at all for [the use of] *Spondees, Troches,* or *Iambics* only; but in irregular Practice grounded on [an] Erroneous Opinion of a few Men; purely to imitate . . . the *French Mode* in Our Nation, in order that the work may sound *sweet,* as they call it."[15] Coward offers a "Table of Quantities," in which he lists the feet that should be employed by the English poet proud of his direct literary descent from the ancients: in addition to the dactyl and the anapest, Coward would like to see such feet used as the molossus, the tribrach, the anti-bacchic, and the bacchic.[16] Coward specifically attacks Dryden for having stated that English verse is restricted to duple-time feet, and he even goes so far as to suggest that such words as "delicate," "moderate," and "generous" might be used without contraction.[17] Despite Coward's rather dubious consistency in some of these points (he wishes the formulation of prescriptive principles for the admission of trisyllabic feet, for example[18]), it is plain that some of the excesses of the conservative prosody had aroused a formidable antagonist. Coward's recourse to the sanctified practices of ancient Greek and Latin verse for illustrations of a desired anti-French prosodic variety suggests that an equation of "neo-classic" with "regularistic" will not always shed much light on the criticism of the early eighteenth century.

In the same year that this outburst of Coward's appeared, Isaac Watts published the second edition of his *Horae Lyricae,* the Preface to which contains an admirable defense of a prosodic system different from the one then obtaining. Watts displays a unique methodology in his approach to the question of the difference between blank verse and the heroic couplet: instead of assuming, as was the fashion, that blank verse is the simple result of heroic couplets "disencumbered . . . from rhyme" (as Dryden had held[19]), Watts proceeds according to the supposition that the heroic couplet is a direct imitation of blank verse (with the addition of rhyme), and that the couplet should display all of the "Variety of Cadence, Comma, and Period" found in blank verse. Watts goes on, "It degrades the Excellency of the best Versification when the lines run on by Couplets, twenty together, just in the same Pace and with the same Pauses. It spoils the noblest Pleasure of the Sound: the Reader is tir'd with the tedious Uniformity, or charm'd to sleep with the unmanly

[15] *Ibid.,* sigs. B7, B7ᵛ.

[16] *Ibid.,* sig. B8ᵛ.

[17] *Ibid.,* p. 54, n. "b"; p. 76, n. "f"; but see above, Chap. III, n. 174, for a contradictory position of Coward's.

[18] *Ibid.,* p. 80, n. "k."

[19] In the Preface to *All for Love.*

Softness of the Numbers, and the perpetual Chime of even Cadences."[20] While Coward had exhorted British patriots to arise and cast off the yoke of the Gallic regularistic prosody, Watts appeals to British manliness: it is characteristic of the early stages of the reaction to the conservative prosody that an address to something non-prosodic about which readers held strong opinions (British virility, for example) was felt necessary for defaming the prevailing prosodic system. A defense of stress irregularity purely for its own sake was still in the future.

In the second decade of the century, John Brightland, in a Grammar often attributed to Steele, opposes trisyllabic feet,[21] but he is in favor of much greater variety of dissyllabic substitution than is permitted by the stress regularists. The strict alternation of stressed and unstressed syllables in the heroic line leaves Brightland quite cold, but still, only a "Master" of the art of versification may venture the bold dissyllabic substitutions required for poetic pleasure.[22] Variety is to Brightland the essence of poetical numbers,

> For the same Sounds perpetually disgust.[23]

Charles Gildon, Bysshe's opponent in the syllable-foot controversy, favors trisyllabic substitution (although he recognizes little of it in existing English verse), and, like Coward, he goes directly to the ancients for illustrations of the use of three and four-syllable feet. After listing the twenty-eight feet available to the ancient poet, Gildon writes, "All these Variations of a long, and a short Syllable did the Application and Industry of the antient Poets find out, to give an agreeable Variety to their Numbers. . . . it being evident, that the *English* Language, as well as the *Greek* and *Latin,* consists of *long* and *short* Syllables; it is as evident that our Poets may, if they wou'd be as curious in this particular, make near Approaches to this wonderful Variety of the Versification, to that of Antiquity."[24] The appeal to classical authority was of course being used at this time by both conservatives and liberals: the stress regularists could always point out that substitution was rare in classical epic and dramatic meters, and was mainly confined to mere lyric and comic poetry, with certain definite regulations even there; while the liberals could, like Gildon, shrewdly confound length with accent and thus draw analogies be-

---

[20] *Horae Lyricae. Poems Chiefly of the Lyric Kind. In Three Books. I. Sacred to Devotion and Piety. II. To Vertue, Honour, and Friendship. III. To the Memory of the Dead.* (2nd ed.; London, 1709), p. xx.

[21] *A Grammar of the English Tongue: With the Arts of Logick, Rhetorick, Poetry, &c. Illustrated with Useful Notes; Giving the Grounds and Reasons of Grammar in General* (7th ed.; London, 1746), p. 160.

[22] *Ibid.,* pp. 160-161.

[23] *Ibid.*

[24] *Complete Art of Poetry,* I, 298. See also pp. 299-300.

tween all the classical feet and their desired English counterparts. Gildon opposes the French-derived "smoothness" which had become the prosodic standard and avers that regularity of stress breeds, "by the perpetual *Sameness* of the Sounds and Quantities, a speedy Satiety. . . . "[25] All this emphasis in 1718 on variety of stress and number of syllables is refreshing, but Gildon's most significant contribution to the cause of prosodic variety reveals more originality. Gildon is probably the first of a long and illustrious line of English prosodists to employ a musical scansion; the poetry-music parallels, of which Temple had been vaguely aware, were apparently growing more and more precise and technical, and Gildon scans as follows:

His   Passion   cast   a   Mist   before   his   Sense.[26]

It will be observed that Gildon's use of the bar-foot analogy is here really undeveloped: by choosing to begin the first "bar" with an unstressed entity, Gildon obscures the possibilities for an equal-time theory which are inherent in the analogy. Had he gone but one step further and scanned thus,

His   Passion   cast   a   Mist   before   his   Sense,

it would have been more plain that, since a musical bar may contain an infinite *number* of notes as long as its *time* is equal to that of the other bars in the same sequence, a foot modelled on its musical analogue may also contain a varied *number* of syllables as long as its *time* is equal to that of each surrounding foot. But this perception of the uses of the bar-foot analogy Gildon left for others.

It has been said that this musical scansion of Gildon's, harmless as it appears, initiated "a course of error which has never yet been stopped,"[27] but most historians of metric would probably agree that the bar-foot analogy, despite the ludicrous excesses to which it has sometimes been carried, was a

[25] *Ibid.*, I, 292. See also William Benson, *Letters Concerning Poetical Translations*, pp. 39; 73-75.

[26] *Complete Art of Poetry*, I, 300.

[27] Saintsbury, *Historical Manual*, p. 245.

useful device for the attack on the syllabic system when it became evident that syllabism was no longer the most fit prosody to express what was to be expressed in poetry. The "course of error" to which the poetry-music analogy has occasionally led in our own time may be observed in a modern scholar's treatment of Gray's *Elegy*. Mr. Henry Lanz, by basing his "notes" on the frequency of each of Gray's vowels as ascertained by the Bell Telephone Laboratories, proceeds to "score" the first stanza of the *Elegy* so that it may be played on piano or tuning forks![28] But during the eighteenth century, few such palpably bizarre or frivolous results arose from the fashionable comparison between the arts of poetry and music. The comparison was found extremely useful in breaking down the syllabic prosody because it furnished "evidence" that the poetic foot, if it began with a stressed syllable as a normal musical bar began with a beat, could like the bar contain an infinite number of separate syllables (cf. "notes") so long as its total time was equal to that of other feet in the same sequence.[29] More will be said about the uses and techniques of the bar-foot analogy as we come upon later and more accomplished practitioners of it.

The third decade of the century saw the publication of another work by Gildon (*The Laws of Poetry* [1721]) in which he carried on his plea for variety, basing it now on the rapidly rising "Uniformity and Variety" principle which was also being discussed by Alison and Hogarth.[30] Here Gildon goes to the verse of Dryden to prove that such structural principles as "the alternation of stressed and unstressed syllables" are violated by the best English poets.[31] Gildon is also aware that, if regularity of numbers is to become accepted as the highest achievement in English verse, such beauties as sound-sense correspondences will largely be forfeited,[32] for, deprived of the device of stress variation, the poet will be left with only minor mechanisms, such as assonance, alliteration, and cesura variations, with which to make his effects.

While by no means the first to support the principle of trisyllabic substitution in opposition to the conservative insistence on "a certain number of syllables," John Dennis is probably the first to misread Dryden's verse in an effort to "demonstrate" that Dryden frequently ignores the syllabic limitation.

[28] Henry Lanz, *The Physical Basis of Rime: An Essay on the Aesthetics of Sound* (Palo Alto, 1931), pp. 24-25.
[29] The general poetry-music parallel is also abetted by Edward Manwaring, *Stichology*, p. 3, and Henry Pemberton, *Observations on Poetry*, p. 107.
[30] See Bate, *From Classic to Romantic*, pp. 102-108.
[31] *Laws of Poetry*, p. 63. See also pp. 316-317.
[32] *Ibid.*, p. 336.

In 1722, Dennis writes, "The Measure of our common *Pentameter* or *Heroick* Verse is usually ten Syllables, but sometimes when there are *Dactyles*, 'tis extended to *eleven* or *twelve*, as in this Verse of Dryden. *Thee Saviour, Thee the Nations Vows Confess.*"[33] Dryden's line is really syllabically regular with a mere initial spondaic substitution, but Dennis, probably reading "Sa-vi-our" or "Na-ti-ons" or both, is able to extend the line past the decasyllabic limit. Dennis' performance at least indicates that a subversive misreading of the syllabic classics was beginning quite early, and that there were a few ears, even during the years when barely any non-syllabic poems were being produced, which were already attuned to the new system of prosody which was yet hidden in the dim future.

Thus from the Restoration until about 1740, we see the beginnings of several significant prosodic currents: first, the poetry-music association which was destined, in time, to compel a strict examination of the similarities between the foot and the bar, and which was finally to produce the equal-time prosodic principle; second, a growing feeling of dissatisfaction with a syllabic system felt to have been formed after French theory and practice, which feeling was not without its strong chauvinistic implications; and third, a re-examination of the nature and extent of trisyllabic substitution in classical meters, as part of an effort to find a solid and authoritative basis for substitution in English verse. Before 1740, however, the small amount of liberal prosodic thought that existed was in the main confused, timorous, and ineffective. It is only in the decade 1740-1750 that these small voices crying in the syllabic wilderness increase in number and volume and finally unite in a resounding clamor against the prevailing Augustan theory.

2. Samuel Say

There seems to me to be little question that Samuel Say is not only one of the major prosodic thinkers of the eighteenth century, comparable in stature and final influence to Bysshe, Johnson, and Joshua Steele, but that he is also one of the great metrical theorists of the whole English literary tradition: because of his sensitivity and his fundamental grasp of the problem of the meaning of meter in English poetry, he deserves a place among such central prosodic theorists as Coventry Patmore, Sidney Lanier, and Robert Bridges. It is indeed difficult to understand why Say has been neglected by modern historians of English metrical theory.[34] His work has been almost

---

[33] James Greenwood, *An Essay towards a Practical English Grammar, Describing the Genius and Nature of the English Tongue* (2nd ed.; London, 1722), p. 267. Dennis contributed to this Grammar only the section on prosody.

[34] See Chap. III, above, n. 59.

unnoticed, and when scholars have called attention to the prosodic essays contained in his *Poems on Several Occasions* (1745), they have seriously underestimated Say's originality and his admirable detachment from prosodic cant and from the prevailing suppositions of his age. Even Say's prose style alone can suggest to the observer that he is not dealing here with just another hack metrist, but instead with a genuine literary sensibility of the upper ranks. It is almost impossible to read the work of Samuel Say in its historical context without a feeling of admiration and a conviction that one has for a change been in the presence of an almost first-rate man of letters.

Say was born in 1676, was educated in the grammar schools of Southwick, Hampshire, and Norwich, and was a student friend of Isaac Watts's. He became a dissenting clergyman and devoted his life to preaching in Ipswich and London.[35] The two prosodic essays in his 1745 book of poems were probably written around 1737.[36] Say died in 1743, and a friend, William Duncombe, assembled his literary remains for publication two years later. Say's *Poems on Several Occasions* contains a brief introductory memoir by Duncombe, dwelling chiefly on Say's piety and on his exceptionally devoted service to his dissenting congregations; a collection of poems ("youthful rubbish," they have been called[37]) ; and the two prosodic essays, the first on metrics in general and the second on the prosody of *Paradise Lost.*

Say's poems are prosodically significant, whatever their final value as poetry. They include four imitations of Horatian epistles in very free blank verse with frequent extrametrical final unstressed syllables after the model of dramatic poetry and with careful marking of unstressed syllables which the conservative reader would be tempted to elide (*e.g.*, "favŏring"). These Horatian imitations were composed as early as 1698 and are an interesting example of the sort of "subversive" poetry which was being all but surreptitiously produced behind drawn curtains during the years when it simply would not have done to have questioned publicly the prevailing syllabic prosody. There are also a few very indifferent love verses in highly conventional prosodic forms and techniques, together with some imitations of the Psalms in iambic tetrameter couplets which display no originality. In general, Say's poems, if not perhaps complete rubbish, are undistinguished, but the evidence they supply of the fact that, as early as 1698, Say was marking and reading

---

[35] *DNB.* And see John Duncombe, ed., *Letters by Several Eminent Persons Deceased. Including the Correspondence of John Hughes, Esq. (Author of the Siege of Damascus) and Several of his Friends, Published from the Originals* (London, 1773), I, 19, n.

[36] According to John Hughes, *ibid.*, III, i. Omond, however, says 1738. (*English Metrists*, p. 50).

[37] *DNB.*

"glittĕring" in opposition to syllabic contraction practice makes them valuable for prosodic study.

According to William Duncombe, the amateur editor of these materials, the two prosodic essays were written at the specific request of "Mr. RICH-ARDSON the Painter, who was pleased with Mr. SAY'S uncommon Way of Thinking on those Subjects."[38] Duncombe also reports that "Mr. SAY, as well as Mr. ADDISON, was a profest Admirer of CHEVY-CHACE"[39] and was "well versed in *Astronomy* and *Natural Philosophy*, had a Taste for *Music* and *Poëtry*, was a good *Critic*, and a Master of the *Classics*. Yet with all these Accomplishments (so great was his Modesty!) his Name was scarce known but to a few select friends."[40] Duncombe concludes his editorial office by dutifully reporting that "Mr. SAY died, after a Week's Illness, of a Morti-fication in the Bowels, on the twelfth Day of *April*, 1743, and in the 68th Year of his Age."[41]

I should now like to focus on Say's two essays on prosody and try to show what it is that requires us to give more than ordinary attention to this small dissenter and dabbler in polite letters. Say's approach to a theory of verse pleasure bears a close resemblance to that held by most subsequent major writers on prosody: the continual opposition of actual sense stress to theoretical or artificial stress is, to Say, the main source of prosodic pleasure. He thus praises certain lines in *Paradise Lost* in which "the Sounds, the Numbers, and the Idéas [*sic*] are . . . set in opposition to one another."[42] This theory of a perpetual tension in the prosodic surface is one of Say's major contributions to English prosody; the assumption that the pleasure of verse structure arises from the perception of the varied approach and retreat of the actual "sense" prosody towards or away from the theoretical artificial pattern is possible only for a man who is scanning strictly according to the prose sense of a verse passage, and who is manfully resisting all his age's manifold pressures to scan ideally or artificially. This theory of tension Say advances when he says that verse must be composed "with a proper Mixture of Uni-formity and Variety." And after analyzing metrical variations in three of Milton's lines (*P.L.*, IV, 254-256), Say rapturously exclaims, "Such is the Variety in such a Uniformity!"[43] As we shall see, the continual employment

---

[38] Samuel Say, *Poems on Several Occasions*, p. iv. See also John Duncombe, ed., *Letters*, III, i.
[39] *Poems on Several Occasions*, p. v.
[40] *Ibid.*, p. vi.
[41] *Ibid.*, p. vii.
[42] *Ibid.*, p. 101.
[43] *Ibid.*, p. 102.

of the "Uniformity and Variety" tag by future prosodists is usually in the interest of advancing this same theory of prosodic tension.

The theory of tension obviously implies that there can be no good verse written with an absolutely regular pattern of stresses, for then there could arise no pleasure from the reader's observation of the subtle variations from the theoretical uniformity. "Imperfect Measures" are thus naturally agreeable to the ear, while "perfect" ones are not even verse.[44] Say's emancipation from the Augustan prejudice against effects of surprise is also clear: the variety absolutely essential to prosody consists of "a proper Mixture, Exchange, Agreement, or Opposition of . . . a Variety of Parts, Sounds, and Numbers; and sometimes a Sudden and Seasonable Start from all Rules to Awaken Attention. . . ."[45]

Say has sufficient natural taste to be repelled by Bentley's misreading and abuse of *Paradise Lost,* and he characterizes Bentley as "a late insolent Editor, equally remarkable for his Dogmatical Temerity, and his Tasteless Notes on This Poëm. . . ."[46] The exquisite variety of the prosody of *Lycidas* Say finds highly pleasing,[47] and he has an equal amount of contempt for *Leonidas*[48] and for Pemberton, its champion.[49]

It will be evident from Say's views on the varied prosody of *Paradise Lost* that he is totally unaffected by the conservative grounding of the regularistic prosody in an ideal theory of art. Instead, Say asserts that "the Numbers, in Every Just Composition, will be as Various as the Passions and Ideas" contained in it and evoked by it.[50] Thus, while the more "active" parts of *Paradise Lost* are expressed in iambic measures, such sections as the Hymns of Adam and Eve, Milton's Hymn to Wedded Love, and the Address to Light avoid iambics and tend to take on a slow spondaic movement, "justly," as Say observes.[51]

We have in this perception the earliest appearance of the "romantic" aesthetic of prosody which we meet in the eighteenth century. Instead of the conservative ideal theory, according to which the matter of the poem adapts

---

[44] *Ibid.,* p. 107. See also pp. 115-116.
[45] *Ibid.,* p. 110.
[46] *Ibid.,* p. 117. The dieresis here is characteristic of Say's technique in prose: he frequently supplies the reader with marks to suggest the precise pronunciation and emphasis he intends. (See, *e.g.,* p. 97).
[47] *Ibid.,* p. 118.
[48] *Ibid.,* p. 141. Speaking of the whole French-influenced "smoothness" cult, Say comments, " . . . the Smoothest Waters are the most *torpid* and *heavy* in their Motion."
[49] *Ibid.,* p. 128.
[50] *Ibid.,* p. 126.
[51] *Ibid.,* p. 127.

and improves itself to fit the archetypal prosodic pattern, Say presents the liberal theory, which holds that the prosody instead must adapt itself to the nature of the poetic material at each passing moment. The prosody is thus actually a "creation" of the poetry's. Say's theory is one which requires that the prosody itself carry its full load of organic meaning; it is a theory which necessitates the sort of subtlety, penetration, and sensitivity to minute effects which the average eighteenth-century reader (if we may assume that the practice of artificial scansion was really as widespread as it appears to have been) was not prepared to bring to the apprehension of poetry. Say's romantic aesthetic of prosody is a theory making an appearance about fifty years before its time, and Say's extremely acute sensibility in perceiving the direction in which metrical theory was to go demands, I think, the attention and respect which genuine originality in the arts will always deserve.

Say's manifest enthusiasm for poetry, and especially for poetry of the highest rank, seems to be more than a merely fashionable affectation of "sensibility": when Say quotes a few lines from *Paradise Lost* (I, 169-177) and then exclaims, "What Majesty! what Rapidity! and, above all, what Propriety may we observe in These Lines!"[52] he is not merely intent on exhibiting his powers as a man of feeling to an admiring sentimental public. "Propriety" here means of course the perfect adaptation of the prosodic pattern to the kinetic sense necessity; to a prosodic conservative, on the other hand, the same word would bear connotations of the adaptation of the sense to fit the universal and inflexible pattern of the static prosody.

The heart of Say's position is contained in the following remarks: " . . . the Greatest Part of Modern Readers, accustom'd to a Smooth and Unvaried Uniformity of Numbers, . . . reject every Syllable which they imagine to be Supernumerary, [and] . . . lay a strong Accent on every Even Syllable in the *English Heroic* Verse . . . in the Bentleian manner. . . . " Say then scans four lines from *Paradise Lost* as they would be read by "the Greatest Part of Modern Readers," Bentley included:

> . . . *Thămmúz* | came néxt | behínd |
> Whose ánn | 'al Wóund | in *Lé* | banón | allúr'd |
> The Sýr | 'an Dám | sels tó | lamént | his Fáte |
> In ám | 'rous Dít | ties áll | a Súm | mer's Dáy. |
> (*P.L.,* I, 446-449)

Of this example of artificial scansion and syllabic contraction, Say comments, "But what Monsters of Sound would *Ann'al* or *An'wal, Syr'an* or *Am'rous*

52 *Ibid.,* p. 129.

be? or does anyone reälly [*sic*] pronounce any otherwise than *ánnŭăl, Sýrĭăn, ámŏrŏus,* in three short, but distinct Syllables? why then does he suffer his *Eyes* to judge for his *Ears?* or suffer Words so agreeable in Sound to be written or printed in a manner he never pronounces? or who would dwell on a Sound naturally short? or lay the Stress of the Voice on an inconsiderable TO or THE, on pretence that the Laws of Versification require it?" Say then scans ·

Ănd thĕ shríll Sóunds răn écchŏĭng róund thĕ Wóods,

and declares that, if most readers had their way, the line would be read,

Ănd THÉ shríll Sóunds răn écch'ĭng róund thĕ Wóods,[53]

with the "ecch'ing" no doubt pronounced "ek-wing." In these remarks, Say is clearly furnishing a new prosody for readers who do not feel the syllabists' impulse towards automatic contraction and their desire to read verse in such a manner as to emphasize its approach to melody. Although we may be fairly certain that almost none of them read him, Say is the spokesman for the new readers who, not syllabists themselves, wish to salvage what they can from existing works written according to syllabic principles. Such readers will require a new mode of declamation to fit their new rhythmic predispositions, and Say is here to be observed supplying them with just such a new mode.

To help break down the principle of syllabic limitation, Say manufactures this couplet in what he imagines to be the essential style of Chaucer and Spenser:

And many an amorous, many a humorous Lay,
Which many a Bard had chanted many a Day.

Say then points out that if the contractions are not taken, the first line contains fourteen and the second twelve syllables, but that each line is "equal" to a strictly decasyllabic line in the time required for its pronunciation.[54] This synthetic couplet attained a great vogue among Say's liberal prosodic successors, and almost every other advanced metrist until the very end of the eighteenth century avails himself of this particular illustration of the "weaknesses" of syllabism. Say reveals a sensibility rather rare for his time when, lashing Bentley for a particularly dogmatic improvement of the meter of *Paradise Lost,* he bursts out, "And why should not the Mind and Judgment of the Reader have some Pleasure in the *Power* and *Variety* of the Numbers, where the Ear is pleas'd to an Excess, and sooth'd with the Sweetness of all

[53] *Ibid.,* pp. 130-131. Apparently Say is now hearing primarily uncontracted forms in colloquial idiom.
[54] *Ibid.,* p. 132.

the Sounds . . . ?"[55] One is reminded of the mode of feeling (and even the vocabulary) of John Keats.

Say naturally approves of full trisyllabic substitution,[56] and occasionally employs Gildon's musical scansion, but with some subtle improvements. Say uses half and whole notes to represent unstressed and stressed syllables, but adds the device of a dotted note to indicate extra stress or cesural pause:

Strong without Rage; without o'erflowing, Full.[57]

The subscription list prefixed to Say's work suggests that its circulation was generally confined to his friends: Dodsley the bookseller took seven copies, and Jonathan Richardson, Isaac Watts, and Jacob Tonson took one copy each, but most of the copies were destined for the hands of such folk as "Aureng-Zebe Hatfield," "William Coussmaker, Brewer," and others of the minor bourgeoisie of Ipswich, Yarmouth, and Harwich.

3. John Mason and other Mid-Century Theorists

Despite its limited circulation, Say's all but revolutionary work reached one John Mason, and by 1749, Mason had his *Essays on Poetical and Prosaic Numbers* on the booksellers' stalls. Mason generally carries on Say's anti-syllabic efforts in the same direction, but, while obviously deeply indebted to Say, he also commits some of the very errors of the Bentley-Pemberton school which he is opposing. Although Mason's discipleship to Say was by no means total, Mason undoubtedly would have been infinitely more conservative had he not had access to Say's work.

Mason's first essay is titled "An Essay on the Power of Numbers and the Principles of Harmony in Poetical Compositions," but Mason's use of the word "Harmony" is far different from Johnson's. To Mason, the word is practically a synonym of Say's "propriety"; it signifies that condition of poetry in which the prosody has perfectly adapted itself to the sense, and the word is thus almost equivalent to "variety."[58] Whenever we see the term "harmony" employed by the liberal prosodists during the 1740's and 1750's, we can be quite certain that there will be loud exhortations to prosodic variety, much trampling on Bentley and Pemberton, and varying degrees of indebtedness, not always acknowledged, to Samuel Say.

[55] *Ibid.*, p. 133.
[56] *Ibid.*, p. 149.
[57] *Ibid.*, p. 153.
[58] *Essays*, p. 61. See also p. 46, n. "a."

Mason makes a great deal of the bar-foot analogy,[59] and is thus enabled to take the position that two unstressed syllables can occupy the same time as a single unstressed one, if only the verse be measured primarily by the length of time occurring between the accents. "Number of syllables," consequently, has nothing to do with the structure of the line, which is strictly a matter of a stated number of equal times. Mason quotes Say's synthetic couplet in illustration of this point, and finds much to praise in the couplet's "sweetness."[60] As will be seen, it is a very short and easy step from this measurement of lines by the number of their equal-time units to a full-fledged romantic accentualism, since the regularly counted stresses, regardless of the number of unstressed syllables that may occur between them, will be the only means by which the number of equal-time units may be perceived. In other words, each accent will serve as a sort of signal flag for its equal-time unit, just as the first beat of a musical bar serves as a signal that an equal-time unit is beginning. The equal-time theory thus serves as an intermediate transitional stage in the development from a syllabic prosody to one primarily accentual.

Mason permits dissyllabic substitution practically anywhere in the line, although the last foot must still be an iamb; such a line as Keats's

Bright star! would I were stedfast as thóu ǎrt———

would strike even Mason as containing too great an irregularity to be countenanced.[61] Say's prosodic aesthetic is carried on by Mason: two successive lines, he says, "should not have exactly the same Order of Feet, unless they have exactly the same Turn of Thought. . . . "[62] That is, the specific prosody of each line must bend and compromise until it is the precise expression of the "content" of the line. Over a century later, Coventry Patmore offers substantially the same theory: "[Variety in the prosody of a poem] must be incessantly inspired by, and expressive of, ever-varying emotion. Every alteration of the position of the grammatical pause, every deviation from the strict and dull iambic rhythm, must be either sense or nonsense. Such [metrical] change is as real a mode of expressing emotion as words themselves are of expressing thought; and when the means exist without reference to their proper ends,

---

[59] *Ibid.*, p. 22.

[60] *Ibid.*, p. 27.

[61] *Ibid.*, p. 47. And see Bridges, *Milton's Prosody*, p. 42. Yvor Winters takes an amusing neo-Augustan attitude towards the meter of this line of Keats's. The fact that the line ends with a trochee is, to Winters, a "blunder" and an "error": the last foot, he finds, "constitutes an unhappy moment." ("The Audible Reading of Poetry," pp. 438-439).

[62] *Essays*, p. 48.

the effect of the 'variety' thereby obtained, is more offensive to a right judgment, than the dulness which is supposed to be avoided."[63] This position of Patmore's stems ultimately from that of Say and Mason, and it is as clear an expression as will probably be found of the romantic aesthetic of prosody, under the principles of which the prosody is assumed to be a kinetic and dynamic aspect (almost "creation") of the poem's total meaning, and not a static and fixed regulating ideal.

Mason agrees with Say that *Leonidas* is a work displaying only "insipid Similarity"[64] of prosody, and he finds that Pemberton's defense of Glover's efforts implies that Pemberton is unable, according to his own principles, to read a page of Milton, Pope, or Young.[65] For all he has learned from Samuel Say, however, Mason is strangely hostile to trisyllabic substitution, and he seems not always aware that his adherence to the bar-foot parallel provides him with a solid theoretical justification for anapestic substitution in iambic lines. Mason censures this Miltonic line,

In thĕir tríplĕ Dĕgrées; Régĭons tŏ whích
(*P.L.*, V, 750)

for bearing too close a resemblance to an anapestic measure. He adds, "The rapid flow of Anapestics, is of all things most contrary to the stately movement of Iambics. And [this] line being a composition of these two contrary Measures, and neither the one nor the other, it is no Verse, but downright Prose."[66] To a thoroughgoing equal-time prosodist, the anapest would seem the foot most similar to the iamb, and the dactyl would be its "most contrary." Mason seems still to be influenced by the conservative antipathy to triple cadences, especially when they make an appearance in verse which aspires to any degree of elevation.

The subtle persistence of the syllabic prosody, even among those who deliberately mustered their powers to put it down, is also apparent in Mason's disapproval of dactylic substitution in trochaic measures. He suggests that the couplet

Paths by meeting paths are crost,
Alleys in winding alleys lost,

the prosody of which is an excellent example of the mutation to romantic cadences, which rely on a mixture of duple and triple measures, "would be more pure" if the second line were altered to

[63] "English Metrical Criticism," p. 159.
[64] *Essays*, p. 49, n. "d."
[65] *Ibid.*, pp. 52-53.
[66] *Ibid.*, p. 59.

Ways in winding ways are lost.[67]

This change naturally makes the two lines equal now in number of syllables and in stress pattern. Mason seems to have forgotten already his earlier insistence that the meaning always dictate the prosody, not the reverse.

Mason would also agree with such a rigorous conservative as Thomas Jefferson that no substitution whatever, even that of an occasional discreet iamb, is permitted in anapestic measures.[68] John Mason's basic position, however, is probably contained in this strikingly Coleridgean summary: "If the ancient [especially Hebrew] Poetry was too lax in its Numbers, the modern is certainly too strict. The just Medium between these two Extremes, seems to be that which Milton hath chosen for his Poems, *viz.* the Penthameter [*sic*] Verse with the mixt Iambic Measure, free from the Shackle of Rhime; in which the Numbers are neither too free nor too confined."[69] Although Coleridge would undoubtedly have chosen Shakespeare as his example of the one poet whose prosody displays this perfect reconciliation of extremes, Mason's whole performance is the sort of attempted compromise between extremes which one expects in the critical writing of Coleridge. It will be noted that Say's theory of prosodic tension is, in essence, simply another way of presenting this notion of "the just Medium."

Say's and Mason's work may be considered the first effective frontal assault against the prevailing prosody, and the years 1745-1750 should be regarded as the period of the first major formal reaction to the syllabic system and to the ideal aesthetic on which that system depended. From 1750 on, the conservatives, whether aware of the fact or not, will really be on the defensive against the equal-time theory (and against the dynamic, organic aesthetic which it represents) which was first formally advanced by these two important theorists of the 1740's.

In 1752, Charles Avison helped carry on the cause of prosodic variety by his comparison of the various arts in *An Essay on Musical Expression.* Comparing painting and music, Avison writes, "As Shades are necessary to relieve the Eye, which is soon tired and disgusted with a level Glare of Light; so Discords are necessary to relieve the Ear, which is otherwise immediately satiated with a continuous, and unvaried Strain of Harmony."[70] The prosodic implications of this position are fairly obvious: using "Harmony" with the conservative connotation of "regularity of rhythmical times" or "perpetual

---

[67] *Ibid.,* p. 65.
[68] *Ibid.,* pp. 68, 72.
[69] *Ibid.,* (Essay on Prose Numbers), p. 47.
[70] *An Essay on Musical Expression* (2nd ed.; London, 1753), p. 23. See also p. 143.

sweetness of the concurrence of tones," Avison's statement could serve as a sanction for such licences as trochaic and trisyllabic substitution in iambic lines. Avison reveals that he is also involved in the Cowley revival which, near the middle of the century, helped popularize the less rigid prosody towards which the age was inclining.[71] Purcell, Avison says, properly combines in his work "harmony" (regularity) with "fancy" (variety), and thus may be placed alongside Cowley as a uniter of the two extremes of uniformity and variety.[72]

The appearance in 1754 of Fortescue's *Pomery-Hill* added to the increasing dissatisfaction with the sort of rhythms which the conservatives' regularistic prosody produced. Fortescue reveals that the British ear is no longer as pleased as it once had been by the contractions necessary to the syllabic system,[73] and he displays a refreshingly inductive temper of mind when he says, "From our great masters of blank verse, Shakespear and Milton, may be framed a rule for its structure: . . . It consists of five feet; in the choice of which the poet is not limited to a certain sort, but may chuse any of those which are used in the ancient lyric poetry."[74] Here again, what is commonly thought of as neo-classicism may be observed working to oppose the "neo-classic" regularistic prosody.

About 1755, Thomas Gray, preparing some notes for his proposed History of English Poetry, produced the essays which are known by the title "Metrum," and which include "Observations on English Metre," "The Measures of Verse," and "Observations on the Pseudo-Rhythmus." These essays were not published until 1814, but they serve to indicate the direction of Gray's thought in prosodic matters once he was released from the obligation of dealing with his own verse or that of his contemporaries. We have already observed that Gray is a very liberal prosodic theorist when dealing with work produced before the ascendancy of syllabism in the Restoration, but that he has no complaints about the prosodic practice of his own time, and that he even accepts wholeheartedly the syllabic principles in the composition of his own verse.

While discussing pre-Restoration poetry, Gray explains, "I call [certain lines] . . . decasyllabic and tetrasyllabic, because they have that effect on

---

[71] See Edmund Gosse, *From Shakespeare to Pope: An Inquiry into the Causes and Phenomena of the Rise of Classical Poetry in England* (New York, 1885), p. 151.

[72] *Essay on Musical Expression*, p. 51, n.

[73] *Pomery-Hill. A Poem*, p. xiii.

[74] *Ibid.*, p. xvi.

the ear: but as they admit of Anapests &c. they have sometimes eleven or five syllables."[75] Gray's phrase "effect on the ear" is of course a hint that he is here proceeding along the lines of a rough equal-time theory. One of the interesting corollaries of the transition from the syllabic to the accentual system during the eighteenth century is this shift from an emphasis primarily visual to one predominantly auditory, and one could probably show that this gradual change in the mode of stating prosodic situations is paralleled by a similar transition from a visual to an auditory emphasis in such matters as poetic imagery, as well as in certain aspects of the art of music. The late-century decline of the Horatian doctrine *ut pictura poesis* as a force on the production of certain types of poetry will suggest itself as a possible parallel to this new emphasis on the appeal of verse to the inner ear instead of to the inner eye. Swinburne's undulating and surfeiting assonances, highly typical of certain prosodic developments of the later nineteenth century, may perhaps be regarded as one of the final products of this innocent attention to "effect on the ear."

Gray is one of the earliest supporters of prosodic variety to reveal by his diction the alliance of some tendencies of the new prosodic theory with aspects of the general pre-romantic and anti-rationalistic current of the later eighteenth century. Gray writes, for example, "The more we attend to the composition of Milton's harmony, the more we shall be sensible how he loved to vary his pauses, his measures [number of syllables?], and his feet, which gives that enchanting air of freedom and wildness to his versification, unconfined by any rules but those which his own feeling and the nature of his subject demanded."[76] Words such as "enchanting," "wildness," and "unconfined" will perhaps suggest that the distance between Gray and Johnson was as wide and as unbridgeable prosodically as it was in other ways. Johnson's reaction to this view of the correct prosody for a religious epic may easily be imagined. Gray's assertion that Milton's "feeling" and "the nature of his subject" provide his sole "rules" of prosody may be taken as another appearance of the aesthetic of the new prosody which Samuel Say had first formulated.

Gray also takes a very liberal view of Spenser's prosody, and singles out for particular admiration Spenser's trisyllabic substitutions, his freedom from the syllabic limitation, and the metrical variety of the "August" Eclogue of the *Shepherd's Calendar*. Gray seems a bit melancholy that contemporary

---

[75] Gosse, ed., *Works*, I, 353.
[76] *Ibid.*, I, 333.

prosody will permit none of these delights.[77]

In 1758, there appeared a book by "Launcelot Temple, Esq.," *Sketches: or Essays on Various Subjects,* which is important as another vigorous reaction to the official metric. The author, John Armstrong, proceeds as if the motto "Variety is the Soul of Versification"[78] were his single guiding principle. Armstrong's ear is particularly offended by Pope's prosody, and he prefers Dryden's air of "masterly negligence" and Spenser's charming variety to the more conservative and rational rhythms dispensed by Pope.

Armstrong is especially in revolt against the French element in syllabic prosody, and he says that if Voltaire (who had confessed himself captivated by Pope's cadences) were really a good judge of such matters, "he would own that there was more Harmony [here, "variety"] in many of the *English* Poets————much more than the *French* Language . . . can attain to, or an Ear debauched by the French Versification is capable of relishing."[79] Armstrong also will be found to be operating under the assumptions of the anti-ideal prosodic aesthetic. One of his favorite complaints against the regularistic prosody, especially as it functions in stage declamation, is that it remains always constant, "without the least Regard of the Variety of Passions, which express themselves in quick or slow, flowing or interrupted, in languishing or impetuous Movements."[80] Armstrong's aesthetic of prosody will be seen to be totally irreconcilable with one which holds that the elevation of the poetic matter to the fixed and regular pattern of the prosodic archetype is the highest beauty. Armstrong also approves of a closer approach to an effect of the colloquial in dramatic poetry; the numbers in dramatic verse "ought for the most part to run somewhat rambling and irregular, and often rapid and subsultory, so as to imitate the natural Cadence and quick Turns of Conversation."[81] This remark suggests how far we have already moved from that theory of prosody which was based on a desire to remove verse as far as possible from the cadence of ordinary speech. Armstrong concludes his attack on the writers of excessively regular dramatic verse by implying that their subservience to French modes reveals a want of patriotism,[82] and that the failings of contemporary dramatic poetry reside in "studied Dignity,"

---

[77] *Ibid.,* I, 339. It may be noted that the "February" Eclogue of the *Shepherd's Calendar,* the prosody of which Gray's ear surely found delightful, is written in precisely the four-stress accentual line used in *Christabel.*

[78] *Sketches: or Essays on Various Subjects* (London, 1758), p. 35.

[79] *Ibid.,* pp. 37-39.

[80] *Ibid.,* p. 39.

[81] *Ibid.,* pp. 40-41.

[82] *Ibid.*

"inflexible Gravity of Pace," "unvaried Exactness of Measure," and "immoveable Hardness and want of Fluctuation in the Lines."[83] All of these characteristics, of course, would seem perfectly just and proper to a conservative prosodist who based his theorizings on an ideal aesthetic.

John Foster, in 1762, is so desirous of promoting the cause of prosodic variety that he discovers, after what tedious hours of travail and misreading we know not, terminal trochees abundantly employed by Pope. The fear that he might be requested to cite some of these non-existent licences undoubtedly prompts Foster's nervous comment, "The beauty of the Trochees in these places is too obvious to need pointing out."[84] In the same year, Daniel Webb, in his *Remarks on the Beauties of Poetry*, submits the Augustan syllabic prosody to a searching critical examination, and finds it founded on erroneous principles, since "a continual repetition of the same movements, must be as tiresome in poetry, as it would be in music."[85] Examining *Windsor Forest*, Webb declares that "the enthusiasm is tamed by the precision of the couplet,"[86] and this strikes him as a bad thing; most conservatives, including Dryden and Johnson, would naturally consider such "taming" of poetical enthusiasm not only a distinct advantage, but also one of the essential functions of the syllabic and regularistic prosody.

Webb proceeds to discover that the prosody of *Cato* is intolerable,[87] and he implies a fundamental disagreement with the whole aesthetic of the heroic couplet when he says that in the couplet "every sentiment, of what nature soever, comes equally recommended to the ear, and of course to our attention."[88] One wonders if Webb was forced into this position by a disgust at hearing couplets intoned according to the accepted techniques of artificial elocution. Like Charles Avison, Webb uses certain techniques of the other arts to illustrate the necessity of prosodic variety: " . . . where a sameness of versification prevails, there can be no degrees, no contrast in the sounds, which, like shades in painting, throw forward, and give a distinction to the superior beauties."[89] Webb's position on prosodic surprise is significant when we recall that one of the main reasons for opposition to medial trochaic substitution by the conservatives was that it occasioned an effect of sudden rhythmical reversal which had no place in the more elevated forms of art. Webb

---

[83] *Ibid.*, p. 42.
[84] *An Essay on the Different Nature of Accent and Quantity*, pp. 46-47.
[85] *Remarks on the Beauties of Poetry*, p. 6.
[86] *Ibid.*, p. 19.
[87] *Ibid.*, p. 13.
[88] *Ibid.*, p. 16.
[89] *Ibid.*, p. 17.

takes precisely the opposite view: comparing Milton's and Pope's metrical techniques, Webb writes, "I must take notice here of a beauty, which finds its place naturally in blank verse, but is almost incompatible with the regular movement of the couplet. I mean those sudden breaks or transitions in the verse, which so strongly characterize the passions; and dart, as it were, a sentiment into the inmost soul of the reader."[90] Surprise is indeed one of the basic premises of the new prosody. As Webb himself puts it, "The distinctive property of Genius is to surprise, either by original Beauty, or Greatness in the idea,"[91] and as he writes a few pages later, "we may judge of the merit of a composition, by the degree of our surprise."[92] It will be evident that the currency of theories of association (and the support they lent the theory of the sublime) was not impeding the spread of such notions as these.

Thomas Sheridan, in 1762, criticizes the contemporary poets for not always adapting the prosody to the poetic subject, and for writing "wholly from ear, and in much the same kind of numbers, whatever be the subject." Sheridan finds this method of poetic composition productive of a uniformity which is "insupportable to the ear, and [which] wearies attention."[93] Here is another appearance of the organic aesthetic of prosody which Samuel Say had first set forth.

In 1763, the anonymous author of the Essay on Versification in the British Magazine, captivated by the infinite possibilities inherent in the new theory of versification, abandons all pretensions to restraint and is hustled into the expression of a series of hyperboles which are almost Elizabethan in their sheer delightful excess: "Spenser, Shakespeare, Milton, Dryden, Pope, and all our poets, abound with dactyls, spondees, trochees, anapests, etc., which they use indiscriminately in all kinds of composition, whether tragic, epic, pastoral, or ode. . . . "[94] It would seem that this writer had just recently discovered that, by reading the contractions of Milton, Dryden, and Pope as if they had been written and printed in full, he could gratify his desire for frequent trisyllabic substitution. The newly invented technique of filling in the intended contractions in reading was evidently proving highly satisfactory

[90] *Ibid.*, pp. 20-21. See also p. 22.
[91] *Ibid.*, p. 65.
[92] *Ibid.*, p. 70.
[93] *Lectures on Elocution*, pp. 165-166. The subscription list prefixed to this work contains the names of such worthies as "James Boswall, Esq.," The Rev. Mr. Dodd, David Garrick, "Hon. Lord Kaims," James Thomson, and "Thomas Wharton, Esq." If "Lord Kaims" actually attended the lectures, his reactions to Sheridan's attacks on Kamesian artificial scansion and elocution must have been worth chronicling by "James Boswall" himself.
[94] Cunningham, ed., *Works of Oliver Goldsmith*, III, 361.

and was productive of some immensely pleasing results to ears grown weary of ideality and regularity. This author's enthusiasm for the new prosody is too limitless to permit him to inquire whether these "abounding" dactyls and anapests are Pope's or simply his own. This same author also supports the validity of the Bysshian syllabic limitation, but he is so excited over the brave new prosodic world which his filling in of the contractions has opened up to him that the inconsistency causes him no feelings of discomfort. The writer of this essay is highly representative of a certain segment of prosodic thought in the middle period of the transition to the new accentual prosody: like a good Elizabethan, he is able to contain multitudes of conflicting and contradictory metrical opinions with a happy innocence that anything is amiss.

In 1763, Dr. John Brown fashionably bemoans the fact that the arts of poetry and music have become separated, and he entertains some hope for a re-alliance. While engaged in this argument, he finds occasion to say that "there is generally a *dead Uniformity* in the Structure of modern Verse," since it conspicuously lacks the variety of feet employed by the ancients in their lyric measures.[95] Brown reveals that he too is thinking along the lines of the new prosodic aesthetic when he says of Dryden's and Pope's St. Cecilia Odes, "In Force of Passion, and Variety of Correspondent Versification, they are admirable." To this he adds a note: a poet composing an ode should use "the Variety of Measure, which often gives a great Energy to the Composition, by the incidental and sudden Intervention of an *abrupt* or *lengthened* Versification."[96] Thus, even prosodic devices of abruptness or surprise are acceptable, so long as they appear to be the direct result of a correspondent transition of thought or feeling in the poem. Or, in terms of the romantic aesthetic of prosody, the meaning of the poem at any point provides the standard of correctness for judging the prosodic pattern: the natural poetic materials need no longer improve their shape to match the invariable standard of metrical acceptability for each poetical *genre*. William Shenstone would agree with Brown that there is nothing inherently offensive about literary abruptness or suddenness, if only it reveal a sufficient and self-evident cause: this sort of suddenness Shenstone terms "genteel abruption," and, in his opinion, "it has a prodigious effect upon the reader."[97] A conservative like Johnson would certainly agree with this last statement, although he would consider the aesthetic-moral value of the prodigiousness in a somewhat different light.

---

[95] *A Dissertation on the Rise, Union, and Power, the Progressions, Separations, and Corruptions of Poetry and Music* (London, 1763), p. 228.
[96] *Ibid.*, pp. 235-236, n. "z."
[97] *Works*, II, 188. ("On Writing and Books").

The appearance in 1765 of Percy's *Reliques of Ancient English Poetry* was both a symptom of the mid-century desire for freer substitution and an important cause of further prosodic liberalism.[98] Under the guise of presenting "Gothick" effects, the imitators of the older ballads were employing trisyllabic substitution at an ever-increasing rate.[99] As George R. Stewart has said, speaking of metrical practice rather than theory, " . . . trisyllabic substitution began hesitatingly as part of the eighteenth-century ballad revival, but concealed itself as rediscovery or restoration. The next step was the transference of trisyllabic technique to verse acknowledged as original, but still looking backward in direct imitation of the ballad form. After the practice had thus, so to speak, worked itself surreptitiously into a special branch of literature, the younger poets were not long in realizing that nothing prevented them from similar practice elsewhere. After substitution had been given its inch in ballad imitation, it soon took the mile, and extended itself to all poetry."[100] But this extension of the practice of trisyllabic substitution to all poetry was slow indeed, and not much before the time of Blake, Hunt, Southey, Coleridge, and Scott do we find frank and open use of anapests for iambs and dactyls for trochees. Despite the impetus which the *Reliques* gave to the extension of the new prosody, the theorists who placed themselves in its defense were still obliged to advance their equal-time notions in the face of very powerful conservative opposition.

John Rice, in 1765, sets forth some radical prosodic views in his *Introduction to the Art of Reading with Energy and Propriety*. Rice was a minor pedagogue of elocution, a Grub-Street hack like William Kenrick, and a man who had no patience whatever with the cant of literary traditionalism or with the standard brand of conservative prosodic dogmatizing. Rice's *Art of Reading* is dedicated to Kenrick, who returned this courtesy by giving the work a very sympathetic review in the *Monthly,* and Rice throughout displays much of the same sort of literary intransigence which was the stock in trade of his slightly more ill-mannered friend.

Rice (who has read Say, and has learned a great deal from him[101]) takes an inductive and anti-authoritarian position towards the problem of English verse structure, and delivers this Baconian announcement of his method: " . . . I shall apply rather . . . to the mechanical Theory of Speech, as founded on Actual Observation, and the Principles and Experiments of

[98] See Gay Wilson Allen, *American Prosody* (New York, 1935), pp. xli, 28.
[99] See Stewart, *Modern Metrical Technique,* pp. 44-45.
[100] *Ibid.,* p. 47.
[101] See *Introduction to the Art of Reading,* pp. 20, 102.

Natural Philosophy, than to the Practices of the Ancients, or Opinions of classical Authority."[102] This is a convenient position for a man to take who probably had had very little grounding in the classics. Rice's opinion of his fellow laborers in the prosodic vineyard is a low one: speaking primarily of the work of Thomas Sheridan, he writes, "It is really amazing to see how a Number of Ingenious Men can successively skim over a Subject, without ever once dipping beyond the Surface, or really enquiring into that Propriety to which they make such pompous Pretensions," and he continues to fulminate in terms of "a Parcel of Sheep" and "pretended Improvements in Literature."[103] Rice is especially contemptuous of those prosodists who have assumed that English prosody bears some necessary relationship to that of the ancients: it must appear ridiculous, he declares, "to People divested of classical Prejudices" (he really means "people without classical learning") "to think that the Prosody of a living Language should be formed upon that of a dead one."[104]

It will seem wholly natural that a man so contemptuous of classical learning as Rice will find few areas of agreement with Samuel Johnson. Rice delivers a resounding blast against Johnson's Bysshian definition of versification in the first edition of the *Dictionary,* the definition based on the ideal theory of harmony: "I should be glad to know from what principle of Nature it is, that the regular alternate Succession of five short and five long Syllables forms a more harmonious line than a different Succession or Disposition of such Syllables."[105] Rice is obviously constitutionally incapable of understanding, let alone embracing, the conservative aesthetic of prosody founded on the premises of universality and ideality. He proceeds to quote Say's manufactured "many a" couplet as an illustration that "harmony" (meaning now something like Say's "propriety") can exist without the conformity of the line to "a certain number of syllables."[106] Trisyllabic substitution is freely sanctioned by Rice, as is the new "full" mode of reading the contractions in syllabic lines: Rice calls the older practice of reading the contractions as printed a "vicious Custom," and his lengthy remarks on this "barbarous" method of reading indicate that the traditional practice was still widespread enough to annoy a prosodist totally unable to understand the rationale of such contractions.[107]

102 *Ibid.,* p. 70. See also p. 135.
103 *Ibid.,* pp. 81-82.
104 *Ibid.,* p. 100.
105 *Ibid.,* p. 111.
106 *Ibid.*
107 *Ibid.,* pp. 111-113.

Rice's commitment to the new prosodic aesthetic seems to underlie his antipathy to poetic contractions. Johnson and his followers, he writes, would scan as follows:

> The wounded Bull
> Rŏar'd béll'wĭng, whĭlst rĕbéll'wĭng ráng thĕ Wóods.

"On the other hand," he continues, "if the Harmony of Verse principally consists, as I conceive it does, in the Consonance or Affinity which the Words of such Verse bear to their Meaning, or in their Propriety or Aptitude to express that Meaning, we should certainly find it [*i.e.*, the "Harmony"] in giving every Syllable of [the quoted] Verse its full Sound and natural Length . . . ," and he suggests this scansion:

> The wounded Bull
> Rŏar'd béllŏwĭng, whĭlst rĕbéllŏwĭng ráng thĕ Wóods.[108]

"Harmony" has thus undergone a change from its conservative meaning, "regularity of stress," to its liberal meaning, "propriety of prosodic adaptation to the poetic matter." Indeed, Rice seems unaware that the term "harmony" has ever carried a different connotation: "I can discover," he says, "but very little Harmony in the mere uniform and alternate Succession of a long and short, or a loud and soft Syllable"; Pope's Homer, most of Addison's poems, and Glover's *Leonidas* are thus without Rice's brand of harmony, and are consequently "intolerably tiresome" in their meter.[109]

Rice is so anxious to discredit the syllabic and regularistic tradition by any available means that he deviously purports to have traced the conservative prosodic theory to Gothic sources, while (ironically enough) "From the classical Source, we deduce . . . the Modulation of Feet and Measure; and the true Method of forming harmonious Periods in general."[110] It is significant that the Gothic was still in such low repute that a liberal (more properly, radical) prosodist could think of defaming a prosodic system he did not approve simply by supplying it with a Gothic ancestry. Rice's opposition to metrical traditionalism[111] is so extreme that he refuses even to employ the customary classical terms for the poetic feet: we find throughout his book no mention of "iambic" or "trochaic." Rice's work has been called "revolutionary,"[112] but the only really unprecedented aspect of Rice's efforts was his extreme anti-classical bias. Say, Mason, Armstrong, and others will be found to have anticipated Rice on almost all other points of any importance, although they

[108] *Ibid.*, p. 115.
[109] *Ibid.*, p. 153.
[110] *Ibid.*, pp. 168-169.
[111] *Ibid.*, p. 308.
[112] Omond, *English Metrists*, p. 68.

could hardly be expected to rival a close friend of Kenrick's in brash contempt for traditional classical prosodic precedents.

Daniel Webb, whose *Remarks on the Beauties of Poetry* had defended prosodic surprise and variety in 1762, aligns himself, in 1769, in support of very free medial trochaic substitution in heroic lines.[113] Webb is another who proceeds in accordance with the new aesthetic of prosody: trochaic substitution for the sake of mere "variety" is nugatory and the definite mark of a minor poet, compared with bold variations from the norm which spring directly "from an elevation in the sentiment."[114] Admitting that "The laws of Art . . . prescribe that our pentameter should terminate in an iambic," Webb nevertheless asserts that "there are beauties of a rank to supersede laws," and thus finds the terminal spondee of

By dead calms that oft lie on those smooth seas

a fine example of prosodic propriety.[115] It will be noticed that the principle of the sound-sense "beauty," generally admitted into the prosodies of even the most rigid conservatives, formed a convenient foundation for the gradual erection of new theories of prosodic variation by the liberals.

The idea of metrical tension, as in Say, is well developed in Webb's prosodic theory: he speaks of the beautiful effect of "opposition" to an iambic movement furnished by spondaic and trochaic substitution,[116] and he implies that it is in this dynamic and perpetual tension between the prosody of uniformity dictated by art and the metrical variety inherent in "nature" that the beauty of English versification consists. Webb's books were very widely circulated, and frequent reference to them by succeeding theorists shows that they had a powerful influence in carrying on the rather "upsetting" metrical principles first advanced by Samuel Say.[117]

*   *   *   *   *

It may be helpful now to pause for a moment and take stock of some of the major tendencies apparent thus far in these reactions to the conservative prosody. The whole movement towards the accentual prosody of the nineteenth century starts from the question of substitution, mainly trochaic and trisyllabic (in iambic lines) ; the new desire for the effects produced by substitution seems intimately allied with certain contemporary tendencies of thought which, at first glance, might appear to have very little to do with

---

[113] *Observations on the Correspondence between Poetry and Music*, p. 102.
[114] *Ibid.*, p. 108.
[115] *Ibid.*, pp. 109-110.
[116] *Ibid.*, p. 110.
[117] Omond, *English Metrists*, pp. 66-67.

the matter of metrical form. The intense patriotic reaction to things French, for example, forced metrists of whatever color largely to abandon the French syllabic line as an authoritative example; the liberals made a rediscovery of the various trisyllabic and dipodic feet of classical lyric verse, and thus found a sanction for substitution in the most esteemed and genuinely universal poetry of all. The conservatives, now somewhat chary of their French line-model, continued to point to the more chaste substitutional practices of classical epic and dramatic verse, but the gradual middle-class loss of interest in the weightier *genres* and the slow revival of the lyrical mode (not impeded by the rediscovery of the ballads) might have told them that these efforts were soon to prove ineffectual.

The poetry-music parallel was pressed hard, and, squeezed to a certain point, it obligingly yielded the bar-foot analogy, which served as precisely the figure needed for an illustration of the rational and "natural" bases of the new equal-time prosodic system. It may be mentioned here that one of the most fascinating phenomena observable in English metrical history is that "rational" grounds for a prosodic change, complete with copious and highly convincing "illustrations," will always appear to present themselves at exactly the proper moment. The ingenuity of the eighteenth-century prosodists, whether of the retrogressive or progressive factions, in searching out acceptable rational bases for their instinctive rhythmical predispositions calls forth a certain amount of admiration from the modern observer.

Certain of the anti-syllabist prosodists like John Rice managed to advance their new theories by the simple expedients of condemning classical authority and of pretending to proceed on the purely inductive pattern popularized, ironically enough, by the very Royal Society which had earlier encouraged certain mathematical characteristics of syllabism. Samuel Say, practically alone in the cause of anti-syllabism in his time, provided in his two essays most of the fundamental premises on which accentualism was eventually to base itself, but Mason and Rice, infinitely more shabby and less original thinkers, popularized his positions and largely received his credit. Finally, Thomas Gray and the author of the *British Magazine* Essay on Versification serve as examples of mid-century metrical schizophrenics; their futile but engaging attempt to embrace syllabism and accentualism simultaneously can shed some light on the nature of the general mid-century aesthetic temper, and can serve to illuminate the cast of thought which lurks behind such phenomena as the Gothic revival and the Ossianic vogue.

It should be emphasized, however, that if John Rice was impudently flaying syllabism in the sixties, the much more widely circulated Kames was giving it his almost unlimited support, and one should remember that even well past the mid-point of the century, the liberals were outnumbered at least two to one by conservative theorists, and about ten to one by conservative common readers. It was to require almost fifty more years of effort on the part of the equal-time theorists and the full-blown accentualists before the British public could take in its hands the fresh copies of Coleridge's poems to struggle with and eventually master the strangely fascinating new rhythms of *Christabel.*

CHAPTER V

1770 AND AFTER: THE ASCENDANCY OF ACCENTUALISM

By 1770, a great deal had been done towards establishing certain liberal prosodic principles which could be assumed to be universally valid by those intent on weakening and finally breaking down the syllabic restriction: the equal-time theory had been well started on its way, abetted by many comparisons between the rhythmical techniques of poetry and music, and the field was now open for the transition to full accentualism.

In the early seventies, the work of William Kenrick, Thomas Warton, and Lord Monboddo, while often ambiguous and not without contradictions, reveals that the tendency towards an accentual theory of prosody was now often lurking more or less unconsciously just below the public surface.[1] Warton, for example, is beginning to perceive that "uniformity of pause" and "regularity of cadence" do not necessarily conduce to "music" in verse,[2] and Lord Monboddo allows himself to brand the syllabic and regularistic heroic couplet "tediously uniform" and thus "intolerable."[3] In fact, to Monboddo, those poets who "break the measure of the verse altogether" (provided they were writing before the Restoration) are infinitely to be preferred to poets who impose on their matter the strict ideal patterns defended by the more conservative theorists.[4] Monboddo, by implication, approaches an advanced position towards substitution when he permits, in anapestic measures, an iamb to replace the conventional initial anapest;[5] if this sort of thing can be sanctioned and enjoyed in triple-time verse, the transference to the principle of trisyllabic substitution in duple-time measures will soon become inviting. In fact, the effect of iambic substitution in anapestic cadences is precisely the equal-time and ultimately accentual effect produced by the correspondent substitution in iambic measures. The sensibility to which this sort of substitution will appeal,

Ĭn súm | mĕr, thĕ bírds | ănd thĕ bées | ĭn thĕ fíelds, |

---

[1] See Kenrick, *New Dictionary of the English Language*, p. 51; Warton, *History of English Poetry*, IV, 67; and Monboddo, *Of the Origin and Progress of Language*, II, 388-389, n.

[2] *History of English Poetry*, IV, 67.

[3] *Of the Origin and Progress of Language*, V, 467-468.

[4] *Ibid.*, II, 388-389, n.

[5] *Ibid.*, II, 395.

will generally be equally gratified by such an exhibition of equal-time equivalence as this:

In thĕ fíelds, | thĕ súm | mĕr bírds | ănd bées | ăppéar. |

But Kenrick, Warton, and Monboddo are small fry compared with
Ramsay, Thomas Sheridan, and Joshua Steele; the work of these three theorists was cf great importance in providing the underpinnings on which
romantic accentualism was to erect itself.

1. *Allan Ramsay the Younger*

Ramsay's unpublished treatise on versification provides a fairly typical
view of the burgeoning accentualism of the seventies. Ramsay, like Gray, is
generally quite strict in his considerations of contemporary (especially heroic)
verse, but he has no objection to initial anapests in iambic tetrameter measures, if only they have been produced before the Restoration. He has high
praise for the use of this device by Henry Stephens, who, Ramsay carefully
points out, wrote some "200 years ago."[6] Taking recourse in the classical
lyric and dramatic sanction, Ramsay is enabled to discover that "The Anapest
is congenial with the Iambus, as the Dactyl is with the Trochy, and may be
mixed with them upon many occasions, with great propriety."[7] Here is
Samuel Say's "propriety" again, with its liberal suggestion, "fitness of prosodic
adaptation to the poetic material at hand."

Ramsay is throughout his treatise exceptionally sensitive to the operations
of the principle of variety in all linguistic phenomena; variety is, in fact, the
humanizing characteristic of language: "Without this diversity human speech
would be a perpetual murmur or drone, less pleasing, and perhaps less in-
telligible than the cries of the brute creation. . . . "[8] This triumph in Ramsay's
thinking of the principle of an underlying variety over that of uniformity
or regularity is implicit in most of his more specific prosodic pronouncements.
Here is his presentation of the equal-time principle: "Rhythm or Cadence
. . . [is] a regular and sensible return, at certain periods, of the same motion[s], which though they are always supposed, with regard to one another
to be of equal length, and measurable by a pendulum; yet with regard to
their internal division may be of different natures."[9] Ramsay makes a great
deal of the illustration of the pendulum, which marks successive rhythmical
beats with no attention to the number of intervening moments (cf. "syllables") ; this pendulum illustration reveals that in Ramsay, accentualism is a

---

[6] "Enquiry into the Principles of English Versification," fol. 16.
[7] *Ibid.*, fol. 19.
[8] *Ibid.*, fol. 10.
[9] *Ibid.*, fol. 14.

very powerful and central principle, and, though occasionally entangled with certain remnants of syllabism, is very near to bursting forth and dominating his whole theory of meter.

The principle of substitution is naturally inherent in this equal-time pendulum theory: once a poetic cadence is begun, substitution may occur freely, and "All that is required is that those cadences, when begun, should be continued by others of the same length and structure."[10] The bar-foot analogy is so well developed in Ramsay's theory that he carries it a step further than its earlier exponents do and always scans as if each poetic foot begins, like a musical bar, with a strong rhythmical beat; in other words, the stress in each poetic foot "must answer to the first note in every bar in modern Musical notation."[11] To Ramsay, the whole English prosodic question "belongs to the Musical art, and must be decided by its rules." Thus, "In Musick each rithmus, foot, or bar, is of a determined length; but this rithmus may be filled up with one, two, three, four, ten, twenty, or any number of notes, provided the accumulated length of them is neither more nor less than the time allowed for the whole rithmus."[12] The equation of notes with syllables and of bars with feet enables Ramsay to advance, in 1775, a theory fully capable of elucidating the metrical basis of *Christabel* and other accentual poems of the early nineteenth century.

Ramsay is still somewhat cautious of applying these principles outright to the sacrosanct English heroic line, although he shows no such hesitation when dealing with other English line-forms. He permits dactylic substitution in trochaic measures[13] and iambic substitution in anapestic measures,[14] but is strangely conservative when he approaches the problem of the degree to which the heroic line may deviate from its pure iambic form.[15] This will indicate how much more secure from the inroads of prosodic innovation of whatever sort the English heroic line was than certain less serious and elegant line-forms; the heroic line was almost the conservatives' very own form, and no matter what compromises their syllabism might have to make in *genres* like the ode and the lyric or song, they retained until very late their control over the principles governing the structure of the heroic line.

Ramsay reveals himself to have been touched by the School of Taste when he observes that "taste" is "a word by which we often mean an observ-

---

[10] *Ibid.*, fols. 14-14ᵛ.
[11] *Ibid.*, fol. 14.
[12] *Ibid.*, fol. 47.
[13] *Ibid.*, fol. 24ᵛ.
[14] *Ibid.*, fols. 35ᵛ-36.
[15] *Ibid.*, fols. 23-25.

ance of rules, that are of too nice a nature, to be communicated by words."[16] He further comments, "In every elegant Art, there is a point beyond which rules cannot carry us. Here the deficiency must be supplied by Taste, which will always advantageously distinguish those artists who happen to be blest with it, and, perhaps nothing tends more to debase any art, and to render it inelegant than an attempt to subject every particular Grace in it to a particular Rule."[17] Ramsay's instinctive use of the word "elegant" while advancing one of the theoretical bases of an anti-Augustan relativistic accentualism will help indicate something of the transitional quality of his prosodic theorizing.

2. Thomas Sheridan: Accentualist Aesthetics and Ethics

Thomas Sheridan's Lectures on the Art of Reading (1775) is another important milestone in the gradual late-century transition to an accentual prosody. Sheridan is extremely conscious of the role of accent in English verse structure, and, to avoid any confusion between length and accent, he rejects the classical foot terminology in favor of his own nomenclature, under which the trochee becomes the "first dissyllabic" foot, the iamb the "second dissyllabic," the spondee the "double dissyllabic," and the pyrrhic the "undissyllabic"; in the same way, the dactyl is the "first trisyllabic," the amphibrach (a foot for which Sheridan entertains an interesting affection) becomes the "second trisyllabic," the anapest the "third trisyllabic," and the tribrach the "un-trisyllabic."[18] Despite all this ingenuity, Sheridan apparently finds it impossible to remember to use these terms in his actual exposition and continually reverts to the more traditional classically derived terminology.

An erroneous conviction that he is a bold pioneer in the reaction to the conservative prosody informs Sheridan's work from beginning to end. The title page of the section of the Art of Reading devoted to "The Art of Reading Verse," for example, contains this little puff: "In Which Also The Whole PROSODY of the English Language, and Art of Versification, are, for the first Time, laid open, and placed in a clear Light."[19] Say, Mason, Rice, Webb, Armstrong, and others would perhaps have felt somewhat badly used by this, and even more by Sheridan's general assumption that every one of his prosodic predecessors has been, in varying degrees, a fool. He self-righteously sets himself with patient hand to unravel "the entanglements of errour formed by early wrong instruction, and knit together by the force of prejudice and habit. . . ."[20] Sheridan repudiates syllabism completely (perceiving as he

[16] Ibid., fol. 41ᵛ.
[17] Ibid., fol. 47.
[18] Lectures on the Art of Reading, p. 214.
[19] Ibid., p. 189.
[20] Ibid., p. 191.

does so the debt of that system to French theory and practice[21]) and turns instead to an equal-time accentualism based on the poetry-music relationship, which proves to be an area in which he is quite competent. "Feet in verse correspond to bars in music,"[22] he announces, and he goes on to point out that Say's fourteen-syllable line,

And many an amorous, many a humorous Lay,

is "equal," in total time, to a line of pure iambics.[23]

Sheridan holds *Leonidas* in the lowest contempt,[24] and he believes that trisyllabic substitution is "one great source of beauty and power in verse."[25] Amphibrachic substitution in particular has some strange lodgment in Sheridan's mind: he scans Say's line above as if it consisted of four amphibrachs and an iamb, in addition to unearthing a multitude of (nonexistent) amphibrachic substitutions in Milton.[26]

Unlike Ramsay, Sheridan is not awed by the sanctity of the heroic line: he advocates the occasional employment of all seven substitute feet in the English heroic measure.[27] Medial trochaic substitution in iambic measures Sheridan is somewhat dubious about, however, for it "interrupts and stops the usual movement, by an opposite one." Yet even this interruption may have its expressive uses, and medial trochaic substitution may now and then take place when obviously called forth as a prosodic expression of the poetic matter.[28]

The new anti-ideal aesthetic of prosody will be discovered to underlie many of Sheridan's positions. Either this new prosodic aesthetic (or something very much like it) was in the air and was occasionally discussed in literary company, or else Sheridan had been reading and borrowing from his predecessors with an assiduity belying his pretensions to originality. To Sheridan,

---

21 *Ibid.,* pp. 192-193, 221, 338, 393.

22 *Ibid.,* p. 213. See also p. 229.

23 *Ibid.,* p. 249.

24 *Ibid.,* p. 218.

25 *Ibid.,* p. 344. By 1775, the newly fashionable doctrine of trisyllabic substitution (often supported by the bar-foot analogy) is being advanced in many other quarters. See, *e.g., Sentimental Fables. Translated from the French, With the Original and Notes. To which is prefixed, An Essay on English Versification* (Brentford, 1775), p. x; Tyrwhitt, ed., *Canterbury Tales,* IV, 92-93, n; and Charles Burney, *A General History of Music, from the Earliest Ages to the Present Period. To which is prefixed, A Dissertation on the Music of the Ancients* (London, 1776-1789), I, 73, n; 77, 78, 82, n; 86.

26 *Lectures on the Art of Reading,* pp. 255-256. It is perhaps significant that to a reader scanning accentually, the amphibrach often seems to be the most frequent English foot. See Bridges, *Milton's Prosody,* p. 99.

27 *Lectures on the Art of Reading,* pp. 215-217.

28 *Ibid.,* pp. 245-246.

"variety" is the name of everything pleasing in prosody: "Variety certainly contains a charm in itself, independent of every other consideration."[29] That the prosodic vocabulary was undergoing drastic and significant changes during the seventies will be plain from Sheridan's definition of "variety" as "the parent of Melody and Harmony,"[30] the two attributes which the conservatives had thought wholly dependent on regularity of stress. The principle of variety within uniformity provides a strong foundation for Sheridan's liberalism, and he disparages Augustan "harmonious" verse which suffers from a lack of equilibrium or tension between these two poles. The pleasure resulting from "simple [i.e., Gloverian] uniformity," he says, is always of a lower order than that arising from "equality and diversity duly intermixed."[31] "The highest ornament of versification," he adds, "arises from disparity in the members, equality in the whole."[32] Sheridan is fond of emphasizing that there must be a "due mixture" of the two elements of variety and uniformity,[33] and he indicates that, as it had seemed to Say, prosodic propriety is the result of the fit adjustment of the prosody to the poetic matter. For "there is no emotion of the mind, however irregular, that may not find a correspondent movement in our verse. . . ."[34] It is to be noted here how far we have moved already from the Johnsonian ethic of prosody, with its emphasis on the power of an imposed regularistic pattern of stresses to order the mind and to purge it of irregular emotions: Sheridan's theory of prosody is one in which these irregular emotions, instead of requiring curbing by a metrical discipline, themselves create their proper and unique prosody in the very act of finding poetic expression; the bold variations of prosody thus become a key to the total poetic meaning. In Sheridan's theory of prosody there is a strong primitivistic implication of the beatitude of original, impetuous, and irregular emotion which seems highly revelatory of the nature of the period during which the theory of accentualism was being developed. An age which regards the free expression of emotion as (at the least) a morally neutral act would seem to require a theory of metric very much like the one Sheridan advances here, and it is clear that such an age cannot continue to employ a prosody designed to coincide with some very different views of morality and aesthetics. This continual re-creation of the meter to help express the feeling and meaning of the poem as it develops is the secret, to Sheridan, of " . . . that magical

[29] Ibid., p. 223.
[30] Ibid., p. 227.
[31] Ibid., p. 280.
[32] Ibid., p. 287.
[33] Ibid., p. 239.
[34] Ibid., p. 345.

power of numbers, which presents the object itself to the imagination."[35]
The Wordsworthian and Coleridgean tendency here is worth noticing: the
object and the imagination must be brought again into an intimate relationship, and, just as the scuttling of Augustan poetic diction and certain invariable
genre conventions can help reunite the imagination and the poetic object,
so the revolution in prosody can allow the poetic material to burst through
the gray, conventional deckings of syllabic and regularistic metric and appear
in fresh, emotion-charged accentual colors.

Thus by 1775 one finds the rising accentual prosody already furnished
with the solid aesthetic and ethic ("unethic" might perhaps be the more
exact term) it required if it was successfully to oust the prosodic system
which had obtained for over a century. Had the accentual prosody been
grounded on nothing more impressive than a banal and merely libertine
desire for more "variety" and "freedom," its establishment might have been
resisted and delayed much longer than it was. But accentualism, like syllabism, is really at bottom an expression of some quite irresistible currents
of thought in wider areas, and just as no amount of repetition of time-honored
cant was capable of turning the French Revolution into something other
than what it was, so no amount of tardy dogmatizing on the part of the
prosodic conservatives could halt the rise to ascendancy of this new prosodic
system, which, with an exquisite propriety (to borrow Say's conception),
expressed in terms of iambs and dactyls, substitutions and irregularities, some
of the basic intellectual and emotional tendencies of a new age in philosophy,
politics, and literature.

3. Joshua Steele

The year 1779 is an important one in the history of the rise of English
accentualism, for in this year was published Joshua Steele's *Prosodia Rationalis*.[36] When his modern reputation is compared with those of some of
his fellow prosodists in the eighteenth century, Steele must be considered
a theorist of quite some fame. Modern opinion of Steele ranges from T. S.
Omond's comments "profoundly original" and "subtle and penetrating"[37]
to George Saintsbury's wry "absolutely no ear for English verse whatever."[38]
An almost total neglect of the bulk of the material I have been examining
in this chapter and the previous one has caused many modern scholars and

[35] *Ibid.*, p. 255.
[36] First published in a somewhat tentative form as *An Essay towards Establishing
the Melody and Measure of Speech* (1775).
[37] *English Metrists*, pp. 93-94.
[38] *Historical Manual*, p. 249.

critics to give Steele much more credit for originality and priority than he deserves. He is really little more than a highly competent and sensitive practitioner of the hoary bar-foot analogy which, as we have seen, various experimenters had been applying since Gildon's first suggestion of it in 1718.

Steele calls a great deal of attention to his fancied inductive method, and it must be admitted that his rejection of prosodic authorities is potentially of a higher type than the sort of ignorant and flamboyant repudiation affected by John Rice. In examining the phenomena of English verse structure, Steele writes, " . . . I resolved to depend neither on hypothesis nor on antient authorities, for my facts which I could ascertain by actual experiment;———— by a pendulum, or by my steps, I can measure the quantities of time."[39] It will be noticed that Steele and Ramsay both use the figure of the pendulum as a marker of the equal-time units.

One of Steele's greatest merits as a prosodic theorist is his rare ability to humanize the stuff of metrical speculation: he is uniquely alert to common rhythmical phenomena occurring continually about him, and he does not hesitate to speculate very engagingly about certain everyday appearances of temporal division and measurement. All men have such a powerful and irresistible inclination to behave rhythmically, Steele conjectures, that everyone's normal speech automatically falls into either duple or triple cadences. This semi-conscious rhythmical impulse in human speech is so strong, Steele believes, that it explains the origin, rise, and universal popularity of profanity in all ages and in all countries, for "cursing, swearing, and many other unmeaning words, so frequently interwoven in common discourse, are merely expletives to fill the measure, and to round each rhythmical period,"[40] he writes, deftly concluding his sentence with a charming triple cadence. Man's instinctive pleasure in both duple and triple measures is a result, according to Steele, of constant habituation to his own walk and to that of his horse, respectively; Steele is observant and clever enough to enjoy adding that lame men probably become more used to triple time than do their unhandicapped fellows.[41] The abundance in Steele's work of these attempts to ground prosodic theorizing in earthy and universal illustrations lends his writing a singular attractiveness and makes it very suggestive of the wider issues always involved, but frequently forgotten, in metrical study.[42]

[39] *Prosodia Rationalis,* pp. 196-197.
[40] *Ibid.,* p. 67.
[41] *Ibid.,* p. 126.
[42] For example, Steele finds it significant that just as all rhythms are divisible into duple or triple time, so all geometrical forms are reducible to either the quadrilateral or the triangular. See *Prosodia Rationalis,* pp. 25-26.

Steele, like many before him, rejects syllabism in favor of an equal-time accentualism,[43] but his individual contribution to poetry-music theory is the part of his work which demands the closest attention. Steele's most enthusiastic desire is to witness, eventually, a reunion of the studies of poetry and music, and he regrets that the two universities have hitherto neglected "to treat the modulation of *speech* as a *genus* of *music* under the rules of *Melopoeia*."[44] Steele's important contribution to the subtlety of the poetry-music parallel is this: by rigidly applying the bar-foot correspondence, he perceives that merely to mark a "bar" division immediately before each stressed syllable is to neglect the "measure" of which the initial unstressed syllable in a pure iambic line is a part. The more conventional bar-foot enthusiasts would scan a typical couplet as follows:

> Thŏse | rúles ŏf | óld, dĭs | cóvĕr'd, | nót dĕ | vísed,
> Ăre | Nátŭre | stíll, bŭt | Nátŭre | méthŏ | dízed;

they would consider that each line (since it consists of five equal-time units, each signalled, as it were, by a stressed syllable) comprises five feet, with one of the feet consisting of both the initial unstressed syllable and the final stressed one. Such a scansion, however, if it is to be wholly consistent with the musical analogy, would have to find another way of accounting for the absence of what should be an initial stressed syllable: the "measures," after all, must begin with stressed syllables, and the iambic line quite obviously does not. Some prosodists solved this problem, as Ramsay did, by considering the initial light syllable the parallel of a silent up-bow performed by a violinist in preparation for a full note on the down-bow.[45] But this is really not a solution at all; the initial syllable is not a parallel of the musical upbeat: it is sounded, and it is an indispensable part of the phonetic material of the poetic line. Steele, aware that some earlier bar-foot analogists had not considered the first light syllable a really functioning part of the line's rhythm, sets forth his solution of the problem by scanning this way:

> | [rést] Thŏse | rúles ŏf | óld, dĭs | cóvĕr'd, | nót dĕ | vísed, [rĕst] |
> | [rést] Ăre | Nátŭre | stíll, bŭt | Nátŭre | méthŏ | dízed. [rĕst] |

The addition of a "stressed rest" at the beginning and an "unstressed" one at the end of each line thus takes care of the initial light syllable, and the heroic line, instead of containing five equal-time units, now contains six, with each syllable accounted for in a thoroughly musical fashion. This refinement on the traditional musical scansion does have the merit of accounting met-

---

[43] *Ibid.*, p. 163.
[44] *Ibid.*, p. xvi.
[45] "Enquiry into the Principles of English Versification," fol. 42ᵛ.

rically for the pause which occurs at the end of the line: the conventional musical scansion, which was content to mark "bars" before each stressed syllable and let it go at that, could be musically consistent only if each line were run into those preceding and following with a speed which the traditional rhymed couplet would, of course, never permit. Steele's scansion represents the poetry-music analogy carried to its logical conclusion, and this ultimate development was potentially inherent in Gildon's first clumsy use of musical symbols for the purposes of scansion in 1718. According to his new method of scansion, Steele explains, " . . . our heroic lines are really hexameters,"[46] and, confounding his readers still further, he adds, as if to clear everything up, " . . . verses of five feet consist at least of six cadences, and commonly those of four feet consist of five."[47] Steele's theory of rests is really, however, relatively simple, if the reader concentrates on ignoring all of Steele's non-pertinent matter, of which there is indeed a great deal.

Steele's approval of trisyllabic substitution takes the same form as that advanced by his many predecessors, that is, equal-time accentualism stemming from the musical analogy, by means of which " . . . the two general modes of times, *common* [*i.e.,* duple] and *triple,* may be intermixed . . . without any alteration in the rhythmus."[48] Steele's only original contribution is his addition of the concept of musical rests to the conventional bar-foot parallel,[49] and even this contribution is not especially important in hastening the arrival of accentualism, although the notion of rests set going by Steele has been a powerful and far-reaching influence in English prosody. The bar-foot analogy alone, with no theory of rests to complicate and obscure it, is a thoroughly sufficient theorem for supporting an accentual prosody, and Steele would be almost as significant as a precursor of pure accentualism if he had never seen fit to confuse the central issue, the conflict between syllabism and accentualism, by adding an embellishment that served mainly to make the theoretical principle of accentualism harder for most readers to grasp. Robert Nares, for example, confesses in 1784, " . . . I found myself utterly unable to follow the ingenious author through his wonderfully acute distinctions," and he voices fears that "his system is too obscure to be of general service, even if right."[50]

By thus initiating inquiry into the time value and structural characteristics

---

[46] *Prosodia Rationalis*, p. 27.
[47] *Ibid.*, p. 31.
[48] *Ibid.*, p. 121. See also p. 217.
[49] See Omond, *English Metrists*, p. 89.
[50] *Elements of Orthoepy*, p. 145, n. See also John Walker, *Key to Classical Pronunciation*, p. 240, n.

of pauses (not the conventional cesuras, but the pauses inherent in the very condition of discrete and separately approached lines of verse), Steele "started a troubling of the prosodic waters which survives even yet."[51] Sidney Lanier's *The Science of English Verse* (1880) is based primarily on Steele's theories, although, as has been pointed out many times, Lanier's specific debt to the earlier work he quite inexplicably fails to acknowledge.[52] Perhaps the latest appearance of Steele's theories is in J. C. Pope's *The Rhythm of Beowulf* (1942), which applies the bar-foot analogy and the theory of musical rests to Old English prosody with very rewarding (if perhaps historically uncertain) results.[53] Steele's book has been called "the first really living work in the evolution of English prosody,"[54] and this valuation is probably true (despite the excessively progressivist implications of "evolution") if by "living" we can agree to mean "influential in the nineteenth and twentieth centuries." But it should be kept in mind that all the essential poetry-music labor necessary for the stabilizing of accentualism had already been done before Steele approached the problem. If we must continue to believe in some sort of pseudo-Darwinian prosodic progress, it is probably more just to consider Steele not primarily as an inventor but as one who mainly called attention by his efforts to theories which had first been advanced quite a bit earlier by minds which would seem, because of their priority, to have been considerably more penetrating.

4. Accentual Theory and Practice after Steele

The reading public had not been receiving all these poetry-music parallels quite as avidly as one might like to assume. William Jackson, in 1783, has had his patience sorely tried by these often facile and superficial comparisons between the arts, and he issues a public call for a moratorium on such analogies, explaining, "I do not deny the *commune quoddam vinculum,* but would keep the principle within its proper bounds."[55] He then proceeds to draw a very entertaining analogy between the art of music and the structure of his shirt, and finally concludes, "a truce with such nonsense.———There are scarce any two things in the world but may be *made* to resemble each other."[56] Jackson's was a healthy reaction to the excesses of some of the more amateur

[51] Allen, *American Prosody,* p. xl.

[52] See Karl Shapiro, *English Prosody and Modern Poetry* (Baltimore, 1947), p. 7.

[53] Pope writes that his own theory "sprang . . . from a study of Sidney Lanier's pioneering [!] work. . . . " (*The Rhythm of Beowulf: An Interpretation of the Normal and Hypermetric Verse-Forms in Old English Poetry* [New Haven, Conn., 1942], p. vii).

[54] Omond, *English Metrists,* p. 94.

[55] *Thirty Letters,* I, 114.

[56] *Ibid.,* I, 117.

poetry-music analogists, but it hardly put a stop to such comparisons which, if anything, rose to an unprecedented number and intensity during the eighties and nineties.

It will perhaps not surprise us that Thomas Jefferson injected some confusion into the poetry-music theorizing. Jefferson, with what appears to be a monumental innocence of musical technique, offers the poetic *line* as an exact analogy of the musical bar. He is apparently wholly unaware that musicians do not make a practice of pausing after each bar. The poet, Jefferson writes, "has discovered that in any rhythmical composition the ear is pleased to find at certain regular intervals a pause where it may rest, by which it may divide the composition into parts, as a piece of music is divided into bars."[57] This fantastic position of Jefferson's will help to show why dissenters from the poetry-music parallel like William Jackson were tiring of such analogies which, in the hands of the more awkward amateurs, could be productive of results so lamentably inept.

James Beattie, in his "Essay on Poetry and Music as they Affect the Mind" (1776), had supported Burney's uniformity and variety principle[58] which could lead only to an ultimate accentualism, and he had permitted a very liberal variety in the heroic line, which to Beattie consisted structurally of five feet which might be any of some thirty types.[59] Beattie presents his views in an even clearer light in his essay "The Theory of Language" (1783). He rejects syllabism completely,[60] encourages (with the aid of Say's illustrative couplet) trisyllabic substitution in the heroic line,[61] and utilizes the musical parallel to show that variety is the "soul of harmony,"[62] with "harmony" now meaning something close to "propriety of prosodic adaptation."[63]

It is important to bear in mind that, in addition to the liberal position maintained by many prosodic theorists during the eighties and nineties, certain poets were now at work opposing syllabism in actual practice. Although

[57] Lipscomb, ed., *Writings*, XVIII, 441-442. A possible explanation of this error of Jefferson's is that, instead of "bar," he had intended to write something like "phrase," and that what we have here represents a mere slip of the pen. To those aware of the eccentricity of some of Jefferson's prosodic positions, however, this explanation of the error may not be acceptable.

[58] *Essays*, pp. 171-172. And see above, n. 25.

[59] *Ibid.*, pp. 299-300.

[60] *Dissertations Moral and Critical*, p. 279.

[61] *Ibid.*, pp. 280, 286, 291.

[62] *Ibid.*, p. 286.

[63] Beattie's antipathy to syllabism and all its concomitants impelled him to publish his early poem *Retirement* (1758) without the traditional apostrophes to mark the syllabic contractions, but this gesture was apparently the result of youthful iconoclasm, for *The Minstrel* (1771, 1774) appeared with all the contractions indicated in the conventional manner. (See Stewart, *Modern Metrical Technique*, p. 30).

Burns's verse displays only a few genuine trisyllabic substitutions, he has been called "the first poet of modern times to put before the public at least a few original poems of great popularity in which metrical freedom was used without subterfuge."[64] And Burns himself writes in the so-called First Commonplace Book in September, 1785, "There is a certain irregularity in the old Scotch Songs, a redundancy of syllables with respect to that exactness of accent and measure which the English Poetry requires, but which glides in most melodiously with the respective tunes to which they are set. . . . There is a degree of wild irregularity in many of the compositions and Fragments which are daily sung [to certain Scotch airs] by my compeers, the common people. . . . "[65] Burns thus still believes that formal English verse owes a compliance to the syllabic principle, but, very much like a sort of bucolic Thomas Gray, he is able to appreciate metrical irregularity when it occurs in folk and popular songs, and "wild irregularity" becomes, in its fit rural context, a distinct prosodic virtue. Certain ballad imitators had been tentatively employing trisyllabic substitution ever since the appearance of the *Reliques*,[66] and the technique was by now very near to bursting its confinement to the slighter *genres* and invading "serious" poetry.

An interesting and important essay "On the Superiority of Dryden's Versification over that of Pope and of the Moderns" was published in 1789 by one Joseph Weston which reveals that the multitude of reactions to the conservative prosody was beginning to bear fruit in the wider area of literary criticism and revaluation. Weston complains that Pope's verse is "marked by an almost total Want of that VARIETY of Pause, Accent, Cadence, and Diction, so eminently conspicuous in his incomparable Predecessor, and so absolutely essential to the Harmony of true Poetry."[67] Weston's opposition to Pope is so extreme that it can be explained only by assuming that he is filling in all of Dryden's contractions and giving his verse the full advantage of a sense scansion, while artificially scanning Pope and reading his contractions exactly as printed.[68]

Erasmus Darwin reveals himself to be an instinctive bar-foot analogist

---

[64] *Ibid.,* p. 44.
[65] David Daiches, *Robert Burns* (New York, 1950), p. 87.
[66] See Stewart, *Modern Metrical Technique,* pp. 21, 43.
[67] "An Essay on the Superiority of Dryden's Versification over that of Pope and of the Moderns," *Records of the Woodmen of Arden from 1785 with Roll of Members of the Society and other Notes Mainly Compiled from the Archives of the Forest* (n.p., 1885), p. 124. This work contains a reprinting *in toto* of John Morfitt's *Philotoxi Ardenae* (Birmingham, 1789), in which Weston's essay first appeared.
[68] See Bate, *Stylistic Development of Keats,* p. 197.

when he speaks of Anstey's *New Bath Guide* as consisting of "dactyle verses."[69] The only way Anstey's anapests could be confounded with dactyls is by the reader's considering every poetic foot as necessarily beginning with a stressed syllable. Darwin must have habitually and unconsciously approached poetic matters from a musical standpoint to have made this error.

Anselm Bayly, although a great admirer of Dr. Johnson, for whose *Rambler* he has almost a scriptural veneration, makes bold to adhere to the bar-foot parallel in his *Alliance of Musick, Poetry, and Oratory* (1789),[70] and he supports trisyllabic substitution and the equal-time principle,[71] but draws the line at free trochaic substitution, permitting it only in the first position and citing as his authority "the author of the *Rambler*."[72] Bayly is another example of a prosodic theorist who attempts to embrace certain contradictory aspects of both the syllabic and the accentual systems, without realizing the fundamental impossibility of reconciling the wholly different aesthetic bases of the two systems.

Blake's *Songs of Innocence* appeared the same year that Jefferson wrote his rather innocent Augustan essay and Bayly attempted to try the new prosody without laying the old aside. His "Nurse's Song," "Little Boy Lost," and "Little Boy Found" provide evidence that he had definitely broken with the syllabic system and was already experimenting in the new prosodic mode. In the "Nurse's Song," in fact, feet of two and three syllables appear in nearly equal proportions. There would seem to be some justification for maintaining that Blake's use of trisyllabic substitution was "the boldest of his time."[73]

The nineties produced several prosodic theorists who in their writings helped to hasten the advance of accentualism. Lindley Murray, despite a bourgeois and utilitarian view of poetry,[74] has been deeply influenced by the "uniformity-variety" theorizing which preceded him,[75] and he permits trisyllabic substitution, although he is forced to mis-scan Milton to produce an example of its employment in English poetry.[76] Murray reveals an indebtedness to Samuel Say by citing one line of Say's accentual couplet, and he points

---

[69] *The Botanic Garden*, p. 125.

[70] *Alliance of Musick, Poetry, and Oratory*, pp. 106-107.

[71] *Ibid.*, pp. 28-29, 112.

[72] *Ibid.*, p. 108.

[73] Stewart, *Modern Metrical Technique*, p. 46.

[74] Murray writes: " . . . there are few persons who do not sometimes read poetical compositions; . . . the perusal of this lively and forcible mode of exhibiting nature and sentiment, may, when chaste and judicious, be an innocent and instructive employment of a moderate portion of our time. . . . " (*English Grammar*, p. 199).

[75] *Ibid.*, p. 210.

[76] *Ibid.*, p. 206.

out admiringly the amphibrachic (really anapestic) substitution which the line exhibits.[77]

Certain essays of Adam Smith's posthumously published in 1795 reveal that Smith had, much earlier, been thinking along rather advanced but confused lines. He quotes Say's couplet with approbation, but still feels a Bysshian necessity to explain the redundancy of syllables by saying that a certain haste of pronunciation causes the extra syllables to "pass as" regularities.[78] A little later in the same essay, however, he seems to reject syllabism and to align himself more or less with the proponents of accentualism: "Both the English and the Italian Heroic Verse, perhaps, are not so properly composed of a certain number of syllables, which vary according to the nature of the rhyme [*i.e.*, whether the rhyme be single or double]; as of a certain number of intervals, (of five invariably,) each of which is equal in length, or time, to two ordinary distinct syllables, though it may sometimes contain more. . . . "[79] Smith's transition within the bounds of a single essay from "a certain number of syllables" to "a certain number of intervals" is, *in parvo*, the same as that which had been going on in English prosodic theory for almost a century, and it is fascinating to observe in this essay the spectacle of the shades of Bysshe and Samuel Say wrestling for possession of Smith's prosodic soul. After Say's victory which we have just witnessed, Smith backslides severely, and finally delivers his tattered allegiance to Bysshe again, explaining that any redundant syllables in a line are somehow "considered as a sort of excrescence of the verse, and are in a manner counted for nothing."[80] It is perhaps this obvious indecision on Smith's part, this uncertain commitment to neither the old nor the new, that prompted Wordsworth to brand Smith as "the worst critic, David Hume not excepted, that Scotland, a soil to which this sort of weed seems natural, has produced."[81]

In 1796, Peter Fogg supports the bar-foot analogy,[82] and writes very sensibly that, in the heroic line, "The amphibrach, the anapest, and the spondee may be substituted for the iambic almost anywhere, provided the greater part of the line remain iambics. . . . "[83] It is interesting that Fogg employs the same prosodic terms which have been found useful a century and a half after his time: he speaks very pertly of "substitution," "compensation,"

[77] *Ibid.*, p. 210.

[78] *Works*, V, 326. ("Of the Affinity between Certain English and Italian Verses").

[79] *Ibid.*, V, 330.

[80] *Ibid.* It should be noted that Smith's sections on Surprise, Wonder, and Novelty in his "History of Astronomy" (*Works*, V, 53-190) are not devoid of prosodic relevance.

[81] Grosart, ed., *Prose Works*, II, 116, n.

[82] *Elementa Anglicana*, II, 187.

[83] *Ibid.*, II, 189.

and "equivalence,"[84] and tries to avoid using such outmoded prosodic labels as "rhythmus" and "numbers."

But that there were still as late as 1798 many old-fashioned ears attuned only to the Augustan cadences will appear from an anecdote related by the grammarian John Walker. Walker discusses the pronunciation of the word "Lupercal" and concludes that it should be sounded "Lupércal." He goes on, "But wherever the antepenultimate accent is adopted in verse, as in Shakespeare's Julius Caesar, where Antony says,

> You all did see that on the *Lúpercal*
> I thrice presented him a kingly crown———

we ought to preserve it.———Mr. Barry, the actor, who was informed by some scholar of the Latin pronunciation of this word, adopted it in this place, and pronounced it *Lupércal,* which grated every ear that heard him."[85] What grated the ears of the audience, and what still is evidently grating Walker's ear, is perhaps the terminal trochee which such a pronunciation of the word produces; it was to be a very long time before this prejudice against the terminal trochee (or, indeed, against any terminal foot but the iamb in a "serious" iambic line) was worn down.

The year 1798 is prosodically memorable for additional reasons than that of the appearance of the first edition of the *Lyrical Ballads.* In this year, the technique of trisyllabic substitution suddenly, and almost as if by some strange conspiracy, bursts into full flower in the work of Southey, Coleridge, "Monk" Lewis, Sir Walter Scott, and John Leyden.[86] It is singular that all these poets seem to have "caught the trick" of trisyllabic substitution at the same time,[87] and it is impossible to tell to what extent they were influenced by the work of the accentual prosodic theorists, or to what degree it simply became obvious to many of the poets at the same time that syllabism would no longer do. The long priority of the theory to the practice here may be offered as an example to those who are convinced that prosodic analysis and theorizing always lag impotently behind poetic practice, and that they are always satisfied to explain observable rhythmical phenomena in contemporary or past verse. As we have seen, the theorists who supported trisyllabic sub-

---

[84] *Ibid.*

[85] *Key to Classical Pronunciation,* p. 60, n.

[86] In the early accentual efforts of Coleridge and Southey, the first position was the favored one for trisyllabic substitution. If generally confined to the initial position, such substitution (like the conventionally sanctioned initial trochee in the heroic line) is much less likely to alter the total metrical effect of the line than if it occurs medially. (See Stewart, *Modern Metrical Technique,* pp. 52-53).

[87] *Ibid.,* pp. 47-49.

stitution anticipated the poets by more than half a century, and were by no means merely expressing in timid academic and analytical terms what the dashing and impulsive romantic poets had previously practiced instinctively. Compared with metrical theorists like Samuel Say and John Rice, the most flamboyant romantic poet must pale as a prosodic innovator, and will appear to have arrived at the principle of equivalence so belatedly as to seem almost a reactionary. Despite the many instances of trisyllabic substitution which began to appear in the work of the poets in 1798, it was not until the publication of *The Lay of the Last Minstrel* (1805) that "the public came to realize that verse was being written contrary to classical rules."[88]

With the technique of trisyllabic substitution now actually in possession of a segment of contemporary poetic practice, the liberal prosodic theorists hammered home their anti-syllabism with a quickened enthusiasm and with an even greater consciousness of rectitude than they had earlier displayed. Richard Mant, editing the poems of Thomas Warton in 1802, writes, "in our pentameter, which is strictly an iambic measure, we not only admit spondaic, but dactylic, anapestic, and trochaic feet. The cause of all which indulgences may be found in the pleasure derived from variety."[89] It will be noted that the "decasyllable" has, over the last few decades, gradually transformed itself into the "pentameter." Mant's permission of dactylic substitution in a line primarily iambic is a radical advance and obviously stems from a parallel with free trochaic substitution. The more easily admissible practice of anapestic substitution will still permit the line to retain a rising rhythm, and the equal-time units will still be marked by stresses almost equally spaced, as in this line:

Thĕ mórn | ĭng sún, | ănd thĕ swéet | lў síng | ĭng bréeze. |

But a dactylic substitution produces a line which is plainly of a totally different type; even the stresses which mark the individual equal-time units display very little temporal equality in such a line as this:

Thĕ mórn | ĭng sún, | swéetlў ĭn | thĕ síng | ĭng bréeze. |

It was just such rhythmical effects which certain of the theorists, anxious to carry on the hard-won principle of trisyllabic substitution to its final implications, were beginning to relish.

William Mitford's *Inquiry into the Principles of Harmony in Language* (1804) had originally appeared in less definitive form in 1774,[90] but he

---

[88] *Ibid.,* p. 49.
[89] *The Poetical Works of the Late Thomas Warton, B. D., Fifth Edition, Corrected and Enlarged* (Oxford, 1802), I, cxxxiii.
[90] As *An Essay on the Harmony of Language.*

revised the work considerably between the two editions, and we must go to
the latest version to examine Mitford's considered opinions on prosodic matters. Mitford believes in approaching the subject of prosody only after a solid
preparation in musical theory, and he even uses the term "analogy": "To
begin . . . with considering the nature and differences of cadences in music,
and then proceed to observe the analogy which the cadences of poetry bear
to them, will be found, I think, the ready . . . way, to a just perception of
the principles of the harmony of language, and of the mechanism of verse."[91]
Mitford associates iambic verse with musical common time (2/4, 4/4, etc.)
and anapestic verse with musical triple time (3/4, 6/8, etc.) : he thus attempts
to avoid the classical foot terminology, and he designates iambic and trochaic
measures "common cadence" and anapestic and dactylic verses "triple cadence."[92] As we should expect, this musical analogy supplies Mitford with
a sanction for trisyllabic substitution on an equal-time basis; he requires only
that the times of the intervals between stresses or beats be, as in music, equal.[93]
(Dactylic substitution in an iambic line, such as Mant advocates, would thus
not be allowed by Mitford.) In addition to the musical analogy, Mitford
avails himself of the uniformity-variety theory and states that all successful
practitioners in either poetry or music have always sought to unite variety
with symmetry.[94] Mitford adamantly denies any resemblance whatever, "in
constitution or mechanism," between French and English heroic verse,[95] and
he says of the structure of the English line, "Deviation from the primary
arrangement [of stresses] is allowed, for the sake of variety, just so far as
not to defeat the purpose of that arrangement, which is time-beating."[96]
The final iambus is still mandatory, however,[97] and liberal as he is with
trisyllabic substitution, Mitford is still not certain about the propriety of
admitting trochaic substitution in the second position, especially in epic
verse.[98] Mitford perceives that once an equal-time theory is assumed, duple
and triple measures can be mixed very freely without disturbing the effect
of a regular succession of beats or accents.

Mitford is a perceptive metrical theorist, and his anti-syllabism contributed, like that of many others, to the gradual consolidation of accentualist

[91] *Inquiry into the Principles of Harmony in Language*, pp. 72-73.
[92] *Ibid.*, pp. 82-83.
[93] *Ibid.*, p. 173. Mitford uses certain poems in the *Reliques* to illustrate the operation
of trisyllabic substitution. See also pp. 105-106.
[94] *Ibid.*, p. 87.
[95] *Ibid.*, p. 287.
[96] *Ibid.*, p. 108.
[97] *Ibid.*, p. 102.
[98] *Ibid.*, p. 128.

gains in the early nineteenth century. To say with Omond that Mitford's work entitles him "to an honourable place among the pioneers of a rational system of scansion"[99] is, however, at once to slight some of Mitford's more original predecessors and to assume that the later nineteenth century somehow represents the absolute pinnacle of rational English prosodic progress. Johnson, we may be certain, would have been justly offended to have heard it implied that his prosodic system was not rational, and it would indeed be very difficult to demonstrate that the prosody of one age is inherently more rational than that of another.

It may be useful to trace the tradition of prosodic liberalism a little further into the new century. *Christabel*, of course, was not published until 1816, but manuscripts had been circulating much earlier, and it is of the meter of the poem in manuscript that Coleridge writes to Byron in 1815: "I count by Beats or accents instead of syllables,————in the belief that a metre might be thus produced sufficiently uniform and far more malleable to the Passion and Meaning."[100] Here we have the essence of the accentual aesthetic, the malleability of the prosody to the "Passion and Meaning" of the poetry, with the inclusion of the customary principle of uniformity to keep the metrical variety within its proper bounds.

In 1816, John Carey, although a rather timid conservative who still displays great suspicion of trisyllabic substitution,[101] offers some interesting hints towards the elucidation of a rather old-fashioned aesthetic of metrical variety. Variety is, to Carey, inherent and essential in "Nature" and in man's condition, and man's love of variety has been implanted in him by the Almighty "for a wise and beneficent purpose";[102] internal trochaic substitution, if used to produce too startling an effect of suddenness, surpasses "variety" and becomes "deformity," and yet "almost every species of poetic deformity may, by skilful management, be occasionally converted into a charm, like the artificial spot on the cheek of Beauty, or the rugged ruin amid the cultured landscape."[103] Thus, in 1816, with the First Reform Bill looming in the foreseeable future and with England already partly transformed into an industrialized behemoth, Carey incongruously finds it useful to rationalize the

---

[99] *English Metrists,* p. 80.

[100] Earl Leslie Griggs, ed., *Unpublished Letters of Samuel Taylor Coleridge* (New Haven, Conn., 1933), II, 148. Charles I. Patterson writes, "One cannot help suspecting that Coleridge has read ... Steele's *Prosodia Rationalis....*" ("An Unidentified Criticism by Coleridge Related to *Christabel,*" PMLA, LXVII [1952], 980, n. 17).

[101] See *Practical English Prosody,* pp. iv, 48-49, 53-56. Carey cites Say's famous couplet, but even at this late date reads it syllabically with all possible contractions (p. 50).

[102] *Ibid.,* p. 39.

[103] *Ibid.,* p. 43.

device of medial trochaic substitution by reference to an aesthetic which had been, by that time, already about fifty years without vitality: Carey, apparently the quintessential die-hard, daintily speaks of beauty spots and Gothic ruins as if time had somehow been standing still since the days of Horace Walpole. With all this rather touching wistfulness, however, Carey's perception of the unique force of English accent (a necessary beginning, of course, for any accentual tendency) is well developed, so much so that he sees no essential difference between falling and rising rhythm, but considers iambic and trochaic lines as of exactly the same structure with only the initial syllable transferred to the end of the line to change the one to the other: "what we call Trochaïcs," he says, "are only defective Iambics. . . . "[104]

When Leigh Hunt, in 1844, advocated accentualism, he too went to the two traditional sanctions for the newer prosody, the bar-foot analogy and the uniformity-variety principle. A heroic line may contain thirteen or fourteen syllables, Hunt declares, "just as musicians put twenty notes in a bar instead of two,"[105] and, he writes, trisyllabic substitution arises from "the principle of Variety in Uniformity by which verse ought to be modulated, and oneness of impression diversely produced. . . . "[106] When we see Hunt using the same two sanctions for accentualism that were actively employed during the 1750's, it is apparent that Hunt's originality has been somewhat overemphasized. If we persist in thinking of Hunt and others like him as romantic metrical innovators, what epithets remain to be applied to genuine originals like Say and Mason, in whose hands these two sanctions had not yet been reduced to the level of virtual clichés?

We have now observed something of the way English accentualism developed out of the Augustan syllabism with the assistance of two major aesthetic premises: first, the analogy with music, which, early in the eighteenth century, was mainly confined to non-technical generalities, but which soon furnished the bar-foot parallel and thus the perfect sanction for trisyllabic substitution;[107] and second, the general theory of variety within uniformity,

[104] *Ibid.*, p. 27, n.

[105] *Imagination and Fancy; or, Selections from the English Poets* (London, 1891), pp. 43-44. ("An Answer to the Question, What is Poetry? Including Remarks on Versification").

[106] *Ibid.*, p. 31. Poe comments, "Of course there is no principle in the case. . . . The 'Uniformity' is the principle————the 'Variety' is but the principle's natural safeguard from self-destruction by excess of self." (Ingram, ed., *Works*, III, 228).

[107] See Draper, "Poetry and Music in Eighteenth-Century Aesthetics," pp. 75, 84; and Herbert M. Schueller, "Literature and Music as Sister Arts: An Aspect of Aesthetic Theory in Eighteenth-Century Britain," *PQ*, XXVI (1947), 196-197, 205.

which was intimately connected with the development of theories of prosodic "tension" and "opposition."

5. The Discovery of the Force of English Accent

The rise of accentual prosody was paralleled from the beginning by a gradually dawning perception that English bore a certain resemblance to the other Germanic tongues, and was thus a language whose prosody would have to take account of a succession of powerful accents as a main structural criterion. It was the neglect of a consideration of the accentual nature of the language which was partly responsible for the triumph of the French-modelled syllabism during the Restoration and the early years of the eighteenth century. Indeed, the idea of stress seldom struck any of the rhetoricians and prosodists of the sixteenth and seventeenth centuries: as has been said, "It occurred to no one to write a Defense of Stress."[108]

This neglect of the element of stress in English (or actual deafness to it) permits Thomas Rymer, in 1674, to announce that "percussion" is stronger in Italian and Spanish than it is in French or English,[109] and Samuel Woodford feels so little stress in blank verse that he sees nothing in its structure to differentiate it from prose.[110] In 1709, an author in the *Muses' Mercury* quotes with approbation and agreement a writer who, failing to perceive the operation of the powerful stresses in *Piers Plowman,* announces that the poem must be written in blank verse.[111] This same disinclination or pure inability to recognize the force of accent undoubtedly lies behind William Coward's uncertainty as to whether blank verse is poetry at all.[112]

Charles Gildon is one of the first whose ear begins to tell him that English is a strongly accented language and that English poetry requires attention to the placement of stresses structurally. Gildon writes that without due attention to the placement of accents, "what you write will be down-right prose, notwithstanding it be tagg'd with rhyme or jingle."[113] Richard Hurd, accustomed to perceiving the accents in English poetry, hears French verse as "only pure prose in rhyme,"[114] and even Lord Monboddo is able to per-

---

[108] Willcock, "Passing Pitefull Hexameters," p. 7.

[109] Spingarn, ed., *Critical Essays,* II, 170. ("Preface" to translation of Rapin's *Reflections*).

[110] *A Paraphrase Upon the Canticles,* sigs. B6ᵛ-B7ᵛ.

[111] Wellek, *Rise of English Literary History,* p. 111.

[112] *Licentia Poetica discuss'd,* p. 65.

[113] *The Laws of Poetry,* p. 342. See also Pemberton, *Observations on Poetry,* p. 124; Say, *Poems on Several Occasions,* p. 144; Newbery, *Art of Poetry on a New Plan,* I, 9; and Rice, *Introduction to the Art of Reading,* pp. 105-106.

[114] Francis Kilvert, *Memoirs of the Life and Writings of the Right Rev. Richard Hurd, D.D., Lord Bishop of Worcester; With a Selection from his Correspondence and other Unpublished Papers* (London, 1860), p. 302.

ceive that the French "want our accents."[115]

After the middle of the century, the revived interest in Old and Middle English poetry had a strong influence on this increasing preoccupation with the accentual nature of English verse. Thomas Tyrwhitt, accustomed by his scholarship to listen carefully for accents as well as number of syllables in older English poetry, is able to apprehend that it is mainly upon accent that the structure of modern English verse depends.[116] Ramsay also insists that "*ictus,* or time beatings," are central in English verse construction, and that accents are the only devices available in English to perform this time-beating function.[117] Thomas Sheridan joins these friends of English accent by pointing out that if English bears a relationship to any modern European language, that language is more likely to be Italian than French, since French displays hardly any accent at all.[118] This new recognition of the strength of accent in the English language is responsible for the statements, of which we have an abundance during the latter part of the century, that English can offer no natural spondees except the word "amen"; minds as far apart as those of Charles Burney[119] and Samuel Taylor Coleridge[120] agree that English is too accentual a tongue to permit the existence of perfect spondees.

It is noteworthy that Robert Burns, his ear sharpened for clear accents, feels none of the Augustan prejudice against poetic monosyllables; he very often sets lines of pure monosyllables going with a rather shambling accentual gait which is very striking:

> It pits me aye as mad's a hare;
> So I can rhyme nor write nae mair.[121]

Lines consisting entirely of monosyllables, in fact, have a universal tendency to overemphasize their accents, and this may have been one reason why the syllabic and French-influenced prosodists of the early eighteenth century, desirous of seeing English verse approximate as closely as possible the placid

---

[115] *Of the Origin and Progress of Language,* II, 327.

[116] *Canterbury Tales,* IV, 75, n; see also 52, n. Cf. Walker, *Elements of Elocution,* II, 150; Blair, *Lectures on Rhetoric and Belles Lettres,* III, 104; Beattie, *Dissertations Moral and Critical,* pp. 278, 271 ("The Theory of Language"); Nares, *Elements of Orthoepy,* p. vii; Fogg, *Elementa Anglicana,* II, 186; and Mitford, *Inquiry into the Principles of Harmony in Language,* p. 81.

[117] "Enquiry into the Principles of English Versification," fol. 43.

[118] *Lectures on the Art of Reading,* p. 209.

[119] *General History of Music,* I, 78, n.

[120] T. M. Raysor, ed., *Coleridge's Shakespearean Criticism* (Cambridge, Mass., 1930), I, 252.

[121] "Epistle to John Rankine," lines 73-74.

syllabic effect of the French prosody, were so severe in their treatment of the "low" monosyllabic line.[122]

Samuel Johnson seems to have been one, however, whose ear was not finely tuned to the recognition of accents. Johnson's characteristically Augustan (and aesthetically, rather paradoxical) failure to feel accents strongly may be one explanation of his customary deprecation of blank verse, which, "left merely to its numbers, has little operation either on the ear or mind."[123] Even "The musick of the English heroick line," to Johnson, "strikes the ear so faintly that it is easily lost, unless all of the syllables of every line co-operate together."[124] It would be easy to refer here to Johnson's deafness, but this handicap would hardly explain an insensitivity to accent which Johnson shared with many earlier theorists who were in full possession of their sense of hearing. Accents simply do not reach Johnson, as they had not reached most of the earlier conservative syllabists, with the extreme force that they present to the later accentualists. There is of course a large element of will involved in this matter of prosodic perceptions, and those who are specifically searching for something in a given metrical situation will usually find it with little trouble. The gradual dawning of a full and public apprehension of powerful accents functioning in poetry seems almost as much a matter of a change of will and emphasis on the part of the perceivers as it is a matter of an actual change in either the nature of the language and pronunciation or the nature of the poetry.

During the last quarter of the eighteenth century, the German influence began to make its impression on both prosodic theory and practice. The transition from syllabism to accentualism may be regarded, in one sense, as a transference of allegiance from French to German models, and from Romance to Germanic linguistic predispositions. The extent of German influence on trisyllabic substitutors like "Monk" Lewis and Coleridge is well known, and German experiments with accentual (instead of the customarily quantitative) imitations of the classical hexameter (leading ultimately to such exhibits as *Evangeline*) began to be noticed during the nineties by Englishmen whose ears were becoming more and more receptive to markedly accentual metrical effects. One William Taylor published in 1796 a "transversion" of a passage

---

[122] See, *e.g.*, Ker, ed., *Essays of John Dryden*, II, 227; Newbery, *Art of Poetry on a New Plan*, I, 17; Monboddo, *Of the Origin and Progress of Language*, II, 375; and Blair, *Lectures on Rhetoric and Belles Lettres*, I, 315.

[123] Hill, ed., *Lives*, I, 237. Cf. "If blank verse be not tumid and gorgeous, it is crippled prose. . . . " (*Lives*, II, 319-320).

[124] *Ibid.*, I, 192.

from Ossian in the new Germanic accentual hexameters,[125] and his seems to be the first attempt to reproduce in English the effect of the classical hexameter by accentual instead of quantitative means. The Germanic contribution to the ascendancy of English accentualism was coming from two directions almost at once: from the fragments of Old English verse which were being eagerly recovered and studied during the century, and directly from contemporary German poets who were capitalizing on the strong accents of German to produce accentual imitations of classical meters. To someone like Bysshe, accent had been so obscure a phenomenon in English verse as barely to deserve mention. The late-century ear was indubitably seeking more accent than the Augustan ear: by 1850 the Anglo-Saxon sensibility had become, in general, so accustomed to being gratified by strong Germanic stresses in poetry that Poe (whose poetic practice reveals that nothing pleased him more in prosody than good strong unmistakable stresses) instinctively finds the French heroic line "the most wretchedly monotonous verse in existence."[126] It is worth noticing that strong accents in music are also a product of the late eighteenth century; the powerful "accentual" rhythms which are characteristic of nineteenth-century music were unknown to the early seventeenth century.[127]

*   *   *   *   *

We have here, then, evidence of a gradual shift of rhythmical taste, from the Restoration to the nineteenth century, in all the arts based on repetition in time instead of space: the process I have sketched in the field of metrical theory could be paralleled by similar developments in the theories of music and dancing. In poetry and metrics, the shift is one from an attention to many minor units of time to a concern with only a few major units: from all syllables, that is, to only accented syllables as the marked and perceived units of temporal measurement.[128] The device of trisyllabic substitution in poetry, by calling attention to the major syllables and leaving the minor syllables to shift as they might, was a necessary step towards the fully accentual system of prosody which flowered at the beginning of the nineteenth century. The decline of syllabism, artificial scansion, and poetic contraction was balanced by the concurrent rise of accentualism and sense scansion, and a new method of both writing and reading poetry gradually emerged.

The lyrics of Heine, Shelley's *Cloud* and *Sensitive Plant,* Lewis' *The Black Canon,* Wordsworth's *White Doe of Rylstone,* Rossetti's *King's Trag-*

---

[125] "English Hexameters Exemplified," *Monthly Magazine,* I (1796), 404-405.
[126] Ingram, ed., *Works,* III, 261.
[127] Donald Ramsay Roberts, "The Music of Milton," *PQ,* XXVI (1947), 332-333.
[128] See Omond, *English Metrists,* p. 109.

edy, Browning's *Statue and the Bust*, Wilde's *Ballad of Reading Gaol:* these are some of the monuments of accentualism which the late eighteenth and nineteenth centuries produced. Their prosody is the result of over a century of earnest effort on the part of poets and metrists alike to produce out of the materials of syllabism a metrical system capable of embodying a new type of poetic material and capable of suggesting new attitudes towards perennial poetic material. The syllabic and the accentual techniques "will not sort together,"[129] in practice or in theory, and, to keep the study of English prosody from growing even more sickly than it is today, one must be aware that the basic metric of the *Essay on Man* is one thing, and that of *The Ancient Mariner* another. Many of the accentualists were undoubtedly unaware that in thirsting for a prosody which might, with propriety, contain the new poetry, they were creating what amounted to a unique metrical system. But that it was indeed unique will, I think, be apparent to those who will investigate without prejudice the implications of the history of metrical theory in the eighteenth and nineteenth centuries. The aesthetic of ideality and universality upon which the conservative syllabism of the eighteenth century had based itself was passing, and a new vitalistic and organic aesthetic was in the process of replacing it. The accentualists I have been considering were, whether they knew it or not, creating a prosodic expression of the new aesthetic, and it is in their writings that we may find some of the first unconscious stirrings of the nineteenth-century aesthetic temper.

6. A Note on Prosodic Study and the Sense of History

"Is the subject of English versification . . . one that has the connotations of a quarrel? It is," says J. W. Bright. "This is because an historical subject is prevailingly treated in an unhistorical manner."[130] The spectacle of metrical historians and theorists continually quarreling and holding each other up to ridicule is hardly elevating, but it must continue to be met with until prosody is approached historically before being considered critically. A multitude of modern errors in scansion and interpretation have resulted from a failure to take into account the theory of prosody under which various poems were composed, and from a tendency to assume that one prosody governs English poetry of whatever period; with the perpetrators of these errors the historian of metric has, I believe, legitimate grounds for a quarrel.

For example, writing of Milton's line

> Doing or suffering; but of this be sure,
> (*P.L.*, I, 158)

---

[129] Bridges, *Milton's Prosody*, p. 119. See also pp. 85 ff.
[130] Review of T. S. Omond's *Study of Metre*, *MLN*, XXXVII (1922), 59.

Brander Matthews tells us that the third foot is "plainly an anapest,"[131] but the student familiar with Restoration and especially with Miltonic prosodic theory and practice will see at once that it is instead a pyrrhic.[132] This is perhaps the sort of error one might expect to encounter in the work of an observer convinced that "versification is only the carved vase which holds the precious wine of poetry";[133] such a position as this not only elevates one abstract type of versification to a generalized position of rule over English (and presumably all other) poetry of all periods, but neglects the fact that, in many poems, prosody and meaning are so intimately allied as to be ultimately inseparable.

Ignorance of the prevalence of syllabic prosody during the eighteenth century permits Henry Lanz to discover thirty-six anapestic substitutions in the first two hundred lines of Pope's *Temple of Fame*,[134] while in actuality there are no anapests at all in these lines, each of them being a strictly decasyllabic affair, in perfect conformity to contemporary prosodic theory.

These are two typical errors arising from a failure to consider the operation of syllabic prosody in the Restoration and early eighteenth century.[135] There also seem to be many theorists and "historians" unaware of the rise and significance of accentualism in the nineteenth century. Richard E. Haswell, for example, writing in 1932, speaks of "the modern system of English prosody—the regular alternation of unaccented and accented syllables," and he announces that "This system . . . has remained the accepted prosody until today."[136] An excursion into late eighteenth-century prosodic theorizing would

---

[131] *A Study of Versification,* p. 239.

[132] Similar mis-scansions of Milton are accomplished by E. W. Scripture, "The Choriambus in English Verse," *PMLA,* XLIII (1928), 320, and by Sir George Young, *An English Prosody on Inductive Lines* (Cambridge, 1928), pp. 45-46.

[133] *A Study of Versification,* p. 6.

[134] *The Physical Basis of Rime,* p. 229. The error of ignoring the contemporary contractions, as Lanz does here, and of working prosodically from modernized texts was pointed out in 1886 by J. Motheré, who writes of the contractions in the original texts, "Ce fait ne saurait être négligé par notre époque, qui professe le respect des documents originaux. Lire, ou du moins scander *th'ideas, t'inclose,* là où Pope a imprimé ainsi (et par des motifs qu'il a lui-même expliqués), ce n'est pas défigurer ses vers, . . . c'est se conformer à sa volonté: autrement on risque de substituer un rhythme nouveau à celui que le poète a voulu." (*Les Théories du Vers Héroïque Anglais et ses Relations avec la Versification Française* [Paris, 1886], p. 10).

[135] See also Donald A. Stauffer's mis-scansions of Dryden and Cowper in *The Nature of Poetry,* pp. 198, 206; Morris W. Croll's misreading of Pope (*Essay on Man,* I, 99), cited by Wellek and Warren, *Theory of Literature,* p. 169; Maurice Johnson's neglect of Augustan contraction theory in his remarks on Swift's use of "handle 'em" and "pendulum" (*The Sin of Wit: Jonathan Swift as a Poet* [Syracuse, 1950], p. 52); and Wallace C. Brown's accentual reading of some of Johnson's verse (*The Triumph of Form,* pp. 71, 75).

[136] *The Heroic Couplet Before Dryden (1550-1675)* (Urbana, Ill., 1932), p. 4. This opinion is evidently shared by Yvor Winters. See "The Audible Reading of Poetry."

have shown Haswell that the accentual system which developed during that period was in direct opposition to the previous syllabism, and that the accentual prosody remained the standard one until late in the nineteenth century (or early in the twentieth), when it was forced to give way to a still different system, the exact nature of which will probably not be clear to anyone for a number of years.[137]

I think that a feeble sense of history also weakens much of the prosodic theorizing of Karl Shapiro, who announces in 1947 (referring to Saintsbury's *History of English Prosody*) that "it has taken about five centuries to work out anything like a complete précis of English metrics, a period in which the richest body of poetry ever known flourished apparently with no more law than its own ear."[138] Shapiro's "apparently" here, one presumes, is to provide some protection against protests that he has ignored the extent to which, in many instances, prosodic theorizing has definitely preceded (one will not venture "caused") certain "advances" in prosodic practice. Perhaps Mr. Shapiro produces his own verse with no more law than his own ear, but the slightest consideration of the eighteenth-century aesthetic of prosody which helped sanction the syllabic theory will show that the poetic method of proceeding in the twentieth century bears no necessary resemblance to that generally obtaining two centuries earlier. A certain temporal provincialism which weakens much of the work of Saintsbury and T. S. Omond seems to be lurking behind Shapiro's statement that "by 1910 English poetry was ready for one of her first great upheavals, and prosody was about ready to undergo its first major mutation since the time of Chaucer."[139] We can only infer from this that Shapiro does not consider the late eighteenth-century "mutation" to accentualism a major one, or that he believes that, until only recently, there has been one English prosody to which all poets from Chaucer to Housman have conformed.

Miss Evelyn Scholl, also assuming that English prosody of whatever historical age is based upon one abiding principle, finds that the one principle is a system of "equal times marked by an accent at the beginning of each period." She goes on to declare, "Since all English metrical verse since 1500 is based upon the same principle, this theory likewise best explains modern English metre."[140] Some might assume that an essential difference between

[137] See Stewart, *Modern Metrical Technique, passim.*
[138] *English Prosody and Modern Poetry*, p. 2.
[139] *Ibid.*
[140] "English Metre Once More," p. 320. And Josiah H. Penniman is to be found believing that all English verse is accentual because Coleridge and Lanier say so. (*A Book about the English Bible* [New York, 1919], p. 88).

the prosodies of, say, *Eloisa to Abelard, Christabel,* and *The Waste Land* or *Mauberley* is really too plain to be missed, but Miss Scholl says in effect that all these poems are constructed according to the same system of prosody, and that this single theory of prosody, operating since 1500, is the same equal-time theory which we have observed emerging only during the last half of the eighteenth century, and emerging for certain specific aesthetic reasons which are directly connected with the unique rhythmical temper of that (and no other) age. Miss Scholl, however, holds that "Most writers, even those who confine their discussion to a single author or a single period, assume that one principle underlies all English metrical verse."[141] Now if "most writers" indeed do so (and I think they really do not), one must state openly that most writers are in error. The search for some dim and mysterious principle of unity behind all English metrical phenomena must be allowed to be an interesting diversion, especially to those metaphysically inclined, but we should be aware that a historical reading of the prosodic documents makes strikingly clear the absence of Miss Scholl's "one principle." Indeed, I wonder why we should expect a single principle to underlie all English prosodies when we do not expect a single intellectual or aesthetic principle to unify English letters when approached from other points of view: when we do not expect to find Swift and D. H. Lawrence, Johnson and Bertrand Russell proceeding in accordance with one ethical and metaphysical principle, what warrant have we for assuming that Dryden, Bysshe, Coleridge, Bridges, and Auden are all (in direct opposition to their own statements on the matter) setting forth in theory and practice one metrical principle? Just as the study of the history of ideas assumes irreconcilable differences between intellectual positions, so the study of the history of prosodic theory and practice must welcome evidence of immense diversity in the possibilities of human thought and feeling. The search for a unified theory of English prosody obscures fundamental distinctions and renders simple and mechanical a subject which historical study reveals to be difficult, paradoxical, and refreshingly humane.

Some suggestions may be made which might help avoid some of these errors in the future, and which might also help restore metrical study as a central and vital discipline in literary scholarship and criticism. What we must do, I believe, is to banish the notion of "English prosody" and to advance the concept of several English prosodies, each having relevance only to its own period and type of poetry.[142] Probably eight or ten different his-

---

[141] "English Metre Once More," p. 295.
[142] Robert Bridges seems to have been thinking of something like this notion of historical prosodies; he writes, in 1921, "just as quantitative verse has its quantitative

torical prosodies can be discriminated; I should suggest the following: Old English, several varieties of Middle English, Renaissance, Metaphysical, Augustan (*i.e.*, syllabic), Romantic (*i.e.*, accentual), Modern (from the Imagist manifesto to 1939?), and Neo-accentual. The point should definitely be made that no one historical prosody (and least of all the latest) should be regarded as "superior" to any of the others: each will be found suitable for its own purposes, and the purpose of each will not necessarily resemble the purposes of the others. One object of the delineation of these historical prosodies would be, of course, the illumination of the sensibilities of the individual poetic periods by an examination of the nature of the prosodic system which each period produced for its own unique purposes.[143]

Next to a natural ear able to distinguish the rhythm of a waltz from that of a march, a healthy suspicion of the validity of the idea of progress in the arts seems to me to be the metrical historian's and theorist's most useful stock in trade. At the present time we have no history of English meters or of English metrical theory which is not distorted in some degree by the assumption that prosody (and by implication, all art) somehow improves with each succeeding age.[144] Considering the extent of the insinuation of this notion into almost all areas of modern metrical history and theory, it is hardly any wonder that modern scholars feel called upon to read into eighteenth-century poetry certain techniques utterly foreign to it, in an effort, one gathers, to make it more modern, and hence, better poetry. While avoiding the perils of the idea of progress, modern prosodic study must also beware of falling into the pit of mere antiquarianism, with its allied corruptions in the direction of pseudo-science and an abandonment of aesthetic and humane concerns.

---

prosody, so syllabic verse has its syllabic prosody, and accentual verse will have its accentual prosody." (*Milton's Prosody*, pp. 110-111). George R. Stewart, in both *The Technique of English Verse* and *Modern Metrical Technique*, Egerton Smith, in his *Principles of English Metre*, J. W. Bright, in his review of Omond's *Study of Metre* in *MLN*, Gay Wilson Allen, in his *American Prosody*, and George A. Kellogg, "Bridges' *Milton's Prosody* and Renaissance Metrical Theory," *PMLA*, LXVIII (1953), 270, n. 8, have all been aware, in varying degrees, of the necessity of delineating historical prosodies, and of the dangers of oversimplification resident in the assumption that English metrical practice can somehow be reduced to a set of universally operative principles.

[143] See the section "The Transcendental Theory of Prosody" in Allen's *American Prosody* (pp. 91-96) for an example of the way a perceptive scholar familiar with the back roads of literary history can deduce a metaphysic from a prosody, and *vice versa*.

[144] It is not difficult, for example, to perceive that T. S. Omond employs the term "evolution" when speaking of prosodic change with a conscious intention of emphasizing the slow but steady march to ultimate perfection of English meters and metrists. See *English Metrists*, p. 94.

For the ultimate goal in all study of metrics must be, I believe, humanistic: the study of prosody should reveal what men, and not what mere accents and syllables *in vacuo,* have done and may be expected to do. I hope that some of the evidence presented in these chapters will suggest the extent to which human considerations are involved in the most superficial prosodic reading of verse, and the degree to which matters of stresses and pauses, regularities and irregularities, are connected with certain purely human presuppositions, expectations, and inclinations. Once prosody departs from this close connection with individual human beings and their responses, it loses most of its value as a literary study. It may then be useful as a scientific exercise, but it can communicate to us little of human relevance except the suspicion that modern scholars engaged in these anxious countings and weighings and measurings are in imminent danger of surrendering up their own humanity.

Another element which seems to me often neglected in prosodic investigations is the subjective one: I mean the degree to which the reader of poetry, by various subtle devices of misreading, actually creates the rhythm that reaches him, instead of merely absorbing the rhythms which the poet intended. Both the eighteenth-century artificial scansionists and certain modern readers who read nineteenth-century trisyllabic substitutions into eighteenth-century syllabic poetry are engaged in an act which is of the greatest importance for metrical study, and yet one which is almost never considered. In addition to historical prosodic studies of the poet-poem relationship, we need more emphasis on the poem-reader relationship. Such questions as these will have to be investigated: to what extent are rhythmical effects originally written into a poem distorted by all readers, even the most proficient, and how deeply does such distortion obscure the total meaning of the poem which the poet wrote? Does the average twentieth-century reader tend to alter the natural rhythms of contemporary verse in the reading (because of certain preconceptions of what these rhythms should be) as much as the eighteenth-century artificial scansionists altered theirs? To how great an extent is such distortion responsible for many readers' "difficulty" with modern (and perhaps all) poetry? What is the source of these particular rhythmical predispositions which influence and often impair a reader's apprehension of a given poem? Until such questions as these are posed and investigated, we shall not be able to say that prosodic study has outlived its usefulness.

The restoration of prosodic study to a vital position in literary scholarship and criticism thus seems to me to depend on its re-alliance with the sense of history. If the prosodies of English poetry can be explored and discriminated with the same tools of objective investigation and documentation which are employed in other areas of literary research, we shall be able to formulate a history of English prosodies which will appear not entirely unrelated to the history of the English people and to the history of their ideas.

INDEX